TV's Image of the Elderly

A Practical Guide for Change

Richard H. Davis
University of Southern California

James A. Davis
University of Maryland

Lexington Books
D.C. Heath and Company/Lexington, Massachusetts/Toronto

Library of Congress Cataloging in Publication Data

Davis, Richard H.
    TV's image of the elderly.

    Includes index.
    1. Aged in television—United States. 2. Television and the aged—United States.
3. Television broadcasting—Social aspects—United States. 4. Television—Vocational
guidance—United States. I. Davis, James A. II. Title.
HQ1063.4.D38   1985   305.2′6′0973   83-47933
ISBN 0-669-06764-4 (alk. paper)

Second printing, May 1986
Published simultaneously in Canada
Printed in the United States of America
Casebound International Standard Book Number: 0-669-06764-4
Library of Congress Catalog Card Number: 83-47933

Contents

10. Guest Appearances: Strategies and Opportunities   183

11. Advocating Your Rights to the Airwaves   203

Appendix A   You and Television   229

Appendix B   Sample Scripts   233

Tables

Foreword

Maggie Kuhn
Founder
National Gray Panthers

Throughout most of the world's history, the aged in society have been revered—and rightfully so. The elders were the survivors, the experienced ones, the ones who had attained wisdom and knowledge through a lifetime of experience that was invaluable to the growth of society.

In recent decades, particularly in America, ageism—or arbitrary discrimination based on chronological age—has drastically altered the status of older people. Instead of being the respected elders, they are the castaways of society. They have been relegated to society's scrapheap as worn-out, used-up, essentially "now-valueless" members of society.

Nowhere has the image been more frequently perpetrated than through the mass media—and in particular, through the electronic medium of television. This same electronic-age medium has been a mixed blessing for old people, even though it has revolutionized our society, providing entertainment, education, and a new awareness of world events at the flick of a switch.

Although this medium has enhanced their lives, it has also done them a disservice. By repeatedly portraying the elderly as senile, useless, and sexless, it has not only encouraged older people to buy into these stereotypes, but has sold a generation of young Americans on the theory that aging is something to be feared rather than revered.

TV's Image of the Elderly is an important step forward in challenging the present mind-set of the television medium. It lays out the problems of this mind-set in graphic detail. It looks at the evolution of television and its effects on the lives of older viewers. It takes a look at how television has chosen to portray older persons and the implications of that portrayal. It shatters some of the major myths by describing older persons as they are: older persons are vital, healthy, active individuals who are having an ever-increasing impact on society; they are people who have individual idiosyncracies, likes and dislikes, and strengths and weaknesses just as do individuals in any other point in the age spectrum.

The book also provides a blueprint to show individual Americans how they can help break this pattern of ageism. Concerned individuals can develop new programming at the local level and can advocate efforts designed to bring about positive change in existing programming. The book not only provides a description of what has been and what is, but an easy-to-follow road map for what can be.

Both authors bring to their work a sensitivity and a wealth of understanding gained through years of work in the field of gerontology and electronic media. Both have been actively involved with the Gray Panthers for years, and through our association I have gained great respect for both of them. For nearly two decades, Dr. Richard Davis has been a leading expert at the Andrus Center in the fields of gerontology and media. Dr. James Davis, who has worked with me on many Gray Panther projects, has contributed significantly to the field of gerontology in the areas of television production, mental health, and senior advocacy. In collaborating on this book, they have increased understanding of how electronic media affect the older generation.

The authors make Americans aware of this prejudice in our society, the role television plays in feeding it, and how we can begin to effect a change.

Gray Panthers welcome the publication of this book. It will strongly support the work of our Media Watch, established over a decade ago to monitor the ways in which TV advertising and programming deal with the issues of age. Viewers of all ages have the right to commend and to complain about television's quality and substance.

Ageism, like sexism and racism, has its roots in our competitive economic system. It will not be eradicated overnight. *TV's Image of the Elderly* is a powerful advocacy tool in pressing for the changes that must be made.

Acknowledgments

It has not been an easy task to collaborate on a book with the two authors separated by several thousand miles. We have each taken responsibility for separate sections of the book, and we wish to acknowledge the help and encouragement of the many people who made our job less arduous.

On the West Coast, Richard Davis is grateful for the help of the following persons. Gerald Jay Westbrook, researcher at the Leonard Davis School of Gerontology at the University of Southern California (USC), consulted as methodologist, contributing to the findings reported in chapter 5. This study conducted by the authors was encouraged and facilitated by Melvin Goldberg, Vice President for Social Research at American Broadcasting Companies, Inc. The Academy of Television Arts and Sciences in Hollywood is recognized for the opportunity given to research Academy materials. Colleague Dr. Robert V. Miller, formerly of DePauw University, now Vice President with Market Vision Research, Inc., collaborated in the compilation of information making up a portion of chapter 6.

Others who aided in the processing of text for the first half of the book are Grace Farwell, Kenneth Kriendler, Loan Loung, Michael Renier, and May Ng, all undergraduate and graduate students at USC.

The contributions of all these people are gratefully acknowledged.

On the East Coast, James Davis wishes to give special thanks to his beloved wife, Lois, for her love, support, assistance and patience; to both sides of his family for their love and support; to Dana Grabiner, David Kobrinetz, Sheila Shueh, Carol Hodges, and Sally Heldrich for their valuable assistance; to Judy and Don Sanders for their friendship and creative inspiration; to Sharon Rubin, Bob Shoenberg, Rita Ryerson, Delores Mulligan, Lorene Hanna, Maggie Kuhn, Edith Giese, Frances Humphreys, and other friends in the Gray Panthers, Carl Carmichael, and Dennis Labuda for their support and friendship; to the staff of Media General Cable in Fairfax, Virginia, to the staff of KVAL-TV and KPNW Radio in Eugene, Oregon, and the UMCP Center for Aging for guidance and support.

Introduction

This book is about television's influence in our society in a special way, in the image it projects of aging. And it is about a special segment of the audience it serves, the elderly.

The numbers of elderly have increased annually over the past several decades. These numbers are projected to continue to increase significantly for the next two decades. Today the population of older people in the United States is larger than ever in our history. This population will grow to be the most influential segment of society by the year 2000. What is even more important, this population will not be passive and dependent, conforming to an outmoded notion of what "old" is.

The definition of "old" is changing. And the community of elderly is growing in fiscal, social, and political power. It is a group that can no longer be ignored.

Television pays attention to what is important, or thought to be important, at any given time in society. There is evidence that older people are being given attention by the electronic media. But we might investigate the quality of that attention as well as the quantity of airtime devoted to both issues in aging and to the elderly themselves. Such an investigation is the first goal of this book.

The second goal of the book is to provide a guide, a manual, for those who wish to use television as a means to reach both the general public and older persons and their service or care providers with information about issues and ideas of concern to the aging.

The book's first part provides the reader with a background for understanding aging as a current social experience as well as for understanding how television works in the public interest and, most important, how it addresses aging concerns and the image of aging in America. The second part of the book presents a "how to" guide for using television to influence the public. Television makes issues important. If an issue receives media attention, it becomes important. This part of the book helps the reader to use this principle to advocate better coverage of the concerns of the elderly and gain access to the airwaves. Guidance is given in dealing with stations and in producing material for broadcasting. A model for the organization of local senior media rights coalitions is also discussed.

As academics who also work within the world of broadcasting, we hope this book will be read by students of sociology, gerontology, and broadcasting. We also hope that it will be used as a sensitizing agent within the broadcast industry. Finally, we hope it will serve as a guide to media watch groups and as a manual for production and community access for those citizens who want to exert influence through this most powerful of communication channels.

Part I
Television and the Aging Audience

1
The Aging Society

The electronic mass media traditionally have targeted their messages toward a broad, somewhat homogenized audience of consumers. For decades the television industry concerned itself almost exclusively with a well-defined slice of the general population. That slice has been limited to the two decades from age 30 to age 50. Of course, there has always been major programming aimed toward clusters of younger consumers; children, teens, and the young adults in the early 20s have been wooed with specialized programming. Until the last decade there has been little or no programming for older viewers.

The elderly population has never been totally ignored, but for the most part programming both about and for older viewers has been relegated to broadcast fringe times. Even children and young adults, whose ages span the years of college and early career building, have not been too interesting to broadcasters because these groups have not been identified as homebodies with heavy investment of time as television viewers and as having a significantly large purchasing power.

After all, the purpose of broadcast programming is to attract an audience for the products advertised. Much market research has shown that the prime consumer audience falls in the age group of roughly 30 to 50. Before 30, concerns other than acquiring possessions and maintaining homes occupy most people. After 50, it is assumed consumers are either thoroughly conditioned in their purchasing habits or they cannot be coerced through persuasive messages. Moreover, it is widely believed that the older market is a slender one since its members are presumed to have little money to spend anyway.

This thinking has worked well enough for the broadcast industry in the past; it has prospered. But society is dynamic and nothing stays the same for very long. The economy changes, social movements cause ripples, and attitudes change, with the consequence that our population cannot be defined in the same manner as it was in the earlier days of radio or television. A major distinction of American society in the 1980s has to do with the increasing numbers of people over age 65 and the decreasing numbers of people under 20. The percentage of people in the Pepsi generation is smaller than ever before. And it does not appear likely to increase dramatically in the next few years.

At the same time the percentage of people in the over-50 market is increasing by leaps and bounds. This is going to make a big difference in the role of television as it markets products, as program content reflects social change, and as its power to influence societal behaviors continues to effect change.

It is true that America is growing older. Today there are approximately 25.5 million people over 65 (11.3 percent of the U.S. population). This is in contrast to 3 million (4 percent) at the turn of the century. There were, simply, very few older consumers in the early days of radio broadcasting, in the 1920s. Even television's advent in the 1940s found a consumer audience that had only a small percentage of older persons. There were valid reasons for not noticing this audience.

Those reasons no longer exist. And that is the justification for this book. The aging society needs to be understood by the people who control media and by the people who are influenced by it. At the same time that the population curve is shifting, the conventional and traditional electronic channels of communication are changing rapidly. These two events are going to interact to contribute to change in the way information is distributed to people, and in the way people look at themselves.

The audiovisual media provide a mirror of society, and by doing so, they contribute to establishing and validating a set of guidelines for social behaviors. The emerging multiplicity of electronic communication channels will have numerous effects upon society. This book attempts to describe the media as they relate to the aging society. It addresses the need for an emerging social role for the media in a gerontocracy, and it suggests guidelines for using the media in a manner that is advantageous to the aging population.

Growing Old in America

For those not familiar with gerontology, the study of aging, a review of the history of aging in America is presented here. This allows for a shared basis of understanding of how America regards the experience of aging and of being old. We are in a time of transition, of social change regarding the concepts of old age. There is ambivalence today in our national and individual attitudes about the elderly. But it has always been this way. Unlike most European cultures, we have not had a long history. Our people have not had centuries to learn how to be comfortable with concepts of old age.

The world image of America has long been one of youthful, robust vigor. Indeed, that is the image Americans have carried of themselves. This image has its basis in fact. It was, after all, mainly the young, rather than the old, who ventured from Europe to settle and tame a rugged and enormously challenging environment. Civilization as it was understood in the Western world had to be carried across the seas to America. The youth entrusted with this mission brought with them the attitudes and conventions of their home society. This may have included a certain respect and veneration for the elders, but in time it was apparent that those who were going to accomplish the task of taming the new world were the young. Consequently youth became a valued human commodity, and age acquired a less utilitarian definition, at least with respect to settling a new world.

Whether in the colonies or in Europe, a long life in the sixteenth and seventeenth centuries was not something granted to the majority. In fact, early colonial census records, which were most often church documentations of village births and deaths, indicate that only about one-tenth of the population reached age 60. Survival beyond childhood was in itself a major accomplishment. Age had different meanings in the beginnings of our country. One assumed adult responsibilities early and could be an elder by age 40.

Of couse, there have always been those who lived to advanced age. Reaching age 70 or 80 did occur in those early days just as it does today, but fewer people achieved that many years then. The number of years humans can attain has not significantly increased since the settling of this country; rather, what has happened is that the numbers of people who reach advanced old age have increased.

Cultural Antecedents to Attitudes about Aging

Ambivalence about growing old and about the elderly themselves is not something exclusively characteristic of modern society. Conflict between the generations is documented in the Western culture from the time of the ancient Greeks. The Bible tells many stories of father–son discord. Shakespeare mirrored attitudes of his time as he drew portraits of the elderly—most of them negative. Victorian literature alludes to the behaviors, appropriate and inappropriate, of old men and women in society.

In the earlier days of our own country, the elderly were paid deference because there were so few of them and they were invested with the wisdom of the community. Even then, just being old alone was not enough to command reverence, however. The older members of the community were also most likely to be those who controlled land and other resources. Their positions of power and authority may have gained them some respect but also caused discord when younger men had to suppress envy and defer ambition.

In time, being wealthy came to be more important in achieving status than did being old. There is evidence that as society became more complex, older persons who had no financial resources were often not extended charity at all. When communal wealth allowed for the distribution of charity, the elderly who behaved in a worthy manner were recipients of that charity. This is quite a different status from those earlier days of the colonies when being old was in itself worthy of respect—not charity.

In a young society where productivity is a measure of a person's worth, the unproductive can quickly lose prestige in the community. The elderly whose strength had waned and whose property was insignificant had little status, if any. The position of older women in colonial days was not at all to be envied unless their husbands had settled a significant estate on them. More often than not the laws of primogeniture prevailed, and the self-interests of the son often excluded the widowed mother from basic necessities, much less luxuries.

Early in our society, then, the majority of the elderly became social burdens. When there was not enough resources to go around, the unproductive were in a humbled position. Being old was not a desirable situation for most to look forward to. These economic conditions, so disadvantageous to the elderly, led to the formation of negative attitudes about old age and the elderly that persist until the present time.

Today's Elderly

The increase in the numbers of older people in today's society is the result of three major factors: birth rate, death rate, and migration. Birth rate (fertility) increased annually in the years of the late nineteenth and early twentieth centuries, and there was a corresponding decrease in the ratio of infant mortality. This means that greater numbers of people survived childhood diseases to grow to maturity. (Remember that today's elderly, those who are 65+, were born in the years spanning roughly 1883 to 1918.)

Add to this fertility factor the great numbers of people who immigrated to this country in the years prior to World War I, and it is easier to understand the seemingly sudden increase in numbers of older people in our society. During the decades of this century, health care technology has become increasingly sophisticated. New drugs and methodologies for treating disease, both acute and chronic, as well as an evolving philosophy for holistic health care have all contributed to keeping greater numbers of people not only alive, but also in a well-functioning state.

According to the White House Conference on Aging demographic fact sheet issued in 1981, the older population (defined in this context as being 75 +, a whole decade older than other definitions of 65 +) has grown from 29 percent of the total population of elderly to 38 percent since 1900. This simply tells us that more people are living longer—that to be 75 years old is no longer extraordinary. The same report projects an expectation for this 75 + age group that it will comprise 45 percent of the total population of elderly in this country by the year 2000.

The 1982 analysis of the older population compiled for the House Committee on Aging is titled "Every Ninth American." The title is a reference to the percentage of our population the elderly constitute: One of every nine Americans is over 65. This report makes vividly clear the mathematics of the increasing numbers of the elderly: 5,200 Americans reach age 65 each day. At the same time about 3,600 Americans who are over age 65 die. This means that each day there is a net increase of about 1,600 persons over 65. The cumulative increment amounts to almost 600,000 older persons a year—a significant number. The elderly make up 11 percent of the current population. The actual number was 26.6 million older persons in this country at the beginning of 1982. Some details will indicate the nature and composition of this large older population.

Sex Ratio. There are more older women than there are older men. It is estimated that there are 146 older women for every 100 older men. As age progresses, that ratio increases. There are 178 women in the over-75 age group for every 100 men. This is quite a change since the turn of the century, when it was estimated that there were slightly more men than women in the older age group (102 to 100). We can speculate on the reasons for this dramatic change in the relative condition of men and women: greater attention to pre- and postnatal care for women perhaps, increased stress on the urbanized males perhaps. Some demographers expect that this trend will persist and that by the year 2000, there will be 150 older women for every 100 older men.

Racial Distribution. It has long been demonstrated that the white population ages with more success, in terms of health and longevity, than the black. Of the entire white population in this country 12 percent are over 65. Blacks have fewer numbers of elderly; 8 percent of the black population lives beyond 65. Even fewer Hispanics survive to be elderly. Four percent of this population reaches age 65 and lives beyond. The failure of more of these minority populations to attain advanced age may also be a result of poor nutrition, economic disadvantages, higher levels of stress, and cultural and societal acceptance of disadvantaged status.

Marital Status. Obviously women in our society can count on being widows for a part of their lives. There are more than five times as many widows as there are widowers. Almost 70 percent of all women over 75 are widows, according to reports drawn up for the White House Conference in 1981. Unlike women, those men who do not reach old age are more likely to be unmarried. This sounds suspect until we realize that census data show that about 35 percent of men who reach old age are married to women who are under age 65. There is also some evidence that men in long-term marriages are less likely to survive the death of their spouse than are the women.

Living Arrangements. Contrary to some popular expectations, most older Americans are likely to live in family settings. Whether it be with spouse or with some other family member, it is estimated that four of every five men and three of every five women live within a family. About 33 percent of the elderly live with unrelated persons or live alone. It is significant in countering one of the myths about the elderly to note that a little less than 5 percent of the elderly reside in long-term care or other health-related institutions.

Most older people are found mainly in just three states: California, New York, and Florida. The warm climate of California and Florida attracts retirees, much of their increased population results from migration. New York has a substantial population that can be assumed to have grown old in place. These three states combine with five others to provide residence for more than half of the older population of this country. (The five others are Pennsylvania, Ohio, Texas, Illinois, and Michigan.)

Health Status. Of course, the elderly are subject to physiologic changes with time. They experience a decrease in function in most organ systems, but this decrease is largely gradual. Of the 500,000 people who reach age 65 each year it is estimated that about 20 percent suffer from serious disabilities. Even so, only about 5 percent of the elderly are institutionalized in some sort of health care facility. When we speak of the elderly as composing a population from 65 up, we may be discussing a 30-year span. Individuals differ greatly in functional decline within this span, aging differently from one another and at different speeds.

Older people do spend a larger percentage of their income on medication and medical attention than do other age groups. Older people take 25 percent of prescription drugs, and, it is estimated, spend an average of $100 each on medication yearly.

Education. It is said that each new generation of the elderly is better educated than the preceding one. This seems logical in our society. Being educated is a condition that we now take for granted. It was not always so.

Earlier generations had to expend most of their energy merely surviving. Going to school was a luxury for many. Even being a high school graduate was not something that people took for granted two generations ago. Many young people left school as soon as they could find employment on the farm or in the mills. The most urgent concern was to provide enough food and shelter for survival. As the economy allowed it, and as families became more prosperous, it was possible for children to receive more education. Today's older population has fewer years of education as a group than their children, and a great deal less than will their grand-children. About 38 percent of the older people today have completed high school, and only 8 percent have college degrees. It is estimated that 9 per-cent have fewer than five years of any schooling at all.

This will not remain the same. Many of the middle-aged children of today's elderly have benefited from government education programs, the various G.I. bills that came after the wars. Their children, the grandchild generation, almost takes a college education as a natural course of events. By the year 2000, it is estimated that about half of all older persons will have at least high school diplomas. That means that today's middle-aged population has a higher rate of college education than their parents. And their children, the elderly of 2020, will make up an older population of the well educated.

Work. In today's tight economy, it is more and more difficult for the over-65 population to remain employed. Still it is estimated that ap-proximately 16 percent of this population remains in the labor force. Of this number, women predominate—a fact reflecting their better health generally, and their longevity. There are many disincentives for remain-ing on the job, and industry offers several plans to encourage early re-tirement. Early retirement is not unusual today. Still, there are those who, for economic reasons or other personal concerns, choose to work into their 70s. In many states retirement cannot be made mandatory, which helps to explain the incentive packages for early retirement. We are seeing more men aged 55 and up retiring even though the economy would not seem to be conducive to early retirement. Fat pension benefits and increased social security rates may contribute to that trend. Older worker "burn-out" may be another factor explaining the male disinclina-tion to continue working. In contrast, more older women are entering the work force after age 55 than ever before.

The Economic Impact of the Elderly on Society

Any statistics that can be reported about the costs of programs for older people, as well as statistics that can be reported about income levels and consumer expenditures have limited use. They reflect the time when the figures were gathered, which is usually several years earlier than when the figures are used to draw conclusions. What we can understand are some generalities about economics and the population.

Figures reported in 1980 on national federal expenditures for the major aging programs indicate that $105.7 billion were spent in 1978. What programs are supported by the federal government? Retirement payments only within the social security budget account for the major portion of that $105.7 billion. The figure for social security retirement totals $52.1 billion. The remainder of this large amount of federal funds is dispersed through Medicare hospital insurance, federal civil service retirement pensions, military retirement pensions, Medicare Supplemental Insurance, Medicaid payments to nursing homes, railroad retirement, and the Older Americans Act, in that order.

The Older Americans Act. Although accounting for only $0.7 billion of the total federal expenditures on the elderly, this program is worth noting. Enacted in 1965, this program stands as a national policy on aging, declaring certain basic rights to the elderly. The Administration on Aging (AoA) has the responsibility for carrying out the objectives of the Older Americans Act. The delivery of services through this Act is facilitated by the State and Area Agencies on Aging. These agencies in turn coordinate the delivery of services within individual communities.

The Social Security Administration. The most well-known of the federal programs, the Social Security Administration provides not only payment of retirement benefits, but also disability and Medicare payments. Also under its aegis is the Supplemental Security Income program, which was designed to replace state welfare programs for the aged. The increasing number of older persons eligible for social security income in various forms, and the decreasing numbers of younger workers paying into the system give rise to concerns about the viability of the system.

Clearly there has been a subtle shift to a welfare system of support for the elderly in our society. This observation always gives rise to speculation about the responsibility of the family versus the responsibility of society (the government) for its members. Federal expenditures for the elderly have risen steadily since the 1960s. This increase is due to the liberalization of benefits (responding perhaps to political pressures), the maturation of existing programs such as the social security system, and the mere fact that the older population has grown so dramatically in numbers.

The Elderly as Consumers. The foregoing paragraphs have summarized the costs to society of the older population. It must be remembered that the elderly are consumers as well, however. They *spend* money, turning back to the economy all of what they receive through benefits and through their own pensions and investments. One of every four consumer households is headed by someone over age 65. Twenty-eight million, or one of every three consumer households, is headed by someone over age 65. The families headed by someone aged 65 or older apportion their expenditures very much like those under age 65. The major divisions of the budget for the elderly are food, housing, and health care. This is not so different from younger families; it is only that the proportions of total income spent in these three categories are greater for the elderly. More than $68 billion is spent annually by these households. According to the 1982 report to the U.S. House of Representatives Select Committee on Aging, half of the more than 9 million older families had incomes of less than $12,881 annually. This may be compared to the reported income of $22,548 for the 51 million families under age 65. Over one-sixth of the older population, more than 4 million, are poor by official definition (income of $4,954 for a couple; $3,941 for an individual).

It must be noted that many older families continue to have high incomes. More than 835,000 (9.1 percent of older families) had 1980 incomes of between $20,000 and $25,000. Fourteen percent of the elderly had incomes between $25,000 and $50,000, and 3 percent had incomes in excess of $50,000. This totals almost 22 percent of the elderly who have higher family incomes than the median for younger families in 1980.

The older population actually accounts for 30 percent of the total personal income in the United States. This group makes 25 percent of all consumer purchases in this country. The elderly consumers are good credit risks. They have the best payment records of all ages, and they have more available collaterals (85 percent own their own homes, usually free and clear of debt). They have, understandably, accumulated and paid for more durable goods than younger consumers. The National Consumer Finance Administration, which represents nearly 800 finance companies, reports that the delinquency rate for people over age 55 is less than 0.5 percent.

Some Projections about Aging in America

Predictions and projections are two different things. Demographers and economists to not make predictions; they attempt projections based on some givens and some degree of speculation. The givens include past and present fertility and mortality rates, migration patterns, economic conditions, the state of technology in general, and political conditions. Thus, a projection is an educated guess about a future condition.

Projections can be made fairly easily about population patterns based on fertility rates. After all, we can count the numbers of persons presently alive in any age group, use actuarial tables to compute the number of probable survivors, and reach an assumption about the numbers of old people at a given point in the future. Projections can also be made regarding percentages of the population involved in a given health problem: cancer, heart conditions, alcoholism, and so forth. Economic forecasts are made regularly which lead to inferences about conditions within the broad population.

Without such projections, planning would be all but impossible. Budgeting is based on projected need; urban development strategy is based on projected growth or decline; programs for the various age segments of the population are planned according to projected numbers and needs.

Birth Rates

During the period following World War II a larger number of babies were born than before or since. Prior to the war, America was in the midst of a great depression, reducing incentives to raise children. More recent decades have also discouraged large families because of economic hardships. But the period of prosperity and optimism in the late 1940s and in the 1950s made families of three, four, and six children not uncommon. This postwar "baby boom" accounts for a population that had an impact on the whole of society from its beginnings. The numbers of children required that whole suburbs spring up, schools be built, and teachers educated. The rearing of this generation became a major interest of behaviorists and of business.

This is the generation that grew to maturity in the 1960s and advocated many social reforms. The generation that would never trust anyone over 30 is now over 30 itself. In fact it is on the verge of middle age. As it ages, this group will continue to influence society. But the baby boom generation has not produced children in enough numbers even to replace itself. Fertility rates since the end of the baby boom have been such that there is now zero population growth. This means that the numbers of people born today are merely replacing those who die. The size of the population is not expected to grow.

There are some obvious consequences to this trend. Because there are fewer children, the median age of the population increases. This means that America is growing into an older society for the first time in history. As the large postwar population grows even older, its numbers remaining large due to increasing life expectancy, we will become a nation with a still more significant percentage of old people. It can be projected that we will be an aging society for several decades with an eventual decline in total population by the middle of the next century.

Some demographers project that the birth rate will increase, but at a very low rate. The birth rate, which had fallen to zero in the early 1970s, has begun to show a slight increase. The U.S. Census Bureau expects this pattern to continue for the next 20 years. Projections in the 1982 Annual Report of the Board of Trustees of the Federal Old-Age and Survivors Insurance and Disability Trust Fund showed that the population is growing slowly from a base of 232.7 million in 1980 to a projected 254.7 million in 1990. Still, in the two decades between 1980 and 2000, the growth rate is expected to fall by 20 percent. As the total population grows slowly, the age composition will change. Two groups are projected to increase between the years of 1980 and 2000: those between ages 20 and 64, and those aged 65 and older.

Death Rates

Demographic patterns indicating an aging society will become still more pronounced as death rate declines. It is projected that by 1990 there will be at least 5 million more elderly than there are today (making a possible total of 30 million older people). At the same time the very young adults, age 18–24, are projected to decrease by about 4 million.

Other projections indicate that the numbers of persons age 75 and older will jump an even larger percentage: about 44 percent, which is higher than the projected increase of 37 percent for all older people. So not only will there be a large population of elderly, the very old will be even greater in numbers than ever before.

As current trends continue and the older live still longer, the percentage of the aged in the United States will continue to rise. As it is currently at about 11 percent, it is projected that will be at 12 percent in the year 2000 and a still more significant increase will bring it to 20 percent by the year 2020. This will bring the median age up. From its current median of 28 years, the projection is that by the year 2000 those aged 35 and older will represent 50 percent of the population. At the same time, the percentage of the population aged 65 and over will have increased 21 percent over the current figure. Within this group the "old-old" (aged 80 +) will constitute 44 percent of the total elderly. This is an increase of nearly 60 percent over the 1980 figure.

In other terms, this means that if today one of every nine citizens is aged 65 and over, by 2000 one of every eight people will be that age. And by the year 2020, one of every six will be 65 or over.

If there continue to be major medical breakthroughs, as they are likely to, the proportion will increase even more. It is anticipated that although the numbers of male babies are increasing, the male–female imbalance will continue.

Some Other Projections Based on Fertility and Mortality Rates

It can be anticipated that future generations of the elderly will be better educated than today's elderly. Each generation for the last several has received more years of education. This translates rather easily into higher economic scales and higher standards of living for each generation. But it is also easy to see that future economic conditions will be greatly influenced by this change in the composition of society. As the mix becomes still more unbalanced, with the elderly, who receive tax-supported social benefits, growing in number, and the young workers, who pay into the system, decreasing in numbers, the dependency ratio will place an increasing economic burden on the young. Various social and budgetary plans will be created to address this inequity.

The U.S. Census Bureau also deals with migratory patterns of the population. They project that by the year of 2000 about six of every ten Americans will be living in the Sunbelt, the states of the southwest, the west, and Florida. Living may be a bit more of an economic challenge, it being anticipated that by the year 2000 both partners in a marriage will be working by necessity. The median family income will not increase in terms of real dollars and it could decline even further in the middle 1980s and 1990s despite this dual income status.

In summary, these projections may be made: By 1990 there will be 30 million persons aged 65 and over. There will be 4 million fewer persons aged 18–24. Of the older population, 61 percent will be female. Fifty-five percent of older persons will have at least a high school education.

By the year 2000 there will be nearly 32 million persons aged 65 and over. This is an increase of 21 percent over the 1980 figure. Of these elderly, 44 percent will be aged 75 and over. This is an increase of 60 percent over today's very old. By this time, 50 percent of the U.S. population will be aged 35 and over.

By the year 2020 approximately 45 million persons will be 65 and over. By this time 30 percent of all Americans will be aged 55 +. The median age of all Americans will be 37. (Interestingly, 582 million persons in the world will be aged 60 and over. So it is not only the American population that is aging.)

Finally, by the year 2030, approximately 55 million persons in the United States will be aged 65 and over. Between 18 and 20 percent of all Americans will be aged 65 and over. The average life expectancy by this time may very possibly rise to the middle 80s.

Of course, the consequences of all this extend in many directions. All of society as we know it today will be profoundly affected. Such changes in the age structure of the population have implications for income and retirement policies. The development of new and the changing of existing technologies in communication and information processing will be influenced. Social and recreational facilities will change, as will types of housing. The health care industry will grow in new directions. There will be a noticeable shifting in product markets and advertising.

Broadcast communication will inevitably reflect these different numbers. The concern of this book is that broadcasting may be lagging behind in its social awareness. Program content and project images of aging may not take into consideration both the changing age patterns of society and the influence of the medium on molding an aging society.

References

1982 Annual Report of the Board of Trustees of the Federal Old-Age and Survivors Insurance and Disability Trust Funds. 1983. Washington, D.C.

Clark, Robert L., and John A. Menefee. 1980. Economic responses to demographic fluctuation. In *Special Study on Economic Change*, Vol. 1, *Human resource demographics: Characteristics of people and policy*. Prepared for the Special Study on Economic Change of the Joint Economic Committee, Congress of the United States. Washington, D.C.: U.S. Government Printing Office.

Demographic Fact Sheet. 1981. The White House Conference on Aging, Washington, D.C.

Every ninth American: An analysis for the Chairman of the Select Committee on Aging. 1982. House of Representatives, 97th Cong., 2nd sess., July. Comm. Pub. No. 97-332. Washington, D.C.: U.S. Government Printing Office.

Information on aging. 1981. *Newsletter of the Institute of Gerontology at Wayne State University 22* (July).

Fisher, David Hackett. 1978. *Growing Old in America*. New York: Oxford University Press.

Nutrition Week. 1983. *Newsletter of the Community Nutrition Institute* (Washington, D.C.) *13* (36).

Soldo, Beth J. 1980. America's elderly in the 1980's. *Population Reference Bureau 35* (4).

Spicker, S.F., K.M. Woodward, and D.D. VanTassel. 1978. *Aging and the Elderly*, Atlantic Highlands, N.J.: Humanities Press.

The 1981 White House Conference on Aging. 1982. *A National Policy on Aging: Final Report*. Washington, D.C.: U.S. Government Printing Office.

2
The Medium and the Messages

Dissemination of information through electronic channels is the most common of mass communication activity. With the popularization of radio in the early 1920s, information not only spread faster through society, but the world seemed to shrink a little. Those living in small communities suddenly became a part of the larger world. Hearing voices that originated in faraway cities and listening to music being played in glamorous big city ballrooms made audiences a part of a larger, more homogeneous group. Reading the newspapers in order to keep informed of national and world affairs began to take second place to listening to news broadcasts. Print media did not disappear, of course; they shifted to fill another information need—that of in-depth, thoughtful analysis of the news—in addition to providing coverage of dramatic events complete with pictures.

Radio brought more than news and big band swing. Radio introduced a new form of entertainment. The radio drama was a specialized format relying on words and sound effects to deliver other worlds to the listener. The listener participated vicariously, stimulated by the words and sounds of the radio drama. Those who were consumers of radio of the 1930s and 1940s will share their recollections of excitement over programs introduced by a squeaking door . . . or the sound of pounding hoofs and a hearty "Hi Ho, Silver!"

In times of national crisis, the entire population tuned the radio for messages from the nation's friends. President Franklin Roosevelt's fireside chats reassured an anxious depression era, prewar population. News print scarcity may have made the newspaper less bulky, but there was no shortage of airtime during the war.

The Second World War interrupted the development for popular consumption of a new electronic communication technology: television. Although developed and made feasible earlier, it was not until the 1950s that the installation of receivers became common in American homes. Prior to that, television was thought of as a sort of novelty, an expensive and exotic toy. Not only were early sets expensive, there was little to watch during the few hours pictures were transmitted. Still, people were fascinated by the prospect of having a machine in the living room that produced moving pictures at the turn of a knob. That the picture was black and white, often grainy and distorted, was a minor inconvenience.

In time, the popularity of television encouraged the creation of more programs and the mass production of receiver sets. With mass production and a competitive market, prices lowered. Eventually, every American family could afford to own a television receiver. From novelty and toy of the wealthy, the television set has become standard equipment in every home, no matter how humble.

The advent of a new and popular technology alters the place of prior existing technologies. Although there are many who cry that the new will destroy the old, this is seldom the case. The introduction of the automobile did not cause horses to become extinct, but it surely did modify the perception of the horse's utility. The introduction of the printing press did not cause pen and ink to have no value, but it did allow for the once penned words to circulate more quickly to a broader audience. Likewise, the mass acquisition of television receivers did not cause manufacturers to stop producing radios, nor programmers to cease producing for radio. But it did take less than 10 years to shift entertainment from radio to television, so that today it is rarely if at all that one can tune a radio to receive drama, comedy, or that one time staple of radio, the soap opera. Such entertainments are all found on television. Radio survives to meet still existing needs and new needs of a changing society. (Radio will be discussed in greater detail in chapter 6.)

The universality of television has made it exceedingly popular with all who wish to influence the public. Politicians have learned it is their most powerful campaign tool, one to be treated with caution and respect. Personalities, performers of all types, authors of books, and a wide range of other self-promoters lay strategies to gain access to television's large audience. Of course, the most obvious of all those who wish to use broadcast channels for gain are the advertisers. Advertising is much maligned, but without it there would be no system of broadcasting as we know it in the United States.

How Broadcasting Works in the United States

In 1982 there were 1,045 television stations on the air. Of these, 774 were commercial stations and 271 were public. Between the two types of broadcast activity more than 5.5 million hours of programming are broadcast annually. (This is based on an assumption of 18 hours for the average commercial broadcast day, and 12 hours for public and educational stations.)

According to Nielsen figures, 43 percent of all television households in the country in 1981 could receive signals of ten or more television stations. (The Nielsen Television Index is a service to the broadcast industry which provides continuing estimates of television viewing, giving the famous "Nielsen ratings," which measure audiences for programs.) This means that there is a broad range of choices in what is to be viewed for most of the audience in the country. When cable service is added to television households, the number of possible stations to choose from grows by a large percentage.

Nielsen further estimated that 81.5 million U.S. households owned at least one television set as of January 1982. Of this number, 86 percent owned color sets. More than half of all television homes own more than one set. Television is everywhere; no longer a novelty, it is integrated into the fabric of our experience.

Television Programming

If we are to understand how social issues are addressed and how television communication can be utilized by nonprofessionals, it is important to understand how programming is created, how it finds its way into the marketplace and how it competes successfully for a place on the schedule.

Television may be thought of as a broadcast system that exists to inform and entertain the population. That notion is true. But it also is a perfect example of private enterprise at work within a democratic society. Television is, first and foremost, a business. The airwaves are public property and some control is exercised over their use. Television, like radio, sends its signals over airwaves. The broadcaster is granted a license by the federal government to send signals over an assigned frequency. Tuning the home set into that frequency, or channel, permits the reception of the signal.

Why should private enterprise want to invest the very large sums of money needed to build, equip, and operate a television station? The answer is that a broadcasting station is allowed by license from the federal government (the Federal Communications Commission) to sell time to advertisers who wish to present their message before the consumer audience. This can be very profitable.

Why should consumers want to purchase a television receiver and spend time being assailed by advertising? They don't—any more than they purchase a newspaper in order to read the advertising only. Consumers may have an interest in what is advertised on television, radio, or in newspapers, but this is secondary to their interest in the entertainment and information that surrounds the advertising. In television and radio, this other fare is "programming," the fare that entices consumers to the channel and captures them for the advertisement.

The fact remains, programming is created for the express purpose of attracting viewers. The Federal Communications Commission (FCC) has traditionally licensed radio and television stations to operate in the "interest, convenience, and necessity" of the public. The easy, and doubtless valid, assumption is that certain information shows broadcast by each station fill that responsibility. Information shows are news and public affairs shows as far as the industry is concerned. However, all shows, regardless of the category label, are information laden.

Other than this somewhat hazy mandate to operate in the public interest, U.S. television is remarkably free of government control. In a society where freedom of speech is highly valued and defended, where private enterprise is the foundation of the economic structure, television content might easily be explored as a reflection of the interests of the public it works to attract.

Of course, such a statement overlooks another interesting argument: that television not only reflects society, it molds it. Proponents of this point of view say that the information individual programs disseminate helps to form public opinion and thereby guide the public's behavior.

The Networks. American television has been dominated by the three big networks: the National Broadcasting Company (NBC), the American Broadcasting Company (ABC), and the Columbia Broadcasting System (CBS). A network is a series of individual stations linked together by technology and legal agreement to carry programming chosen by the network and distributed by it. A network has the advantage of direct control of several stations it owns and operates. These "O&O" stations are located in the major markets and are a source of prime revenue for the networks.

The network makes money by selling advertising time during its network program hours. It buys shows to broadcast which it believes will attract the most viewers to the products advertised. Network affiliates agree to air network programs that it gets at an agreed upon price. The advantage to the affiliate is that it can attract audiences through the superior offerings of network programs and it can sell local time spots for advertising income.

About 90 percent of privately owned stations are network affiliates. The remaining 10 percent of stations are local independent operations. Sometimes these are bound together in a loose syndication or in a smaller network of regional natures. Westinghouse and Metromedia Corporation, with stations in major markets, are two examples of important independent operations.

Independent broadcasters often program original material, even cooperating to fund an occasional miniseries or made-for-television movie. However, their staple fare is usually reruns of programming first introduced on the three major networks. One contribution of the local independent is that it quite frequently focuses more seriously on issues of local nature and may provide easier access to airtime by the public.

The third system to be aware of is public television. Public television is like commercial television in that it is part of a national distributing system. Stations are affiliated through the Public Broadcasting System (PBS) to carry special program offerings. This system was intended to be an alternative information system. It grew out of early educational television, programming reflecting the premise that culture and artistic achievement would not be served adequately through commercial broadcasting channels.

Although free of commercial sponsorship in the strict sense of the word, public broadcasting has been beholden to the public for federal funds through the Corporation for Public Broadcasting and also for funds acquired through private donation. Support is provided by major corporations who do not run advertising messages as are seen on commercial stations, but instead have a discrete message: "The following program was brought to you through a grant from the "Triple X Corporation."

Although it has been possible to persuade public broadcasting stations to attend to social issues, such as the aging society, to a greater extent than commercial broadcasters, it is also true that public broadcasting has always attracted only a small fraction of the viewing audience. Therefore, its influence on the public is assumed to be less than that of the three major commercial networks.

Federal Regulation of Broadcasting

The FCC is the controlling body for regulating broadcasting. Even so, the FCC is mostly concerned with granting licenses and renewing them. It allocates space in the broadcast spectrum and determines the conditions of licensing. The guideline for decision making is the phrase from the Federal Communications Act of 1934 quoted earlier: "the public interest, convenience and necessity." Guarding the public interest necessitates monitoring of broadcast operations. Station licenses are renewed every three years. It is up to a station to demonstrate that it has, indeed, operated in the public interest. This is done through presentation of a log of program operations. Periodic surveys of the public served by a given station are made to determine what are the major concerns of the public. These concerns are then addressed through broadcast activity during the ensuing year. This is known as public service programming. The public service activity may take the form of specials, ongoing public forums, or public service messages informing the community of a given issue or event.

It is in the area of public service that we often see issues of general concern to society given air time. Unfortunately, this programming is most often seen at early morning hours, or on Sunday afternoon. These are times proven to attract fewer numbers of viewers, therefore commanding less revenue from advertisers. Still, the station can demonstrate that it does truly attend to the issues of interest and concern to the public—and no matter that the attention might be given at 6:00 A.M.

Licenses are renewed fairly routinely. Citizen groups might protest the renewal of a license. But usually citizens are unaware or indifferent to license renewals.

Federal agencies are constrained by the principle of free speech from interfering in programming. The government does, however, influence program practice through its investigation of such matters as the effects on children of violence seen on television. Senate hearings are inquiries not wholly welcomed by the broadcast industry.

The industry attempts to monitor and regulate itself through its own organization: the National Association of Broadcasters (NAB). This association formulates and enforces codes of broadcast principles to which broadcasters adhere in setting policy regarding program content. Such self-regulation forestalls intervention by the government. The NAB Television Code is subscribed to by the networks and most independent stations. This Code sets standards regarding controversial issues in program material: violence, sexual behaviors, language, and even commercial length and number within a given time segment.

Even though this is an attempt at self-regulation, there are no provisions for punishment should a member not conform to stated policy. It is left up to what is known at the broadcast standards department in each network to police program content. The department interprets the NAB code and enforces it by reviewing scripts and finished video products. This powerful department within a network can determine what is and is not acceptable for broadcasting.

Program Production

Details of production are usually of interest to the public; even so, there is much misunderstanding of the manner in which a program moves from concept to final airing. Occasionally, programs are produced by stations themselves (this is where we find most public service programming), but most programs are produced by agencies outside the station and even outside the network. It has been ruled that production and distribution of material by the same entity is in violation of antitrust statutes. Therefore, the major part of what we see on television is produced by other sources, known as "production houses."

Production houses are creative entities that supply the dramas, comedies, talk shows, game shows, soap operas—in short, the majority of what we see on television. Production houses, or companies, are quite often film studios. Once known primarily for their production of theatrical features distributed as "movies" throughout the land, film studios now diversify into production of television programs, movies made for television, video cassettes, and a variety of industrial and educational 16-millimeter film projects. Major film studios such as Warner Brothers, Columbia, Fox, Paramount, and Universal all have divisions devoted to television production. In fact, television activity on any one of these lots is likely to be greater than theater film production on any given day.

Most studios today operate as production centers. And although some production personnel may be kept under contract, it is usually for a shorter period of time than was the case when making theater films was a major, full-time industry. Now talent may be under contract at a studio only for the duration of a series or a single project. Independent producers rent necessary space from the major studios for the production of a television program or series.

These independents are in large part responsible for the fare that reaches the television screen. Examples of such operations known to many because of their product include Tandem and TAT ("All in the Family" and a string of iconoclastic masterpieces that changed television content forever) and MTM ("The Mary Tyler Moore Show," which gave a new freedom to the portrayal of modern women). Other outstanding examples, among many, are Filmways, Lorimar, and Aaron Spelling Productions.

All these entities work in the milieu of film making. The contest between television and theater film has diminished in recent years. The industry is united in creating products to entertain the public and creative people move easily between the two media.

What is Produced? Production houses and the networks themselves in some instances produce the complete variety of shows that make up a broadcast schedule. These include talk shows, game shows, and soap operas primarily for daytime programming. "Prime time" is the designation for that part of the day when most people are available to view, from 7:00 to 10:00 P.M., a time that commands higher prices when sold to advertisers. Nighttime programming is the most expensive to produce; because it is prime time, more money is invested in programs for these hours in order to lure the largest possible audience. Prime time programming is usually series programs.

The series is not like a serial, which is what soap opera is. The serial has a continuing cast of characters with a plot that extends from segment to segment, with lack of resolution deliberate at the end of each segment so that the audience will "tune in tomorrow." In contrast, the prime time series is episodic in nature. Each segment, even though it may have the same characters from week to week, is complete unto itself. Each segment is a single story, usually revolving around central characters, but with resolution at the end of each show. "M*A*S*H" is an example of series format. "Dallas" breaks the convention and is more of a prime time soap opera, but the expensive production values are more typical of prime time show budgeting than daytime soaps.

The series stems from an idea usually promoted to networks by a successful production house. Many a production house has begun with one series that has been successful and provided seed money for the evolution of subsequent series. "All in the Family" allowed Tandem Productions to spin off several other successful series for prime time.

Series may be either dramas or comedies. A few generalizations may be made about the genre. Dramas are likely to be adventure shows and to be filmed outside. Comedies are likely to be domestic shows and to be videotaped inside. Men are likely to be given lead roles in the filmed adventure series, while women are seen more often as leads in the domestic comedies. Since a series depends on a succession of viable story ideas to extend its life beyond one season, it is likely that all social issues will at one time or another be tackled as program subject matter.

Movies made for television and miniseries dramatization of a popular novel are more and more often seen on as video fare. These are specially produced and financed activities, often released as theatrical fare overseas.

The products made for distribution via broadcast networks are created by companies who are, in effect, suppliers. They create an idea, a story line, and present this to a network for financing. If the network anticipates that the project is a good bet for placing in its program schedule in a future season, it finances a pilot program. If the project succeeds at pilot level, it will receive financing for series production. It then is distributed through the network. It is the network's task to sell time around the program to sponsors, and, of course, to sell the mass audience on the new program.

Of course, all this process is much more detailed and complicated than is indicated here; nevertheless, this limited description of the process of placing programs that influence millions of viewers on network television allows for a better understanding of why the television broadcasters don't always program the way critics would have it. Television is big business and a lot of people have decision-making powers in any one project.

Program Content

So many systems and people are involved in passing judgment on a program idea that it is a wonder any series reaches the home screen in any semblance of cohesive unity. The regulatory agencies, the networks who are the primary buyers of programs, the marketing staff selling airtime either nationally or locally, and the considerable creative talent pool, all have input into content of a given program.

The term *gatekeeper* has good application in this context. A gatekeeper in information systems is any individual or bureaucracy empowered to stop or permit information flow. Certain decision makers or decision-making bodies can allow or disallow any piece of audio or visual information to be in a given program. We have some understanding now of the motivating interest of the FCC and NAB in monitoring program content. Let us look now at the other individuals and groups that have gatekeeper power and can influence program content.

First, consider that the term *industry* is regularly applied to the business of creating television programming. It is commonly regarded as an industry because there is an end product, just as there is in manufacturing automobiles or some other item for popular consumption. There are those within the business who debate the existence of television as an art form. If it is to be so considered, it must be understood that it is a popular art, a creative endeavor that aims to appeal to a mass audience. Further, it is an activity that results in mass production of a standardized product by profit-minded entrepreneurs solely for the gratification of consumers.

It is easy, therefore, to charge that television fare panders to the lowest common denominator. Critics say that in its concern that no one be offended by program content, television creativity is squelched. A bland product with no real evidence of (disturbing) artistry is the ultimate goal. The successful series is one that entertains all and distresses none. Of course, there are many examples of programs that achieve just exactly that (or at least almost that).

And there are many examples of programs that belie that charge. The history of television programs abounds with artistic, innovative, creative, and successfully unconventional shows. For every mindless, escapist adventure series, there is an example of a program that has sensitively portrayed the human condition.

A successful television series is one that is heavily sponsored; it pays well to all concerned. Another definition of a successful series is one that makes a statement about life and about people that moves and enriches the viewer. It is difficult to do this on a weekly basis, but even within a series there are episodes that reach this height. Because television consumes hours and hours of material, the quality will, of necessity, vary.

Who, then, are some of the gatekeepers responsible for that variable quality of program content? Basically, they are the producers, directors, writers, actors, and a number of technicians. They work together as a team, each contributing talent to the project.

The Producer. Perhaps the most powerful of the gatekeepers is the producer. The producer controls the story development, the casting, and the editing—three major creative elements. It is the on-line producer who has the responsibility for daily operations. An executive producer may be based at one of the major studios, or head an independent production house. He or she may be in overall charge of several shows or series. The producer's power is related to the number of series or movies he or she has on the air. Producers sell the networks on ideas for programs. The idea may come from other sources, sometimes the networks themselves, and sometimes from a creative group of people under contract to the production company.

The working on-line producer is concerned with not only creating a show, but keeping it on the air. In television, a producer may also be the director, or the writer. Producers who serve in such double capacity work very closely with the writer and the director to see that the original concept that won them the contract is carried out successfully.

The producer's power is not absolute. Within the bureaucracy of a network or studio there are officials who can, and do, release an on-line producer from contract when there is disagreement.

The Writer. It is the writer who might most justifiably complain about stifled creativity. The story is basic to the success of a show. Yet, the writer works under a multitude of inhibiting conditions. Writers often feel that their work and creative talents are kept limited. Interviews with writers tend to indicate that by and large they identify themselves as artists. The writer is the educator who often has a message to deliver to the public. When that message is buried inside frivolous program context, the writer can feel thwarted.

Writers are considered wordsmiths; they write dialogue and invent situations. Usually action pivots around the character of a series lead. Series formats that allow for action to occur in a setting where a variety of things can happen (a hospital, for example) offer the writer more leeway than writing for a series where the action is limited to the living room (of the Jefferson family, for example). Regardless of setting, the script for dialogue becomes the property of the production company, and therefore it can be rewritten and changed without permission of the writer. Few if any writers have contractual control over their product. Scripts can be, and are, changed for a number of valid reasons by story editors, producers, network officials, directors, and even the actors.

The Actors. In the broad sense of the word *gatekeeper*, the actor has more power than the writer or director. Yet this is not always understood or acknowledged. The drawing power of a personality often is the key to success of a series. In fact, the series is often thought of by the public as a show of a particular actor. That actor is so identified with the character of the series that he is irreplaceable—thus his power as gatekeeper.

Television creates instant stars. But we must redefine "star" in this medium. The concept of a star performer as was known in the days of powerful motion picture studios does not apply to television. One seldom sees film "stars" appearing on television regularly. When there is a guest appearance by a bona fide film star, much is made of it. Television series stars are simply those people who have lead roles, perhaps title roles in a series. Since series often fade after a season, so do the series "stars."

Still, in a successful series the star provides enormous drawing power. Alan Alda, Mary Tyler Moore, and Carroll O'Connor all exemplify this drawing power. (They may also be examples of performers whom the public will accept in only one role.) These stars put their own stamp on a role, on a show, and thereby exercise control over what can be said or done. Dialogue or actions that are out of character or less than believable simply have no place on the show.

Supporting actors are less powerful. They are not necessarily indispensable to the continuation of the series. They can be written out and replaced with a character of greater drawing power. When a supporting actor evidences great popularity with the public, a spin-off series is often created. The "Maude," "Phyllis," and "Lou Grant" shows are examples of this phenomenon.

Other production people are contributors to the gatekeeper phenomenon. Anyone whose work becomes a part of what is seen and heard has some control. Since they work following the director's dictate, their individual function as gatekeepers is minimal. These people are part of the larger creative team: the camerman, the set designer, the costumer, the makeup artist, the lighting director, and so forth.

The Impact of Television Programs on Society

Understanding how programs are created—or better, *why* they are created, is prerequisite to understanding their impact upon the public.

Remember, the creation of program material is a group effort designed to result in a product that returns high profits. Therefore program decision makers are very concerned about building appeal into program content to attract large audiences.

In the U.S. system of broadcasting it is popularity measured by the "ratings" that determines whether a program remains on the air or not. Hence constant surveillance of the numbers of viewers attracted to a given show is maintained.

It is not size of the audience alone that is of interest to the network or station. It is composition of audience that determines how much can be charged for advertising at any given time. The advertisers compete to draw the 18- to 55-year-old audience, this segment of the population being assumed to have the most per capita income. Each network, and at the local level, each station, competes for the lion's share of the market. The product offered is the means of attracting audiences.

When this product is examined by broadcasters (and it is incessantly examined), point of view is a criterion. The broadcasters evaluate the show's track record for attracting and retaining viewers. They want to know clearly what the elements are within the show that appeal to the viewers. Then they wish to keep those elements intact. This becomes the formula for the show; and the formula isn't tampered with. (Don't disturb a good thing.)

When the product is examined by social scientists (and it is incessantly examined), another point of view prevails. Identifying the element of attraction is pertinent, but equally pertinent is the question: what is the impact? Chapter 5 examines the impact of programming on older viewers and upon all viewers in the context of issues in aging. For now, it is important to look at the impact of television on society in general.

Television and the Family

The Nielsen ratings report on television use in "TV households." The number of hours a receiver is turned on within a home is broken down by age, but it is recognized that a television set may be turned on and viewed by any numbers of different kinds of people. Television within the family is often part of the audiovisual environment. It may be turned on as a routine early in the day and left on for hours. People may wander in and out of the area and pay varying amounts of attention to what is being broadcast. Still, it remains an environmental influence.

More than half of the homes in America are equipped with more than one television set. This means that members of a family might be (and most likely are) viewing at the same time but not together. The television experience may be a shared one, but there is little evidence that it promotes interaction among family members. In fact, there is some speculation that viewing is essentially a solitary experience even when done in the company of others. Some research indicates that the presence of television reduces the time spent in conversation within a family.

The presence of more than one set in a household further fractionates the family. Adults may watch together, but children will watch the set in their separate quarters. (This behavior also reflects the change in family environment and behavior due to the increased affluence of the postwar years.) It seems that it is rare that the different generations come together *because* of television. Some researchers contend that television aids the separation of adults and children within a family. The television is well known as the electronic baby-sitter. The consumer protection group called ACT (Action for Children's Television) monitors content of children's programs and publishes guidelines for viewing. The parent–teachers associations and other similar organizations encourage parent–child interaction about what is seen on television.

The issue of violence in television programming and its effects on children has occupied the attention of behaviorists for years. Books are written on the subject, and it has commanded the attention of Congress. Extensive investigations have included numerous laboratory experiments. The conclusions of such research as well as less formal observations are mixed. On the one hand there is some evidence that viewing of televised violence results in an increased likelihood of aggressive behavior of children; on the other hand there is no conclusive evidence that such viewing contributes to criminal acts by the young adult the child becomes.

The more alarming notion is that the presence of televised violence witnessed by viewers over a period of time may contribute to a desensitization to real violence. When what is seen on television becomes accepted as a norm, then social attitudes, opinion, and behaviors do indeed alter to adjust to the new norms. This has implications for expectations about families, about marriage, about work, sex roles, and age roles.

Television and Sex Role Socialization

Television exigencies seldom permit accurate, factual portrayals of all the people who populate the parade of programs. Consider that there are small segments of time in order to tell a story. Thirty, 60, or 90 minutes is the time available to tell a story. How much of this time can be given to the delineation of character? When the character is the story (for example, "The Autobiography of Miss Jane Pittman"), then the viewer is offered deeper insight into the human being. Usually, however, the character is established quickly so that the action can begin. This leads to something less than the development of fully rounded characters.

In a series format it is necessary for the lead characters to be given identity early on. And this identity is a sort of shorthand for easy viewer identification: Archie is a lovable bigot; Edith is a cheerful, forbearing mate; Dr. Welby is the conscientious and caring hospital administrator; and so on. The series takes this simple premise about a character and hangs many a plot on it. Once the lead character has established a personality with the viewers, the role can be played with consistency while the introduction of guest players in weekly episodes provides new character interest.

Still, the audience does not have time to be given more information than it needs about a given character within a given situation. The multidimensional and sometimes contradictory nature of people is not useful in telling a story. Such character conventions are not the creation of television. As long as stories have been told and dramas have been played, characters have been restricted to the personality aspects needed in the drama.

In the world as depicted by television, this necessary restriction leads to sex role stereotyping. Especially restricted in definition are supporting roles. Numbers of people who must walk in and out of the thread of comedy or drama must do so with only superficial characterization. This results in what is termed "stock characters": the butlers, schoolteachers, old maids, Irish cops, rural bumpkins, and on and on, who enrich the texture of the drama, but who give skewed information about particular identities.

Viewers for whom television supplies role models may receive a distorted view of what it means to be a man or woman of any age in today's society. One of the major findings of all research in this area is that women appear about one-third as often as do men on the screen. Women have been appearing in lead roles in recent years, reflecting their increased status in the world of work. The behavior of female television characters transmits a special set of messages. Women are most often seen in comedy and family dramas, soap operas, and, of course, in commercials. They are rarely seen in adventure and crime drama, except as adjuncts to male heroes. When they are present, they are often victims. Female characters appear even less frequently in the world of Saturday morning cartoons.

Women carry the responsibility for marriage and family on television. Men are infrequently given these dimensions of life because it serves plot better to have men portrayed as active, virile, struggling, fighting, winning. Women are more often passive, seductive, the prize to be gained, and of course, the possessors of sensitivity and emotions of love.

Men demonstrate needs for physical support and women appear to be the ones needing emotional support. It seems also that it is men who give physical support and women who give emotional support.

Sex role stereotyping is clear and persistent. This is one of the most obvious examples of the efficiency of writing characters who are uncomplicated. The viewer does not want to be confused by the unexpected. Caring men and hard-driving women may exist in the real world, but they do not have much utility in the world of television.

In one study of the choices of sixth grade children of what television characters they "would like to be when they grow up," 27 percent of the girls chose a male character. No boys crossed over to choose a female character. This may reflect the predominance of males in the television population. It may also reflect the comparative desirability of male traits in the value systems promoted on by television.

Television and the World of Work

It is unavoidable that work roles be considered extensions of sex roles, since the two are intertwined. In the world portrayed by television, there are jobs that men do and jobs that women do. That law is seldom altered, with one exception: Women are given men's jobs in medicine and law enforcement (two major acceptable careers on television), though men are never given jobs of women.

By and large it is the male characters in the world of television who hold the most desirable jobs, who do the most interesting work. This is explained by the nature of plotting in program content. Most programs are action oriented, conflict oriented. Although there are women who work where such activity exists, they only occasionally appear in such jobs on television. Men are more likely to be in law enforcement, while the women are cast as lawbreakers or victims. Authority figures are usually male: lawyers, businessmen, doctors. The women play supporting roles: clerks, secretaries, nurses, entertainers.

Other messages sent to viewers are that the man has the most prestigious standing in the community of work. He is the chief of staff, senior administrator, supervisor. And those he supervises are more likely to be female. Further, men are more likely to be the order givers and women the followers. The exception to this is during daytime programming, where women are more likely to be giving orders or to have dominant positions in the social structure.

Again and again it is made clear that there are two worlds: the real one and the world of television. It is in the area of work that this is readily apparent. A division of the labor force depicted on television would show that about one-third employees are at the professional and managerial level. The situation is even more distorted in daytime programming. Here 62 percent of the females on the shows and 89 percent of the males are in the top three status occupational categories. In the real world only 19 percent of the women and 30 percent of the men have this status.

Television does not offer many job opportunities to its characters. It virtually ignores low-pay, low-status jobs, even though in the real world such jobs are held by the majority of viewers. It would appear that many characters on television make their living in health care or law enforcement. Even those who are cast as criminals are likely to demonstrate age bias, being more often than not mature rather than young—whereas statistics indicate that the majority of criminals are under 20.

Television as a Socializing Instrument

Television can and does play a strong role in socialization of its audience. Children are not the only ones influenced in their perception of the world because of their television viewing. All viewers are to varying degrees given specially formulated and arranged presentations of reality. J. Saltzman (1983) writes:

> Some of us realize that everything we see on television, from news to documentaries to dramas to situation comedies to soap operas, is based on someone's point of view or someone's creative concept. Some of us also realize that most of the images we hold of the world come from television: these images may be reinforced by other media and by friends, family, and teachers, but it is television that gives millions of Americans their basic idea of reality. (p. 43)

This brings us back to the recognition of the gatekeeper's function and power. It is the gatekeeper who is the "someone" referred to by Saltzman. This someone—writer, director, producer, station executive—has an individual point of view to guide his or her interpretation of reality. He or she is also constrained by budget, time, and a myriad of inhibitions that prohibit an accurate portrayal of reality.

Even if the someone were to portray reality with absolute accuracy, no one would watch what was produced. Reality gives us too much information to fit into a story. So only that information which is pertinent, and which is appealing to the audience, and which is interesting to the creative talent producing the story is used. As a result, the viewer is given a distorted version of reality.

Television is not the only influence in the process of socializing. After all, we know there are other jobs than law enforcement and medicine. In fact, many of us may not be able to count even one member of either of those two professions among our circle of acquaintances. And we all encounter men and women who are mixes of those traits we identify simplistically as masculine or feminine. We experience family configurations that are many times more complex than those we observe on television. So there is major input from many sources into individual and group socialization.

We experience this, know this, yet television continues to be a major source of ideas about what life is—or should be. We want our heroes and heroines to be more beautiful than *we* are, live more exciting lives, have more money, and experience greater emotional heights. Television, after all, is the most convenient means of escape. No longer is the romantic or adventure novel the only path to entertainment away from our daily routines. No longer must we plan time to drive to a local theater for an hour and a half of escape from working at the shop or coping with the children. Now we need only walk across the room, punch a button, dial a channel to have a neatly packaged hour of escape to Hawaii or some similarly exotic locale where we can look at beautiful people involved in adventures we would never dream of encountering while at the shop or with the children.

So why should there be any concern about such an innocent pastime? What harm is done by such relaxation? Mightn't it even be therapeutic—giving us relief from daily pressures? These are good arguments, and probably true as far as they go, but let's consider something more basic to an understanding of life's experiences.

Television as Communication Medium

Television is one means of communication; it is part of a system of mass communication that facilitates the flow of information through our society. A review of communication theory, and especially of mass communication models will be helpful in establishing that television must be taken seriously as a major element of socialization.

Communications as a discipline is an aspect of the behavioral sciences. Communications incorporates thinking from linguistics, sociology, psychology, and physiology. Add to this mathematical and electronic engineering sciences, and you have communication pushed into the new world of electronics—certainly a part of television technology.

Communication is a social experience, and as such is governed by too few absolutes. Humans act in uncertain, vague, and nonspecific ways. It cannot be assumed that people are programmed as are machines to perform in absolutely predictable and constant ways. However, communication theorists have attempted to make models of the experience to help us understand the process. Since this understanding is preliminary to understanding mass communication, a brief review is pertinent.

Communication Theory

Basic links in the communication chain are labeled *sender, message,* and *receiver.* These are three elements necessary to be in place for communication to occur. Communication is the transfer of information. The information is not so much within the message, but within the sender. In order to get that information into the recipient, the sender must encode the message into symbols. The idea inside the sender's head must be encoded into signals, a form that can be transmitted. The receiver is able to decode the symbols. If both sending and receiving is done successfully, the idea has passed from one to the other.

The common symbol used in human communication is the word. The most common manner for the transmission of words is through spoken conversation. In fact, this is the most successful mode of information transmission. The one-to-one experience has the highest chance of successful completion of the encode–decode act. This basic communication experience is helped by nonverbal communication: body language, pauses, emphasis, varying degrees of volume, and so forth.

Ideas may also be communicated in other ways. They can be encoded into print. That is what is happening now. These ideas about communication and television as a socializing agent are being encoded into printed words by me, the author. You, the reader, are now decoding. Assuming that the sender (writer) is choosing the best words, and that the reader (recipient) brings enough skills to the experience, information is exchanged.

Ideas may also be encoded into audio and audiovisual modes such as records, tapes, videocassettes, and film. When ideas are thus encoded, it is said that they are *mediated*; that is, something has intervened between the sender and receiver to carry the message. Thus "media," the paths or channels for communication, becomes a better understood word. The mediated message is removed from the speaker through coding it into a form other than the spoken word. Now the recipient must decode without that body language and other messages from the original sender.

Pause to consider that the communication experience is something more than the three elements given above. There is a fourth link: feedback, or response. Harold Lasswell's classic communication model (1972) involves sender, message, receiver, and response: who says what to whom with what effect.

When we are involved in transmission of information through conversation, we can measure effectiveness quickly through noting response. If we are not understood the first time, we can modify the message, repeat it in several ways until we are understood. Most messages go beyond the immediate stimulus–response model; some messages are intended to indoctrinate people with philosophical values to guide their behavior. Response to such messages is not measured immediately, but from time to time when individuals are placed in situations where values are tested. Much of mass media communication falls into the category of value-building.

In mass communication, the channel or medium chosen to transmit the message becomes an intervening variable. The channel intervenes, comes between, the two parties: sender and receiver. The experience of direct communication is lessened and immediate feedback is not measured. In mass media communication, each element is composed of several factors. As shown in this chapter, the sender is not just one person, it is a team. The channel, when it is television, provides a range of audio and visual messages at one time, and the recipient is not one unique individual, it is a mass of people with as many differences as there are similarities.

In 1948 sociologist Bernard Berelson wrote that "some kinds of communication on some kinds of issues, brought to the attention of some kinds of people . . . under some kinds of condition, have some kinds of effects." (p. 184) This tells us that there is no certain and proven method of guaranteeing that the information transmitted via television is sent or received in the exact manner any one of the participants anticipates. Knowing that misunderstanding occurs frequently and easily in one-to-one communication, it is no wonder that misunderstanding is likely to be compounded in mediated communication.

There are too many variables operating in too many combinations and in unison in the mass media communication process. Therefore, it is not possible to create an absolute model that guarantees that sending message A will evoke the desired response, the anticipated message B. If this were so, if there were a set of scientific absolutes about communication, then advertisers, politicians, and playwrights would not face the creative challenges they do.

Most communication is persuasive in nature. Its intent is to persuade someone to accept a point of view and act on it. In advertising we are aware that this intent is overt and there is little subtlety. However, there is a large body of communication which is also persuasive and which contributes to the building of value systems within a society. It is the contribution of television to the structuring of commonly held values that interests social scientists. For the values held by people determine their behavior.

Social Values Communicated by Television

In many ways American society has become homogenized. One can travel about the country and find the same store fronts in every city and village. There are almost no regional differences in dress. The work pants that once characterized cowboys and ranchers are now ubiquitous and even high fashion. Increased mobility results in a blending of speech patterns so that it is more and more difficult to know someone's origin by speech.

While there are a number of reasons for this, mass communication is a major contributor to social homogenization. When the majority of people are subjected to the same messages, they are going to hold similar information. When these messages are strong and are repeated, then the majority of people are going to begin to think alike about the subject, and if action is called for, or is encouraged, they are going to act alike.

After all, this is the basis for thinking that a message promoting the virtues of a product will make masses of people believe in those virtues—and, most important to television's sponsors, purchase the product. This is the basis for thinking that if a politician gets enough media exposure for his or her campaign platform, masses of people will understand that platform, share the beliefs espoused, and elect the politician.

At another level—one more subtle and pervasive—television is also successful at creating values. It is still more successful in promulgating established values, reinforcing commonly held social beliefs. A value system is a complex, multidimensional structure. It involves the individual ego, the self-image. It is what we believe; therefore, it determines how we act.

Mass media messages are screened through the individual's value system. That which threatens it, offering potential damage to the ego or self-concept, is rejected. Broadcast communicators, knowing this, do not intentionally send messages that threaten the collective value system. They send messages most likely not to be screened out.

The result is a series of messages that tend to reinforce some fairly basic American values. Often the social values reflected in the subject matter of television programs may seem to be for the general good. When looked at closely, however, some disadvantages to some segments of the population are seen.

Social Values in the Fictive World of Television

Self-reliance. Perhaps more than any other concept, self-reliance is core to the American identity of self. In the beginning, this country depended on the adventurous, the self-reliant, to open up the wilderness for settlement. Our folklore has glorified those who settled along the eastern shores, blazed trails into the woods, crossed the mountains, plowed meadows and plains for farming, laid rails, created new businesses, survived against the odds. Such character attributes as independence, endurance, stamina, and self-sufficiency have become admired components of self-reliance. We have come to believe these are the attributes of success in business and, indeed, in life. Those early settlers and pioneers were, for the most part, young people. They were adventurers, and even desperados, who immigrated to this country for a new start. They had little choice but to be self-reliant. There were no developed social support systems.

Independence has been our national byword. We sought it from the beginning; we value it and fight for it as a nation. On the personal level, it is demonstrated in our need to take care of ourselves, be without obligation to a stronger source. We think less of ourselves when we must turn to charity, or even to others, for help.

The fictive heroes and heroines of television exemplify this value. The truly strong succeed by their own efforts and over terrible odds. We are given them as models for being. We learn that in order to be valued in this society, the individual must strive for independence; he or she must be self-reliant.

The Human as Commodity. Work, what we do to earn a living, how much we do, where we do it, what the title of our job may be, and how much we are paid are all indicators of our value in society. It hasn't always been so. In the early days of this country each person had the opportunity to exercise self-reliance in a very basic way; the pioneers acquired land and raised what they needed to survive on that land. In time, as the country became industrialized and urbanized, there was less opportunity to own land and make a living from it, and there was less need to do so. Surplus productivity allowed foodstuffs to be mass marketed. Industry was growing and it needed workers; the need was filled by waves of immigrants, many of whom had never tilled the soil in their homeland. People now could market themselves to a buyer who would pay for their skills, or strength. Rather than produce their own food, clothing, and shelter, people could work for others and purchase those necessities. The higher the price they could get for their labor, the better quality and more quantity of goods they could purchase.

Thus working became a value indicator. Human beings marketed themselves. Leisure time meant time when there was no work to do. Leisure became somewhat of an embarrassment, so that even today many workers approach retirement in some panic because it means a loss of value in the society.

The vocation of television's lead characters—especially male—often supplies the raison d'être for the program as well as the character. Even when characters are not shown often in the environment of their work, it is alluded to and certainly the financial gain from that work is made evident. We learn through television that in order to be valued in this society, the individual must be employed in "meaningful" and often highly recompensed work.

Control over Nature. Associated with the American concern for self-reliance is the concern for dominating the environment. There is a historical assumption that human beings must master their environment. This is not solely an American concern; it has been a human concern from the beginning of time. As humans mastered the elements, they survived. We have gone far beyond utilization of fire, water, and air to give us fuel and power. We now wrestle with elements of overwhelming magnitude. Politically, the position is that the nation that controls certain vital elements controls the world.

There is the perception that the universe is mechanistic and therefore is controllable. Humans overcome nature and structure their own environment. When nature demonstrates its capriciousness, humans overcome the natural disasters and rise above it all. They are even moving into outer space.

The struggle to master the environment is a valued dramatic device. The strong succeed. There has even been an assumption in television programming that people can go beyond making the world better technically, they can make themselves, the human race, better; witness the bionic man, woman, boy and even dog of a few seasons back. We learn through television that in order to be valued in this society the individual must be able to control nature—and by extension, natural beings, the human body and mind.

Physical Beauty. That concept of control or mastery extends to the individual. Personal physical appeal, sometimes confused with worth, is measured on a value scale of attractiveness. It is basic to television's attractiveness to the public that it offers opportunity to see other human beings whom we are encouraged to believe typify our society's ideal of beauty. The countless commercials promoting physical appeal further emphasize that value. Television advertising tries to persuade viewers that serving a certain brand of coffee or using a particular household cleaner will make them more attractive, that driving a particular car, wearing a certain perfume, or drinking a certain wine can contribute to making them more beautiful and desirable.

Countless models of youth and beauty populate the airways. The message is too obvious: youth and beauty are combined so that one is not possible without the other. There is a double standard, of course; women are more highly valued for their beauty than are men, and they disappear from programs when they move too far beyond 30. Men have been promoted in recent seasons as being valued as much for their good looks as for their athletic ability. For men, physical attractiveness in films and television lingers longer. Men are cast as leads in television, and probably in real life, for longer periods of time than are women. Their aging female counterparts, however, are relegated to selling floor polish and coffee to younger housewives. We learn through television that in order to be valued in this society, the individual must be physically attractive (and we also learn that is a purchasable status).

Future Orientation. Finally, we accept that a major value in American life is a trust and faith in the future. This country has its roots in future-building. The purpose of today is to prepare for tomorrow. In our value system tomorrow is going to be better—if we make it so. The acquisition of material advantages is worked for; plans are laid and carried out for education, for business expansion, and for retirement. These future-oriented activities help to give purpose to the present.

Television promotes next year's model. The newest, the best, the most improved are all presented to a consumer population that begins to suspect that if yesterday's acquisition has less value, therefore, its owner has less value. This kind of message works on a still subtler level. Those who have value in television program plots are those who have something important at stake in the future: a romance, a business win, a birth, a major gain of some sort. Those interesting enough to be the concern of television drama are those with a lot of future.

Through these quite conscious ways television programs promote the values with which the public feels most comfortable. There is a reinforcement for the familiar and for rationales that structure our behaviors. This list of social value systems could be extended, but enough is presented here to make the point: Attitudes (reflective of value systems) that fit with long-established cultural precepts are reinforced by television programming.

If the human being is a commodity, if society cares for the individual so long as he is profitable for the group, if being physically attractive is basic to being accepted socially, and if being dependent on few, if any, systems or people is the ultimate in value, then many people are going to be social rejects. All these precepts are surely disadvantageous to the elderly, who, in general, are dependent, have reduced or no market value, are not young and firm, have a limited future, and obviously have not controlled nature.

References

Berelson, B. 1948. Communication and public opinion. In W. Schramm, ed., *Communication in Modern Society.* Urbana: University of Illinois Press, pp. 167–85.

Bogart, L. 1956. *The Age of Television.* New York: Frederick Ungar.

Cantor, M.G. 1982. The organization and production of prime-time television. In D. Pearl, L. Bouthilet, and J. Lazar, eds., *Television and Behavior.* Vol. 2: *Technical Reviews.* DHHS Publication No. (AOM) 82-1196. Rockville, Md.: National Institute of Mental Health.

Cantor, M.G. 1982. *Prime-Time Television: Content and Control.* Beverly Hills, Calif.: Sage.

Comstock, G.A. 1980. *Television in America.* Beverly Hills, Calif.: Sage.

Comstock, G.A, S. Chaffee, N. Kautzman, M. McCombs, and D. Roberts. 1980. *Television and Human Behavior.* New York: Columbia University Press.

Davis, R. 1980. *Television and the Aging Audience.* Lexington, Mass.: Lexington Books.

Davis, R.H. 1982. Television and the elderly: A search for values. *Media and Values* 19:8–9.

Gerbner, G., L. Gross, N. Signorielli, and M. Morgan. 1980. Aging with television: Images on television drama and concepts of social reality. *Journal of Communication* 30(1):37–47.

Greenberg, B.S. 1982. Television and role socialization: An overview. In D. Pearl, L. Bouthilet, and J. Lazar, eds., *Television and Behavior.* Vol. 2: *Technical Reviews.* DHHS Publication No. (AOM) 82-1196. Rockville, Md.: National Institute of Mental Health.

Katzman, N. 1972. Television soap operas: What's been going on anyway? *Public Opinion Quarterly* 36:200–12.

Lasswell, H. 1972. The structure and function of communication in society. In W. Schramm and D.F. Roberts, ed., *The Process and Effects of Mass Communication.* Urbana: University of Illinois Press, pp. 84–89.

Miller, M., and B. Reeves. 1972. Dramatic TV content and children's sex-role stereotypes. *Journal of Broadcasting* 20:35–50.

Nielson, A.C., Co. 1982. '82 *Nielson Television* (1982 Nielson Report). New York.

Saltzman, J. 1983. Fact vs. fiction. *Emmy* 4(4):42–7, 118–19.

3
Television's Image of Age

Analyzing any aspect of television content is like analyzing a Rorschach ink blot: Different things are visible to different viewers. In the last decade or more, many researchers have been occupied with counting numbers of representatives of ethnic and racial groups appearing on television. The portrayal of women as characters in scripted drama and comedy, as well as their appearance on news and public affairs shows has been well analyzed. Children, blue collar workers, executives, and teenagers have been counted and their roles analyzed. Questions have been asked about the honesty of males as models on the myriad of action and adventure shows. Criticism has been leveled at producers of "jiggle" shows because of the way they have exploited young women. The image of older Americans has been a concern of sociologists, too. Especially during the last decade television's projected image of this group has come under scrutiny.

Because television is credited with the portrayal of role models of all sorts, its critics are concerned about the honesty of those role models. What are people learning about certain professions, about being male or being female, about being a young person, middle-aged person, or an old person? There is legitimate cause for concern about the television's image of growing old and being old.

Television is not the only socializing agent. We learn about professions, ethnic groups, cultures, the sexes, and various age groups through a variety of experiences. First-hand, primary experiences have the strongest impact, of course. When we know someone well who is different from ourselves, we have a certain understanding of that individual and his or her differences. Since we are not able to have primary experiences that cover all areas, we have to rely on secondary experiences. We may not know, for example, a female immigrant from a third world culture. But we can read about such a person and become acquainted with her life in her home country and the travails of immigration to this society. In so doing we gain an increase of understanding. Likewise, our understanding increases even more so when we are exposed to such a person and are given insights into her life through a film drama or in a public affairs report on television.

Once again, these are secondary experiences. They are mediated experiences, depending on print or moving image channels to deliver the information. Although they do not have the impact of primary experiences, they are invaluable in their ability to educate. A large percentage of our perception of the world comes through mediated experiences.

As children we may have been told stories that gave us an idea of the larger world. That those stories might have misinformed us is something that we dealt with as we matured. We continue to get information about things outside our immediate experience from other persons. Often our world is enlarged through reading fiction and nonfiction. More than likely, however, an important source of information continues to be films and television.

Depending on our generational identity, a surprisingly large number of hours of our lives have been spent with television. If we were adults when television became commonplace, we have an entirely different frame of reference about the world than if we were born after 1950 and grew up with television as an established part of the home environment and an accepted source of knowledge.

Preschoolers spend a great percentage of their day with television. As they move into a larger society, that time diminishes. As the child matures and more activities occupy him, television consumes even less time. The individual in his late teens and early 20s is less interested in viewing television than at any other time in life. He is simply too busy doing interesting things outside the home. He returns to television following marriage and with the advent of children.

So those early, very impressionable years allow for hours and hours of instruction about what the world is like and what people are like. The conditioning to accept the world of television as a reflection of the real world happens early and remains strong.

Television has demonstrated time and again its power to influence, to set standards, to create models for being, to set norms for evaluating behavior, appearance, and social worth. When we look into the world of television to find information about aging, guidelines for our own evolution, or instruction on how to be old in this society, what do we discover?

Old People on Television

Frequency of Appearance

The world of television displays a demographic profile that reflects its structure. No people appear in that television world who are purposeless. Each person on camera has a reason for being there: The plot calls for it. This is true in public affairs shows as well as series comedies and dramas. This is true in documentary specials and movies of the week. It is true as well in news panels.

The population of the television world reflects the values of that world. In addition, the length of time any one person (or type, or age) appears on screen also reflects the values of the special world of television.

So it is possible to do a content analysis of programming which is actually a head count. A census can be taken of the population of television's fictive world. Government census counts allow us to know how many men, women, and children and of what ages populate the real world. Does the world of television reflect the demographic facts accurately? Numbers of studies have made such counts, and the answer is a resounding *no*.

How Is Age Determined?

Before counts are taken there has to be a set of criteria established for the designating of on camera characters as old. Researcher Mary Cassata directed a content analysis of thirteen daytime television serials for a two-week period during the summer of 1978. Characters were determined to be older when content defined them as being age 55 or older, they were seen as being the eldest of at least three generations, a grandparent, a resident of an institution for the aged, a retired person, or any character who *appeared* elderly. If the actual age of the actor or actress playing the character was known, that, too, was taken as an indicator that the character was old (if, of course, the actual age was "old" according to the researchers).

In 1981 Joyce Elliott did a similar survey of daytime television— specifically soap operas. She monitored thirteen daytime television serial dramas over a four-week period. For this study an older adult was distinguished by being "about" 65 years old or older, a judgment made on the basis of appearance. In addition, old people were in roles of great-grandparent, parent of a child 30 years old or older, or designated as retired. If the character had lines that self-described him or her as older, or if others described him as older, he was tabulated as being old. Again, if the actual age of the actor or actress was known, this qualified for inclusion in the old category.

Obviously a certain amount of subjectivity is employed on the part of coders on such a survey. In most such studies, coders are carefully coached so that there is consensus on their image of old on television. Often, more than one coding person is assigned to view the same program. One acts as a check against the other.

The Body Count

Several studies have counted old people in various segments of the broadcast day.

Aronoff analyzed data pertaining to age of 2,741 characters in prime time network television drama sampled between 1969 and 1971. From this large number of characters, Aronoff identified 98 older males and 36 older females. Each comprised 4.9 percent of the sample for their sex. It is interesting to note that of the total (television) population, men (regardless of age) numbered 2,017 and women (regardless of age) numbered 724.

Harris and Feinberg gathered data on frequency and type of characterization of the elderly. They used a four-hour random sampling of four time segments during the broadcast day. The programs were selected in a random basis over a six-week period from all seven days of the week and from all three networks. A total of 312 characters were observed and rated. Of these, 24 were classified as being between age 60 and 70. Only two were identified as over 70.

Using a much smaller sample, Peterson analyzed 30 network half hours of prime time in 1972. She counted all people who were known to be at least 65 and who were themselves on the show. In addition, she counted those playing roles she judged to be at least 65. She found 32 people, three of whom were women. This amounted to 13 percent of the television population reviewed.

Ansello analyzed 238 half-hour segments of programs as well as commercials in 1977 and 1978. He found that 6 percent of this population could be identified as elderly.

Commercials are a special genre and will be discussed later. But it is interesting to note that of the sample of 100 television commercials Francher looked at in 1973, only two included an older character.

In 1974 Northcott did a content analysis of prime time drama on the three networks. All role portrayals lasting two minutes or longer were analyzed. This amounted to 464 role portrayals. Of these only seven, or 1.5 percent appeared to be over 65 years of age.

Children's Saturday morning programs have also contributed to these population surveys: Gerbner's group identified only 1.4 percent of all weekend daytime characters being 65 or older. In 1973 Richard Levinson found 4 percent of the human characters in Saturday cartoons to be old. Also looking at cartoons, Bishop and Krause found 7 percent of the characters to be elderly.

Greenberg, Korzenny, and Atkin surveyed for character age (among other variables) in programming in the fall of 1975, 1976, and 1977. Those over age 65 comprised 4 percent of the characters in the first year,

3 percent of the second, and 2 percent of the third. This group analyzed more than 3,500 characters over the three years of the study. Barely 100, or 3 percent, were in the old age bracket.

In the Cassatta study of soap operas, 365 characters were monitored. Of these, 58, or 15.9 percent, were judged to be 55 or older. The majority of these older characters (55 percent) were judged to be in their 60s.

Finally, Elliott's study of daytime soap opera (1981) analyzed 723 characters. Fifty-eight people were determined to be age 60 and above; this constitutes 8 percent of the study population. Estimated as 12.6 percent of the study population were characters who seemed to be in late middle age, age 50 to 59.

Implications

What do these findings tell us? It is obvious that the numbers of older people appearing on television do not correlate with the numbers of older people in society. Of course, there is no rule or regulation that says there should be a correlation between fiction and reality. Indeed, such an "equal rights" regulation would cause havoc with the various program decision makers, who would then be forced into contriving plots that included percentages of all kinds of people and all kinds of ages. It would be foolish.

The problem, however, with skewed distribution of the elderly rests in the awareness that what is important in our society finds its way onto television. And if an issue or a person appears on television, then by virtue of appearance alone, the issue or person becomes important. When increasing age equals increasing invisibility on television, the message is clear: To be old is to be without importance.

When the elderly are seldom seen on television, this may translate into their seldom being seen in society. Viewers are sensitized to the prevalence of certain physical types as their success on television encourages proliferation of these types. This is evident in the real world, where people strive to resemble the currently popular model. For example, at the height of the popularity of a TV adventure serial, "Charlie's Angels," one could see Farah Fawcett lookalikes on every street. When there are few if any older persons on television, they might, in fact, be on the streets in significant numbers, but remain unseen.

Women on Television

It appears that women are more likely to be seen on television if they are in their 20s, and to be seen less frequently with each succeeding decade.

The situation differs with males, most of whom are seen in the general age span of 35 to 49. About 20 percent of men on television are in the over-50 category. Content studies identify less than 10 percent females in this category. When a count is made of persons over age 65, this population is more than 90 percent male. We know this does not represent distribution in the real world.

Gerbner's studies show that the likelihood is that older men on television will have a higher level job and a higher socioeconomic status than younger ones. In general, most depiction of the elderly in scripted shows is not that of poverty. In contrast, however, the emphasis in public affairs specials on the elderly is too often on the poor and severely deprived.

Gerbner also finds that the elderly tend to be shown as more comical, stubborn, eccentric, and foolish than other characters. They are more likely to be treated with disrespect. The latter is more true in prime time programming than daytime serials.

Because of the generally negative portrayal of older women, and especially because of their near invisibility on television, several concerns have been raised. Peterson's study indicated that one might expect to see an older man on television every 22 minutes, but an old woman would be seen only every 4 to 5 hours. Gerbner's content analysis shows older women to be in general: silly, stubborn, sexually inactive, and eccentric. And in crime dramas they are the ones killed, almost never the ones doing the killing.

These illustrations of woman's place in the world of television reinforce the generally accepted notion that woman's place in the real world is basically one of romantic interest. Further, it is made clear on television that woman as a romantic partner is more desirable when young than at any other time. In fact, women are portrayed with increasing sexlessness as they age, while men are often attributed enhanced sexual allure. This male attractiveness is based in their having been ascribed power. Men are usually, if not always, depicted as somewhat older and usually smarter in the ways that count than their female companions. The female, according to Beck's 1978 study of older women in television programming, is usually 10 years younger than the lead male, and becomes increasingly unimportant to the plot as she ages. Her role becomes one of adoring attendant upon the "rocking chair sage," or she is cast as a nag.

Past female characters who are "old" come to mind. "Maude," who carried her own show, and Edith Bunker, cheerful mate to the insufferable Archie, were highly visible models of middle age. But what kind of women were these as images to copy for young women who had been listening to the rhetoric of the women's movement for the last 10 years?

The grandmother generation fared no better. In past years, Grandma Walton epitomized the patient, enduring, faithful companion, but other older women and mothers-in-law were too often silly to the point of ludicrousness.

In more recent television series the picture of the matriarch has been presented on several series. They seem to fill the role of commentator on the events in the lives of their offspring. They do a lot of warning, shaking of the head, and being generally critical.

This sort of older woman is seen more often in daytime programming. Also the studies of this genre find that the older woman is treated much more favorably than on prime time drama. Although older women may be shown in conventional role behaviors, that is, as housewives or in nonauthoritarian jobs, they are portrayed with respect and sympathetically. Both Downing and Elliott in their extensive studies of older characters on soap operas report that the women tend to be perceived by the coders as being more attractive than people of similar age in the general public. (Being "more attractive" would seem to be a requisite for all performers on soap opera, if not television in general.) Elliott also noted that the greater percentage of older females were widowed, which was not the case for the older males who appeared in the serials. Further, the older females tend to live in family settings and to be from the middle to upper classes.

Elliott's soap opera older women were also cast as official and informal advisors. Their male counterparts were authorities in the world of business, so their advising was seen as official. Although older women in these programs tended to have closer friendships with men than with women, their romantic involvement was nil compared to that of younger women. The older women were more likely to be nurturing than were the older men; again, this is true of men and women in general in the fictive world of television.

Implications

What we learn about behaviors of older men and women in television program content is very much like what we learn about other adult males and females on television drama. Women appear less often and in more passive roles. Men hold the power and are active in physical, political, and business senses of the word. Men tend to have interesting and productive roles in the drama of life much longer than do women. For the most part, women act as useful accoutrements to males. They provide romantic interest, and when young they populate the television world in great numbers. They tend to disappear after age 30, except in soap operas, where their numbers diminish after age 50.

Perhaps once again television reinforces commonly held and there-fore comfortable stereotypes. The way to behave as males and the way to behave as females is shown over and over again. This cannot help but influence all viewers as they attempt to be socially acceptable persons.

Young people who want to know what the next age stage of life is like and what models there are to pattern themselves after may have some troubles adjusting to harsher realities as they find that human be-ings are not as simplistically put together as their television heroes and heroines. If they should be curious about what life is like for those in mature adulthood and old age, they will get some input about older males (that is, age 40 and up), but they will have little or no useful infor-mation about older women.

Perhaps the most disturbing implication to be drawn from tele-vision's presentation of older role models, or rather the lack of role models, is that a disadvantageous stereotype of women is reinforced. As women are instructed to deny their own aging and attempt to create the il-lusion of youthful appearance and behaviors, they are setting themselves up for some depressing confrontations in later life. As men are conditioned to see older women as second-class citizens through their portrayals on television, they will have difficulty being supportive of the unavoidable consequences of aging in their mates, and in themselves.

Images of Health and the Elderly

In the world of television, poor health is often more interesting to the plot than is good health. There are numbers of shows wherein the ac-tion is centered in hospitals. The sick person will be the center of atten-tion. In daytime programming health problems often provide a major source of drama. Not all these ill people in both day and night program-ming are old people. Harris and Feinberg's study showed that a signifi-cant percentage of older characters demonstrate moderate to high physical activity. In this study 14 percent of the characters between ages 50 and 60, and 12.5 percent of those aged 60 to 70 were tabulated as engaged in highly physical pursuits. Peterson also found that the majority of older characters in programs she reviewed were active, in good health, and independent.

The Harris study charted ill health and age factors showing that poor health increased with age. In the below-50 category, only about 6 percent had health problems; in the 50–60 category, 14 percent showed health problems; and in the 60–70 category, 25 percent of the population had poor health. Harris remarks that, while it is true that in real life, health problems increase with age, it is significant that television chooses to focus on this, the failure aspect, rather than on success in business and politics, which is also demonstrable.

In the world of the soap opera, where it is already demonstrated that the elderly have roles of greater respect and authority than in prime time, it is also indicated that they enjoy better health. It has been pointed out the characters on soap operas do not have diseases and illnesses that viewers are likely to have. This is probably deliberate on the part of writers in order to make the programs nonthreatening. It is doubtful, for example, that any soap opera character battles obesity, much less general excess poundage. Further, not all the illnesses on these kinds of programs are even classified. Cassata found only one-fourth of the illnesses to be classifiable and that they were responsible for only one-fifth of the deaths in the programs. People, it seems, are more likely to recover than to die in soap opera. Death may be reserved for those characters who, for one reason or another, must be written out of the script.

Older people on television, therefore, are not necessarily victims of disease, or even holders of disease. In fact, Cassata and Downing both find that over 90 percent of the older characters were in remarkably good health. It is those characters between ages 22 and 45 who have the most health problems.

It is the observation of both Davis and Kubey that television may tend to present a distorted image of health among the aged through a tendency to focus on the exceptional. Calling this "reversed stereotying," Kubey explains that older people are often seen riding motorcycles, dancing with abandon, or referring to their highly active sex lives. These "exotics" make good video subjects because they are seen doing things thought to be extraordinary for older persons. When young people hang-glide or surf, no one pays much attention. When a 60-year-old does the same thing, it becomes a news item. When a 70-year-old does it, he or she may well become the star of a 10-minute segment of "Real People."

Kubey suggests that when such reverse stereotypes are presented in prime time comedy it is intended to be comical. It is accepted as a joke, and thereby negative stereotypes continue to be reinforced.

In contrast, the usual public affairs special about old people in the community is likely to focus on the visible elderly who have multiple health losses. As the subject of aging has gained media acceptability, public affairs programs are produced and presented almost every season. Since audiences tend to respond to the unusual more readily than the usual, to the tragic rather than joyous circumstance, and to the appalling more than to the appealing, a show about old people easily allows this response to be facilitated. Every city has its derelicts, the down and outers who may look years older than they are. These people make for good "visuals." Most cities have a park where older people come together for a variety of highly valid and useful reasons. Allowing the camera to pan the assembled elderly while a voice-over comments on the pathetic lot of those who do not commute daily to single-family dwellings in the suburbs is a common part of many "community interest" programs.

These two sets of images, the very ill and the very active, are two ends of a spectrum of health in the elderly population. When that is all that is seen, another set of stereotypes is reinforced.

Fortunately, there are also some more realistic images of aging and health available on television. "Over Easy" was a long-running daily half-hour program on the Public Broadcasting System. The program format featured thematic examinations of critical issues. Major segment categories included health, nutrition, and exercise. Health segments presented information about heart disease, cataracts, podiatry, stroke, and other pertinent problems. Prevention, detection, and treatment were stressed. Exercise and nutrition segments featured how-to information.

A program analysis of the 1981 season for "Over Easy" represents a typical broadcast year and indicates that there are more segments about the general topic of health than on any other issue. This is because other themes addressed in the programs are closely linked with issues of health and well-being. Family relations, philosophy, psychology, and social issues are all definite aspects of a holistic approach to health maintenance and aging.

Health and the image of aging will receive more positive attention as new broadcast systems search for viable program material. As illustration, the Cable Health Network, which began programming in 1982 devotes all its program schedule to health related issues. Programming for this network follows a thematic concept. Of eleven themes, one is devoted to the health of older persons. Titled "Getting Older, Feeling Younger," this series of programs is designed to contribute to the well-being, fitness, nutrition, medical care, and emotional health of older Americans. It may be assumed that older persons seen in this program and on this cable system will project healthy images.

These two examples, however excellent they may be, still were available only to those who view either public broadcasting or a specialized cable service. Unfortunately, this is not the majority of the viewing population.

Implications

Brotman's report lists the problems of ill health among the elderly, problems of which he says only 14 percent of all older Americans are afflicted. They include arthritis, 44 percent of that group; hearing impairments, 29 percent; and vision impairments, hypertension, and heart conditions, each about 20 percent. Except for the heart conditions, these health problems do not make for very interesting television fare. Since the young populate the world of television, it would be highly unusual (although quite possible) to have a young arthritic admitted to the hospital cast of characters. Most shows deal with acute, not chronic, problems in the first place. In the second place, those problems must have enough elements of the unusual to make for good drama.

Senile behaviors are not mentioned in soap opera, and when used in evening programming, they are usually material for a joke. Other diseases that make life difficult for the elderly are ignored because those who have them do not play central roles in the programs. It is easy to conclude, if one is gathering information about life from television's presentation of it, that there is no midground of health for the elderly. One either suffers from multiple debilitating losses or from none at all. Either way, a rude confrontation with reality is in store.

Images of Age in Children's Programming

Children are heavy viewers of television. This is especially so of the very young. When they are given a picture of the world and the people who populate it that is biased, then the perception they are forming of reality is likely to be equally biased. In studying a sample of shows viewed by children, Jantz et al. found that not only were older women, children, and minority groups underrepresented, but out of 85 half-hour segments there were only four child–elderly interactions. The researchers concluded that children were not being provided with realistic and accurate portrayals of the elderly.

Other studies of children's attitudes toward the elderly are equally alarming when they show that children say they do not want to be like the elderly or to grow old themselves. Seefeldt surveyed the attitudes of 180 elementary school children in 1978. The children were drawn from a variety of racial, ethnic, and socioeconomic backgrounds. They found that the children stereotyped the elderly, identifying them as being sick, tired, and ugly. The children saw old people as being unable to do anything but sit and rock, go to church, or be pushed in wheelchairs. The physical characteristics of age—white hair, wrinkles, and false teeth—were viewed with horror by the children.

We know that the elderly have a low representation on prime time and evening special shows. This representation is even lower in those weekend daytime televison shows that are designed especially for children. The Gerbner figures and those provided by Greenberg indicate weekend shows are mostly populated by characters who are under 20 years of age. This is the age group that is not particularly visible on the usual prime time shows.

The old are seldom seen in cartoon programs. This is a genre specifically targeting younger children. It is concerned with the struggles that children have between one another and with authority. Authority is usually held by the parent generation, not the grandparent generation. So not only are old adults not likely to be seen in cartoon land, but when they are there, they are benign. Negative roles are assigned to younger adults, or to nonhumans who are not old. These findings of content analysis done by Bishop and Krause demonstrate that aging and old age are not dominant themes, or even subordinate themes, in the Saturday morning television programming. This absence of any image at all contributes to the general invisibility of the elderly in the world of children.

Implications

It is estimated that a typical child has watched between 10,000 and 15,000 hours of television by the time he is 16. Children draw on this mediated experience for information to acquaint themselves with the world and to equip themselves to function well within it. There is reason for concern about children's attitudes toward older persons which goes beyond their acceptance of the negative stereotypes and myths that abound in our society. Questions have been raised about the influence of such beliefs on the child's developing self-image and about the effect of such conditioning on productive intergenerational relationships.

Age-segregated housing, dispersed family, and other social conditions tend to isolate today's children from the realities of growing old. This alienation is reinforced by our educational system, as evidenced in the limited curricula on aging. Negative attitudes about aging were present in 90 percent of the sample studied by Seefeldt. The children are quoted as saying they would feel "awful if they were old." They voiced denial, "Oh no, not me, I'm not getting old," and "I won't grow old; it's too terrible."

Mobility has meant that children have fewer opportunities for interaction with aged family members. In addition, for many children, contact with their grandparents means involvement with a relatively young person, someone in their 40s, 50s, or early 60s. Furthermore, because of the proliferation of age-segregated communities, children have limited exposure to older persons outside their family. Children deprived of experiences with a diversity of older persons in a variety of settings may never learn to question the stereotypes they hold about aging.

The Elderly in Television Commercials

When television becomes the primary source of contact with older persons, as is the situation for many children, negative attitudes toward aging are further reinforced. The Gerbner researchers concluded that the main results are clear and consistent: The more young people watch television, the more they tend to perceive old people in generally negative and unfavorable terms.

In the eight televised commercials monitored in the in-depth analysis by Harris and Feinberg, 10.6 percent of the total characters were over 60. This a different and somewhat larger percentage than others have noted in actual program content. But like program content, the number of males increased as age increased, while the number of females decreased with age increase. The study also indicated that physical activity decreased and health problems increased with age. Statistically, the elderly in commercials experienced ten times the health problems of the young. Even though there is evidence that the elderly are healthy in many important ways, their counterparts in televised commercials do not reflect this.

Commercials often feature advice givers. Older advice givers tend to be male and tend to be celebrities. Older public figures are utilized to enhance a sales message; however, older characters are seldom given that responsibility when cast in story commercials.

Francher's study of television commercials showed that when a single character is used within the commercial it is likely to be a young, very attractive, and usually sexy female. Men are useful in advertising without as much regard to age. In fact, older men with graying temples and a certain macho image of virility and sexual appeal are often valuable to be associated with some products. However, Francher also concluded that older people are more likely to be used when the commercial is either humorous in tone or when there is a health product especially targeting the older age group.

The elderly often function to give reliability to a product. Their presence implies that the product meets the high standards of quality set decades ago. The inference is that only the older person would have the experience to be able to endorse the product.

The words *old* and *older* are seldom used in advertising. The words *young* and *younger*, however, often are used. The message is obvious, the product may be shown with a middle-aged face or an older one, but the words heard or read are those "young" words. The product, it is announced, makes one "younger." This is especially true of beauty products. The promise of youth is the major appeal. And this is a promise made to all those women who don't want people to know they have passed age 30. Younger women sell the beauty products. Older women sell digestion aids, laxatives, denture fixatives, and arthritis remedies.

Implications

The point is well made by this time: The image of aging in all areas of television programming is subject to criticism. However, nowhere might that negative image projection be more damaging than in commercials. Here is where promises are made. That one can buy youth, or at least youthful appearance, endows that state and quality with high value. Television commercials present to a consumer society all that is worth owning. The message inherent in advertising is that we are what we buy. This is what causes resentment and discontent among the disadvantaged, who cannot purchase "the good life." Similar resentments and discontent are likely among those who cannot afford to buy youth, those who find the promises empty; youth cannot be purchased anywhere. The glorification of youth, the Pepsi generation bouncing about the beaches of America, leaves a large majority without validation through the world of television advertising.

Stereotyping: Consequences and Countermeasures

In this discussion of images, it is apparent that what is being dealt with is clusters of stereotypes about men and women and about various age groups. Stereotypes are those conceptions and images which are simplified and inaccurate but which have become standardized and are commonly held. Stereotypes are categorizations. It is a way of thinking that aids in organizing one's world. Psychologists tell us that people find it useful to think in terms of categories, to classify both experiences and people symbolically through language (that is, by using descriptive words). Then these symbolic classifications are used as though they were real and represent truth.

These categorizations then, help to organize human actions toward a particular place, event, or person, regardless of the actual truth. The simplistic ordering of identities enables us to make decisions about how we are going to react to a given situation populated by people about whom we do not have a quantity of personal level experience. For example, when in a neighborhood largely composed of an ethnic group different from our own, we may feel threatened because we believe that all such persons are capable of and even desirous of inflicting harm upon us. If we find ourselves at an entertainment function largely attended by members of another age group than our own, we may feel uneasy because of our conception of them (if they are younger) as irresponsible drug users; or, if they are older, we may feel uneasy because of our conception of them as fragile and humorless. As drivers, we have a set of notions about other drivers and their highway behavior dependent on their age, their sex, their ethnicity, and possibly the kind of car they are driving.

We make decisions about how we are going to behave in each of these situations. More often than not, the motivation for this behavior is fear and mistrust for that which is "different."

In spite of all the statistics we have about aging and being old that would promote a positive image of age, it is evident that these facts are not generally known, or perhaps not generally attended to. Our society perpetuates a mythology about being old. It is possible that some of this mythology is a consequence of truth as it may have existed in decades long past, but which no longer stands as fact. This tells us that much information is passed by word of mouth from generation to generation and given much more validity than what is read in the papers. What we are told at an early age by the authorities in our environment stays with us. Parents and grandparents may pass on information gathered from their parents and grandparents. They may also instruct us through actions even more strongly than through verbalizations. So we are given a set of attitudes about aging, about being old. These attitudes are difficult to overcome even when presented with subsequent packages of more intellectualized information.

The Mythologies of Age

There are numerous commonly held generalities about the elderly. The most common examples are listed here.

1. Old people are rigid and inflexible.
2. Old people decline in intelligence.
3. Old people are less productive as workers.
4. Old people are institutionalized and dependent.
5. Old people are senile.
6. Old people are sexless.

Evidence countering these assertions has been presented in chapter 1, but not everyone has read such evidence.

The Gray Panthers is a national advocacy organization whose members include not only the elderly but young people and middle-aged people. This organization has voiced much concern over media images of aging. They have mounted a "Media Watch" to record evidences of discrimination toward old people. The group has developed a list of characteristis that it considers stereotypes, to guide them in spotting offenses in television program content. The Gray Panthers' list includes the following characteristics.

Appearance. The face is blank and expressionless, and the body is always bent over and infirm.

Clothing. Ill-fitting garments.

Speech. Halting and high-pitched.

Personality. The dominant characteristics are stubbornness, rigidity, and forgetfulness. The "rocking chair" image predominates.

The Gray Panthers pose a series of questions for television's gatekeepers to use in checking against possible distortions of fact:

1. Are older people depicted as intruders or meddlers in the relationships of others?
2. Are older people ridiculed when they show sexual feelings?
3. When there is an age difference in romantic relationships, are older women accorded the same respect as older men?
4. Are old people patronized and treated as children?
5. Are the oppressive conditions under which older people must live in society analyzed? Are alternatives to the existing conditions presented?
6. In any discussion of social and economic issues, are the perspectives of older people included?
7. Are older people directly involved in writing, directing, and producing the program?
8. How about the acting? Are there valid reasons for young actors to play the roles of older people?

These questions asked by the Gray Panthers might cause smiles among network and other programming officials, whose concern is not to act as a public relations agent for any group. Their concern is to present a story that has enough audience appeal to attract large numbers of viewers. They might attend to these guidelines for content review if they thought that by doing so, they would not alienate a significant audience. Nevertheless, such sensitizing of producers, directors, and writers will have eventual results. After all, it is doubtful that any of these creative people deliberately set out to offend through poor taste.

Another set of guidelines has been published by Coronet, a company producing both print and film educational materials. Coronet's target audience is young people, for whom they produce educational materials. The booklet, titled *Guidelines for Creating Positive Images of Persons and Groups*, lists suggestions for the treatment of older persons, including the following:

1. Older adults and children will be included in materials at all levels in all curriculum areas. They will be included both as central characters and as group members.
2. Older citizens will be featured as vital, independent functioning adults. They will be shown living independently, as being successful, doing interesting things, and having interests that are shared by others.
3. Older people will be shown relating positively with each other in realistic, believable situations. Viewers will be shown some positive aspects of a relationship, such as helpfulness, romantic interest, etc. They will be allowed the full range of human emotions, hopes, and desires. Viewers will be given a feeling that they would like to know characters portrayed.
4. Older adults will be shown as economically productive citizens within a community. They will be shown gainfully employed, participating in community affairs, and as reasonable people to work with.
5. Older persons will be portrayed in positive roles within a family. Their opinions will be respected and their accumulated wisdom will be valued and sought. Their status will be shown as an asset. Families with more than two generations will be shown.
6. Older citizens will be featured interacting in positive relationships with children. Grandparents or foster grandparents will be shown teaching children how to do some task. They will be shown passing on family traditions and values.

A third set of guidelines are those developed by the National Council on Aging by its executive director, Geneva Mathiesen. These guidelines are intended for use in directing program people toward positive depictions of older people. Mathiason asks that the media portray the current generation of the elderly, not reflect the past in stereotype.

1. Show older people in their current environments and with their current mind sets.
2. Don't portray institutionalization as an inevitable adjunct to old age.
3. Don't give the impression that old people are separated and/or alienated from—and neglected by—their families.

4. Combat the fallacy that emotional or mental departures from the norms by the elderly are evidence of "senility."
5. Don't exaggerate symptoms of mental confusion manifested by older people; they affect people of all age groups.
6. Please, no more cheap jokes about sex in old age.
7. Old people sitting on park benches or in rocking chairs are not prototypes of older people, most of whom are, in fact, busy, active, and useful.
8. Portray the growing significance of the elderly as a political force.
9. Continue an advocacy role on behalf of those elderly who are poor, sick, alone, and afraid, unable to hold their own in a fast-paced society inclined to ignore or to victimize them.
10. Among the many programs depicting violence, dramatize the muggings and murders of the old by youthful gangs or identified bullies, often only for their meager dollars or maintenance checks.
11. To eliminate stereotypes, portray old people as personalities, not types.

All these guidelines help creative people to understand the nature of positive role-modeling in educating about aging. Television decision makers who would not characterize themselves as producers of educational material might still find inspiration in such a set of advisories.

What is important in the mass media is that a balance of images be presented. It is true that some elderly have unappealing mannerisms. The same is true of all ages. It would be reverse stereotyping to present a whitewashed picture. At one time it was acceptable for many minorities to be ridiculed. The handicapped, alcoholics, and members of racial and ethnic minorities were used as the butt of humor. Public awareness has grown so that alcoholic behavior is no longer considered funny, nor is stuttering, limping, or being mentally retarded. As a consequence, there has been a decline in that form of humor. Using the elderly as objects of ridicule is equally inappropriate. But public awareness and sensitivity has yet to rise to the level of expressing concern and limiting such attacks. The Gray Panthers are attempting to do for the elderly what "Black Power" advocates did for blacks. Jamieson's 1977 report to the Senate Committee on Aging says that this sort of activity will "transform the pejorative into the positive while replacing the assumption of powerlessness with the assertion of power."

Effecting Change through Shifting Attitudes

The promotion and maintenance of stereotypes about aging through inappropriate or biased modeling of characters on television has obvious consequences. Aging, a natural process, is made undesirable. Being old is made an unwanted state because of the conviction that it necessarily includes diminished participation in life events and diminished satisfaction. Such thinking may be a self-fulfilling prophecy. If one is convinced that a certain time of life is to be a bad experience, events may very well be manipulated to make it so. We usually find our expectations about others, and about ourselves, fulfilled.

If the commonly held notions of aging that are stereotypical in nature are to be altered, then the basic or underlying attitudes about growing older must be changed. Attitudes are not easily influenced. Using the media to change attitudes means that we are dealing with persuasive messages to influence opinion on a mass scale. Now we are talking about opinion, rather than attitude. Public opinion is usually a set of conclusions on a proposal involving social change. Bogardus defines mass opinion as being generalized judgment of a considerable number of people on a particular aspect of social life.

This is what advertising is all about. Advertising is an attempt to influence judgment of a considerable number of people about a particular product or activity. "It will be good to see this movie, or "It will be good to own this car" are examples of opinions advertising attempts to establish.

We know what opinions a person holds because we hear them verbalized. Sometimes we can know the range of a person's opinions through some sort of survey. For example, surveys are frequently taken to determine the public's favorable or unfavorable opinion of a political leader. Such opinions are considered to be reflections of individual beliefs. An opinion is an overt, or measurable, response. An opinion may reflect an attitude. Attitudes, however, are covert; they are not themselves heard or on checklists.

Opinions, heard or checked, may or may not truly reflect an individual's attitude. It often happens that a person will express an opinion that does not reflect his or her true attitude. Such an opinion may more accurately reflect a wish to conform to social pressure, to maintain facade, or to protect the speaker from criticism or harm. In this case, overt verbalization of opinion is being altered for social acceptability. It does not reflect attitude. Nor can we realistically assume that verbalized opinion is going to indicate probable action.

Attitudes are more accurately expressed in nonverbal behavior. Attitudes might be thought of as the evaluation by the individual of some aspect of his world in a favorable or unfavorable manner. Clusters of attitudes, or specific attitudes linked together in an organized hierarchical structure, become value systems.

More simply stated, an individual's value system is his collection of attitudes about a given issue or subject. The array of value systems held by an individual become his or her identity.

It is this value system of the recipient of mass media messages that we wish to influence when we try to alter attitude. Value systems are complex, multidimensional structures. The message to the communicator are clear: to effect change in complex, multidimensional structures, the persuasive messages must be within the field of the recipient's cognition (he must understand the message) and it must be easily incorporated into the existing value structure without excessive threat to the individual's self-image. As the value system is a reflection of the self-image, there is an ego resistance to any possibility of alteration of the value system that does not operate to improve that image.

Any persuasive communication, one designed to change attitude about aging, for instance, exposes the recipient to the possibility of accepting or rejecting a recommended opinion. (Can we get acceptability for "Old is beautiful" in the same way that "Black is beautiful" became both a rallying cry and a facilitator for change in attitude about black people?)

Hovland says that, when exposed to a recommended opinion, individuals have two responses; they think of their own answer to a question and of the answer suggested by the communicator. This process of weighing the two opinions is now within the cognitive frame of reference. What is involved now is the selection of the one opinion that fits most desirably within the individual's value system.

The successful persuasive communication alters attitude when the recipients learn that the new opinion helps them achieve value-goals that reflect their desired self-image. Because broadcasters wish to attract and retain viewers, reinforcement of opinion and attitude is more common than conversion to a new idea or another attitude, however.

Finally, let us remember that mass communication functions not as an isolated phenomenon, but within a complex social and psychological structure subject to a myriad of mediating factors and influences. This makes persuasive messages disseminated via television contributing agents to change, not the sole agent. But it is important to remember the strong impact of television in this society and to recognize that, although it is but one agent for change, it is a most powerful one.

References

Ansello, E. 1978. Broadcast images: The older woman in television. Paper presented at the meeting of the Gerontological Society, Dallas.

Aronoff, C. 1974. Old age in prime time. *Journal of Communication* 24(1):86–87.

Beck, K. 1978. Television and the older woman. *Television Quarterly* 15(Summer):47–49.

Berelson, B. 1948. Communication and public opinion. In W. Schramm, ed., *Communications in Modern Society.* Urbana: University of Illinois Press, pp. 167–85.

Bogardus, E. 1951. *The Making of Public Opinion.* New York: Associated Press.

Brotman, H. 1978. The aging of America: A demographic profile. *National Journal 10*(7):1622–27.

Cassata, B., P. Anderson, and T. Skill. 1980. The older adult in daytime serial drama. *Journal of Communication 30*:48–49.

Coronet Film's Guidelines for Creating Positive Images of Persons and Groups. 1978. Chicago.

Davis, R.H. 1978. Advocacy: Using media to change attitude. *The Gerontologist 18*(4):408.

Davis, R.H. 1983. Television health messages: What are they telling us? *Generations 3*(5):43–45.

Downing, M. 1974. Heroine of the daytime serial. *Journal of Communication 24*: 130–37.

Elliott, J.C. 1981. Images of older adult characters on daytime television serial drama. Unpublished Ed.D. dissertation, Teachers' College, Columbia University, New York.

Francher, J.S. 1973. "It's the Pepsi generation . . .' Accelerated aging and the television commercial." *International Journal of Aging and Human Development 4*:245–55.

Gerbner, G., L. Gross, N. Signorielli, and M. Morgan. 1980. Aging with television: Images on television drama and conceptions of social reality. *Journal of Communication 30*:37–47.

Greenberg, B.S., F. Korzenny, and C. Atkin. 1979. The portrayal of the aging: Trends on commercial television. *Research on Aging 1*:319–34.

Harris, A., and J. Feinberg. 1977. Television and aging: Is what you see what you get? *Gerontologist 17*:464–68.

Hovland, C., H. Janis, and H. Kelley. 1953. *Communication and Persuasion.* New Haven, Conn.: Yale University Press.

Jamieson, K. 1977. Age stereotyping and television. Staff review prepared for the hearing before the Select Committee on Aging, House of Representatives, 95th Cong. Washington, D.C., September 8.

Jantz, R.K., C. Seefeldt, J. Cunningham, and K. Serock. 1978. Children's attitudes toward the elderly. Unpublished report, University of Maryland.

KQED (Public Television), Rector, R. (producer). 1981. *Over Easy: An Analysis of Content, The Fifth Season.* film. San Francisco.

Kubey, R. 1980. Television and aging: Past, present, and future. *Gerontologist 20*: 16–35.

Levinson, R.M. 1973. From Olive Oyle to Sweet Polly Purebread: Sex role stereotypes and televised cartoons. *Journal of Popular Culture 9*:561–72.

Mathiesen, G. 1973. It's time for fair play. *Perspective on Aging 6*:17–22. Published by The National Council on the Aging, Inc., Washington, D.C.

Northcott, H.C. 1975. Too young, too old: Aging in the world of television. *The Gerontologist 15*:184–86.

Peterson, M. 1973. The visibility and image of old people on television. *Journalism Quarterly 50*:569–73.

Seefeldt, C. 1977. Young and old together. *Children Today 6*(1):22.

4
Discovery of the Older Audience

Older people have not always been appreciated as consumers. Only recently have special marketing efforts been made by enough advertising agencies that it can be recognized that the older buyer is being wooed. Edith Gilson, quoted in a 1984 *New York Times* article, calls advertising campaigns for the elderly "a little bit fashionable." Gilson is a senior vice-president in charge of research at J. Walter Thompson advertising agency and is in a position to know about trends in advertising. She believes that, regardless of the apparently new awareness of the older consumer, advertisers are not going to make a major shift toward marketing to the elderly. There is still strong reason to spend the bulk of advertising dollars wooing the 20- to 49-year-old consumers.

Nevertheless, enough special advertising targeting an older market is becoming evident so that it would, indeed, appear that advertisers have just recently discovered the older consumer. This discovery is reflected in part by increased appearances of older people in commercials, and the addition of older characters in programs and—most important—by the emphasis on products catering specifically to the needs and wants of the elderly.

Age-specific products are not a sudden phenomenon. As early as 1964 the older market was discussed in the *Journal of Marketing*. In this journal, Reinecke discussed variations in amount and type of expenditures and explored the differences due to lower income and the small size of the older population. By 1969 *Forbes*, the business magazine, featured an article titled "The Forgotten Generation." The article identified the market at an expenditure figure of $40 million (in 1969), but as being virtually ignored by manufacturers. The reason for this was offered by spokespersons from cosmetics and dress manufacturing industries. They did not want to be identified as being "connected only with older women." In 1969 one of the few national companies deliberately wooing the older consumer was the Greyhound Bus Company. This company indicated that about 75 percent of its business was from older persons and that this patronage was actively pursued.

In 1971 *Business Week* ran a special report on the power of the older consumer group. The report identified the elderly as a $60 million market—up $20 million since the 1960 estimate. The article sets forth the argument that marketing will reflect the demands of the older consumer group, who "refuse to be ignored as consumers any longer." By the mid-1980s it is obvious that the older consumer is definitely not ignored. As advertisers compete for this market, the image of age as depicted in copy, both for print and electronic media, will contribute to the building of new attitudes and new images.

The Older Consumer

Even in times of economic difficulty, today's older population has quite a different economic profile than their counterpart of two or more decades past. As expected, this population also has a different income and expenditure pattern from younger population groups.

Retirement has not always been an expectation of American workers. Participation in the labor force among those 65 and older dropped and has continued to drop since the great depression of the 1930s. The passage of the Social Security Act in 1936 contributed to the withdrawal of older persons from full employment. More recently the phenomenon of early retirement (that is, prior to age 62 and, in some instances, as early as age 55) has grown. Early retirement has been encouraged by some businesses and industries as a cost-cutting measure. Financial bonuses and other incentives have been offered to effect a reduction in costs associated with top-heavy management and the price of long-term employees. In spite of generally reduced income experienced by the individual who retires before 65, early retirement is less and less an unusual event.

Finally, despite laws against age discrimination, finding a new work position after age 55 remains a challenge for most people. This is true for managers as well as for those laid off the assembly line. Many factors, then, contribute to the decreased numbers of older people still employed.

Their participation in the work force being lessened, it is not surprising that income for the older population on the average is only about half that of the under-65 age group. In 1980 the median income of older families (those headed by a person age 65 or older) was $12,881. This may be compared to the median of $22,548 for families headed by persons under age 65. The mean income for older families was only $10,918, the 31.3 percent increase over the median income reflecting the impact of small but important numbers of high-income older families.

Median *individual* income, as opposed to family income, in 1980 was $5,095. The mean (or arithmetic average) for older individuals in 1980 was $7,176. It must be noted that more than 1.2 million (or over 15.3 percent) of the older *individual* population had incomes between

$10,000 and $25,000 per year. Only 190,000, or 2.4 percent of that population, had incomes in excess of $25,000.

The income figures for *families* with heads over age 65 are higher than for individuals over 65. According to 1980 figures, 9.1 percent of such families had incomes between $20,000 and $25,000. Fourteen percent had incomes between $25,000 and $50,000. Another 3.3 percent (or an actual count of 397,000 families) had incomes higher than $50,000. So there *is* an affluent market.

In contrast, 3.9 million older persons (over one-sixth of the entire older population) had incomes below the poverty line in 1980. To be poor, according to the federal definition, is to have a family income in an older couple household of $4,954 and less, and of $3,941 or less as an individual.

Regardless of all too true income problems of the older population as a whole, this is a market with enough significance in purchasing power that it cannot be ignored. After all, older people are not, as a rule, spending money raising children, acquiring and establishing homes, or consuming considerable amounts of foodstuffs. They may have smaller incomes, but for many there is a larger percentage of discretionary income than ever before. It is estimated that about 70 percent of older people own their homes, and that most of these are free of mortgage. Older persons in some communities get a break in property taxes. So less money is spent on housing than is spent by younger people.

Rena Bartos, writing in the *Harvard Business Review* identifies the older market as starting at age 49, which does not coincide with the gerontologists' concept of where old age begins (60 +). This gives a certain advantage in profiling "older" consumer spending patterns. Most people are still working and probably earning their largest incomes from age 50 until retirement. Bartos divides this age group as follows: active affluents (comprising 40 percent of the older consumer population); homemakers (22 percent); active retired (15 percent); the disadvantaged (17 percent); those in poor health (1 percent); and others (6 percent). It is the "active affluents" who are most targeted by advertising, because these are the ones who are most likely still to be working and who have the largest amount of money to spend on extras. Bartos reminds marketing people that these active affluents eventually become the active retired and continue to spend money past age 65. These are the people who do not lose their interest in comforts and luxuries. They will buy big cars and take expensive cruises.

Carole B. Allan heads a Washington, D.C., based marketing group. She has written numbers of articles about the older market and is considered an authority in this area. She informs the business world that the older market begins at age 55 and that it is an impressive one. She reports that households headed by a person 55 or over account for $400 billion of annual income—and this was in 1978! Further, they spend 28 percent of all discretionary money. This is much more than is spent by younger households.

How the Money is Spent

Again, the market is best divided into two consumer groups if we are to understand spending patterns: the younger (age 55–64) and the older (age 65 +). Since this book is concerned primarily with the latter group, only a brief discussion of the essentially middle-aged consumer is appropriate. The middle-aged are still working and are at the peak of their earning power. They have raised their children, purchased a home, and now have money to spend on luxuries. They are more likely to buy new cars, to take airplane trips, and to use cosmetics than are either older or younger consumers. They spend more money on diet products, drugs and other health-related products, travel packages, new clothes, liquor, gourmet foods, vacation homes, high-priced electronic equipment, and stocks than do either older or younger populations.

Allan reports that this age group buys 25 percent of all cosmetics and bath products, pays for almost 50 percent of women's care services at beauty parlors, buys 50 percent of all coffee sold, and buys from 25 to 33 percent of all alcoholic beverages.

The 65 + Market

Although consumers at this age are no longer likely to be bringing home monthly salary checks, they have incomes that allow most of them to consume beyond the bare necessities. Because there has always been a mythology about the poor elderly, it has been easy to assume that there was no money to be spent by the retired, therefore, there was no attempt to market to them. Of course, there are the economically deprived; but there are also the economically advantaged. Manufacturers are just beginning to discover them. As long ago as a decade past, it was estimated by the Bureau of Labor Statistics that consumer expenditures of the over-65 group exceeded $68 billion. By 1983 this amount has increasd, reflecting the better economic circumstances of this generation of elderly, and an increased liberal attitude toward indulging oneself through living "the good life."

What do they purchase? They purchase more drugs and health care products than does the general population. Specifically, asthma remedies, laxatives, sleeping tablets, vitamins, and denture cleaners are purchased in greater quantity. They purchase personal care items in significant quantity, but much less so than does the 55–64 age group. They spend more on foods to be consumed at home than do younger groups. They are larger consumers of coffee (which may explain the long-time use of aging actor Robert Young as television salesman for decaffeinated coffee). Understandably, this older market also spends more on home fuel and on household supplies than do younger groups, who spend less time at home. They do not spend money on away-from-home purchases such as eating out, movies, theater, and on automobile gasoline. They are still a significant market for new automobiles and for travel, especially scheduled tours by plane and boat cruises.

Marketing to the Older Adult

With the increased awareness of this older market has come a concern for merchandising to them. No one has seemed secure in a knowledge of how to tap into this purchasing power. There just has not been a significant bloc of experience, and most agencies have few, if any, advertising personnel much beyond the age of 35. Nevertheless, most agencies have been doing their homework. They are researching this audience of television viewers, who are subsequent buyers of what they see advertised there.

Advertising agencies are much maligned in our society. There is a general negative image of "the hucksters." From a sociological perspective the advertising business reflects and molds many behaviors and sets social patterns that contribute to role definition. In a consumer society it often seems that one's purchases help to define who or what one is. Advertising, then, is a social force aiding in structuring society along certain dimensions.

In a 1978 presentation by the J. Walter Thompson Company to the New York Society for Security Analysts, advertising was defended as being vital to the economic balance of society. It was said to influence consumption patterns, which in turn influence levels of production and employment. Advertising creates demand, which in turn contributes to improvement of products and to the reduction of prices through competition. It is interesting to note that the J. Walter Thompson Company has been operating for 120 years. Advertising is not a modern innovation. With advertising in one form or another people have been promoting goods as long as there have been competitive markets.

If consumers do in large measure define themselves (at least for the observer of externals) by what they purchase, then advertisers can help to create role definition. Automobile advertising provides a good illustration of this. Observe the difference in the ways a sporty little car and a four-door luxury sedan are advertised. The entire projection of image is geared toward a specific market. And that market is age-related—not so much by overt depiction as by implication. The sports car can surely be purchased by anyone who has the price, but its quality in the televised ad is more often than not projected by appeal to young drivers. In contrast, the larger luxury sedan is presented as appealing to those who have earned enough money to let the world know of their success by the very expensive car they drive. This market is a more mature one, the implication being that older consumers have a different message to project by the cars they drive than do younger ones.

It is true that there are products designed to appeal to a specific age group. After all, denture products have an age-limited market. Does a soft drink? Will there always be a "Pepsi generation" of young people who seem to spend their time on the beach playing volleyball? Yes, there will always be such a generation. But whether it will always be large enough to warrant the expenditure of large amounts to market them is doubtful.

So advertising agencies are finding that they can no longer ignore older markets. In 1976 one of the major agencies, Ogilvy and Mather, prepared a comprehensive report on the older consumer. It was titled "The Oldsters" and subtitled "Who They Are, What They Buy, How To Reach Them." The designation "oldsters" would not be approved by certain advocacy groups today, but when the report was written no one in advertising was quite sure how to label this market. Today the euphemistic term "mature market" seems to have more acceptability. The Ogilvy and Mather report was intended to give their copywriters insight into the demographics of the elderly, their product usage, and their media consumption characteristics. (In 1978 academic studies of media behavior of the elderly had just about reached a peak, coincidently.) This is one of the first really comprehensive surveys for advertising use that attempted to assess the population so that policy could be established regarding marketing and advertising techniques and media selection for placing advertising.

The agency concluded that consumption of most products by the elderly was at a lower level than most of the adult population. The exceptions to that were coffee, diet products, larger automobiles, some health products, travel, and some home products such as soap. (It is easy to assume that these are the same items that would appear on a current list.) They concluded that older adults were less likely to try new products than other adult consumers.

In the years ensuing since the Ogilvy and Mather report that last opinion has been both disregarded and disproved. New products have been created for the mature market and advertising has focused on the older consumer as it has never done before.

Creating advertising for the older market has been an especially difficult challenge. Certain products may have appeal only to older persons, and certain products can appeal to a broader range of consumers. In creating the copy, sensitivity has to be exercised since it is assumed that most people do not want to be appealed to through their age status primarily. Although being old is not something that bothers all people, it can be assumed, being catered to or patronized because of being old is something that does bother most people.

The advertising copy as well as the visual images need to incorporate elements of appeal to all ages, or at least to a broad spectrum. Good advertising ideas appeal widely and override any associated age images. One of the most popular fast food commercials on television in 1984 featured a "little old lady" who in the company of two equally elderly companions complained about the quality of the beef in the hamburger of an unnamed competitor of the sponsor. Her line, "Where's the beef?" became popular instantly and was used by everyone from talk show hosts to Walter Mondale, campaigning for the Democratic presidential nomination. Wendy's, the fast food chain sponsoring the commercial, increased its sales to all age groups—including the older consumer.

Advertising that demeans the elderly (or any other group for that matter) is less and less evident. We no longer find infirmity or disabilities funny. An illustration of advertising that failed and even brought criticism to the makers of the product is a television spot for a lemonade mix that features an old man. The old man was deaf and his repeated inability to understand the lines about the product was not perceived as entertaining. The advertisement was dropped as complaints were filed and decreased sales evidenced rejection of the approach.

Hiring older copywriters would seem to be one solution to reaching the mature market. It is difficult, if not impossible, for a young man or woman, no matter how bright, to understand the psychology of the older consumer. More mature individuals might at least consult on the creation of marketing strategies for products designed for the elderly. This approach has proven successful in the magazine field, where several new magazines have been launched and proven successful in reaching the older market.

Magazines such as *Modern Maturity, Seniority,* and *50 Plus* have wide circulation. *Modern Maturity* is the fourth largest magazine in circulation in America. (It follows *Reader's Digest, TV Guide,* and *National Geographic.* This may be due to the fact that it is the official magazine for members of the American Association of Retired Persons.) Regardless, with a circulation in excess of 8.5 million, it commands attention from those who wish to reach the older market.

Television cannot be considered in the same advertising framework as magazines. Everyone watches television, while not everyone reads

Modern Maturity. Certain products are more easily advertised on television if the market is not made specific to the elderly. Oil of Olay is an example of a skin care product that is advertised to appeal to all women who want to "keep their skin looking young." There is an age taboo in the cosmetics industry, but the industry also knows that it is the aging woman who is the best customer. Manufacturers of beauty products tend to sell women on the idea that they look 10 years younger than they are. The "Who would believe I was over 30?" sort of approach is really pitched at the woman who is over 40. The woman over 50 is pleased to be regarded as in her 40s and the woman over 60 thinks of herself as in her 50s.

Such vanity is not exclusively a feminine trait. Regard the highly successful advertising for "Grecian Formula," a hair coloring product for men. The approach here is an obvious attempt to make the male look younger and to enable the male to retain the competitive edge of youth in the business arena.

New products are being developed at a rapid rate and are advertised carefully to capture the mature market. Golf clubs have been designed to allow the older player to have a better grip and consequently play a better game. Clothing for the older individual has long been an ignored product need. Noticeable today is more than one line that copies the success of the Levi Strauss Company. Their product for men, "Levis for Men," and for women, "Bend Over Jeans for Women" are both promoted for easy wear for the "mature figure." These two products have in common a fuller cut through the hips and across the bottom. (You know you are growing older when you can no longer buy clothes in the collegiate shop. And this happens long before age 65!)

Food products are being marketed for the older consumer. Cereals with high fiber content, instant and decaffeinated coffees, low cholesterol cheeses, and even a product called Freedent Gum made especially for denture wearers who like to chew gum without the embarrassment of displacing their dentures, are all examples of new products.

Linking the product to something other than age is still the major approach to marketing products that in reality do target the elderly. Since products that can be advertised as bringing benefits to people because of health needs, the market captures the older consumer as it is broadened to include others. Such items as low-sodium food products, low-fat products, high-fiber products are examples of goods that lend themselves to this sort of marketing strategy. Other items are blood pressure machines, scales, bed boards, and similar health care appliances.

Advertising for these items is more likely to be seen in the print media than in television. Television advertising is vastly more expensive to produce and has to appeal to a larger market. Therefore, the elderly are seldom targeted with television advertising for these products. There are exceptions, of course. And these products are understandably seen advertised around the evening news segments. What do we see? Health care products, denture products, automobiles, and flight plans prevail.

And we see older persons portrayed in insurance advertising, food products, fast food chains, and all sorts of consumer promotions. The older person is not being overlooked in today's advertising. As recent evidence of this, guidelines for effective advertising to the elderly were presented at the 1982 Conference of the Advertising Research Foundation in New York. The presenter was a senior vice-president, director of research for Oxtoby-Smith, an advertising agency. The principles outlined for communicating with the older population involve more detailed and more sophisticated analysis than the 1976 Ogilvy and Mather paper on the same subject. Agency awareness has greatly increased in the past several years. Advertising creative personnel are now given information about the older consumer from financial profiles to understanding of vision, hearing, and cognitive processing.

Further evidence of awareness of this market and increased sophistication in approaching it is found in a 1984 article in the *Journal of Advertising Record*, Stephen and Warrens reported here on research directed toward understanding "Advertising Frequency Requirements for Older Adults." Clearly, advertising is responding to the realities of an aging market.

Television Programs about and for Older People

As advertising reflects a new awareness of the older consumer, so will television programming. The older person is a consumer of television fare as well as services and goods. Although this is discussed in other places in this book, some specific examples of programming will be helpful to illustrate the medium's responsiveness to the older market.

Programming *for* older people (as opposed to programs *about* older people) is difficult to find and awkward to identify. We can find programs for preschoolers ("Mr. Roger's Neighborhood," for example), and programs that usually appear on Saturday mornings, which we can easily assume are for children who are somewhere between Mr. Roger's friends and fans of the "Fonz" on reruns of "Happy Days." But there are few adult-oriented programs about which one can say, "These target older viewers." After all, older viewers are not necessarily greatly different in their interests than other adult viewers. There are programs for older viewers, but they are few and far between on commercial television.

On public broadcasting stations until recently older viewers could relate to "Over Easy," the daily program with a magazine format that presented information on a variety of subjects from health to life-styles. This highly successful show probably presented more information about aging issues to more people over its six-year life than any other show on the air. Packaged as specials, "Over Easy—Prime Time" continues to disseminate information on an occasional basis. Nothing of the scope of this series has been created to fill the void left by its absence.

Public television has also been the showcase for other program series targeting older viewers: "Prime Time" a miniseries on retirement life styles aired in the late 1970s, and Fred Rogers of the children's series also created a short-lived series about older people and intergenerational relationships. Titled "Old Friends, New Friends," it provided viewers with insights into various styles of coping and surviving well in old age.

These shows are no longer on the air. Does that mean that public broadcasting has declared aging to be an issue no longer? What is more likely reflected is the economic troubles of public broadcasting in general. In public television dramatic series production, aging dealt with from time to time. But there are no nationally distributed series about aging on public television today.

In commercial broadcasting the situation is no different. Few, if any, series about aging have survived on commercial television. Aging as an issue understandably most often dealt with in the genre of public affairs broadcasting. Every station feels an obligation to program a certain percentage of airtime with material in "the public interest, convenience, and necessity." This demonstrates their concern to serve their public for its betterment. Public affairs shows are often segments of the newscast, but they also appear as talk shows, panels, documentaries, and special reports. They may be shown at any time during the broadcast day, but most often are found outside of prime time hours. In fact, many such shows are often seen on weekends or early on weekday mornings.

"New Wrinkles in Aging": Program Topics

An example that may stand as a model for such broadcasts is a 1977 NBC 20-part series titled "New Wrinkles in Aging." This was created by Los Angeles station KNBC and presented in the NBC major markets through their early morning "Knowledge" series. The series featured a host who presented a number of knowledgeable guests for in-studio discussion. The twenty topics covered the gamut of subjects most often presented in such series and are listed here as an example of what may be expected as topics in almost all the specials and talk shows dealing with aging.

1. "Use it or lose it." Reviewing the multiple areas of research activity in the pursuit of knowledge about human aging.

2. "Attitudes and myths on aging." Debunking ageist stereotypes.
3. "Retirement—the pros and cons." Guidelines for preretirement and retirement planning.
4. "The faces of aging." Attitudes and treatment of various ethnic minority aged.
5. "Sex after seventy." Sexuality in later life.
6. "The fountain of youth." Research findings regarding extending the life span.
7. "Employment for the aged." How to get a job and launch a second career in midlife and beyond.
8. "Service groups." Service groups that offer aid to the elderly.
9. "Counseling for the elderly." Dealing with the special psychological problems of the elderly.
10. "A good age." Living life fully throughout the lifespan.
11. "The law and the elderly." Legal rights and legal assistance.
12. "Extending your life span." Guidelines for a healthy, happy old age.
13. "The middle years." Moving through midlife toward a healthier, wealthier old age.
14. "The myth of senility." Understanding senile behaviors and how the memory works.
15. "Don't die broke." Preparing financially for the older years.
16. "The Gray Panthers." Report on the national group of militant activist elderly.
17. "The test of time." Health practices to increase life expectancy.
18. "You and your aging parents." The aging relative and the nuclear family.
19. "Dealing with death." Reducing the fear of death and dealing with bereavement.
20. "The elite society." Guidelines from centenarians and those who exemplify the best of being old.

Another example of a commercial station's endeavor is a 1983 project by Los Angeles Station KHJ-TV, an RKO General station. Under the umbrella title "The Changing Family," a one-hour public affairs show was produced that dealt with aging issues. Created as a documentary special, "May to December" focused on aging, retirement, and social security. What made this program outstanding is that it was given a large budget. This is not usually the case with locally produced public affairs shows. However, Los Angeles is a major and very competitive market, so this production stands as an example of shows created by major stations in major markets. More modest productions are discussed later in this chapter.

"May to December" was augmented by printed study and discussion guides that were made available to public service organizations and to the schools in Los Angeles. A "Human Services Directory" was also printed and made available to viewers who called in to request it. This was a cooperative venture with the social service agencies in the five-county area covered by the KHJ broadcast signal. Another special aspect of this production was that it was followed up by an half-hour in-studio discussion with a panel of gerontologists and service providers. These people interacted with a host of the program and with the studio audience, and with viewers who phoned in their questions. This is an ambitious program for an independent station to undertake, but is not entirely unusual. On a more modest scale it is possible to cite similar programs at various station levels around the country.

Commercial television is in the business of entertaining. Programs are presented with enough appeals that a hoped-for mass audience will be available for the commercial messages surrounding and interrupting the programs themselves. The series or weekly comedy or drama has proved successful in attracting viewers. Such shows are usually built around the situations involving a major character. They may be action-adventure, comedy, comedy-drama, or any workable mix of entertaining elements. Usually one or two characters are created around whom the action occurs. Television's successful series types change from time to time, but basically they remain the same in drawing viewer interest to either situation or personality. Examples of personality programs viewers have supported with their time are those such as "All in the Family," "The Mary Tyler Moore Show," "One Day at a Time," "The Lou Grant Show," among many sharing the approach of involving the central character in concerns of other people. Such shows have lent themselves well to addressing issues in aging. Each one has run one or more segments involving a crisis in the life of an older person.

The action show is less likely to focus on the human condition as dramatic material when the human involved is an old person. We are not likely to see such a topic on "Magnum P.I." or "Simon and Simon," for example. But "Hill Street Blues" would find "the plight of the elderly" an appropriate subject to address.

Dramatic specials such as "movie of the week" two-hour blocks of program time have dealt with the subject of aging more often than other program types. Here we see such stars of the screen as Bette Davis, Henry Fonda, George Burns, Art Carney, and others of a similar age as featured players. There are some good reasons for this. Older actors have long plied their craft through rigorous training in the days of being contracted to the major motion picture studios. They know how to deliver a good day's work without going into overtime. They have a drawing power that ensures good audience numbers. Examples of such television movies in recent seasons include "Two of a Kind" with George Burns, a story of a grandson who works to bring his grandfather's interest in life back to the point where he can leave the shelter of a nursing home and live independently once again. "Right of Way," starring Bette Davis and Jimmy Stewart, was produced for exclusive airing on HBO (Home Box Office Cable System). This story bravely addresses the subject of self-determination of life's ending. The two elderly persons agree upon and carry out a suicide pact in the face of community agency and family opposition.

"A Doctor's Story" uses all the dramatic elements of a hospital setting to show the dedication of a young resident in working to save the lives of and make healthier several old people in the geriatric ward. This film features Art Carney as an old man who has been diagnosed as "senile" and who is "cured" when the doctor takes him off certain drugs and helps him to deal with the emotional problems following the death of his wife.

These movies have in common a certain sentimental approach to being old. Nevertheless, they work as dramatic entertainment fare. The plot situations are not unreal; the events depicted do occur in real life. Most important, films such as these have drawn large viewing audiences, further educating the general public on issues in aging.

Programming at the Local Level: The New World of Cable

The public affairs programs mentioned above are examples of programs developed for a large market—Los Angeles. Similar programs are aired yearly in every large market. The smaller stations deal with aging issues in their talk format shows and other community affairs programs. However, some of the most exciting and innovative programming in the country today is appearing on community cable systems. Here is an opportunity for air time that is just not available on traditional commercial station operations.

Many cable systems are community access stations. Persons within the community have free time made available to them as part of their responsibility as a chartered or community-franchised cable system. Many programs are not only produced for older people, but by them. Since this book's second part is devoted to how to access television for advocacy activity, it is appropriate to list and describe significant examples of such television programs here.

This kind of program activity information has been made available through the efforts of Area Agency on Aging (District V) in La Crosse, Wisconsin, and the Department of Health and Human Services in Kansas City, Missouri. These government agencies have allocated staff support to the dissemination of information through television. These examples of cable activity are taken from their compilations.

Creekside Teleproductions in Bloomington, Minnesota, has been using a volunteer group of men and women from age 55 through the late 70s to produce video programs for the last 5 years. The group is responsible for the basic design of the shows and arranges for talent, scripts, camera, control room, and studio set-up. The technical set-up and color balancing is done by the cable operator staff. They produce the following shows: "The Bloomington Connection," a panel discussing issues ranging from drunk driving to estate planning; "Speeding Along at Fifty Five and Over," a 28-minute weekly information series on topics of interest to older persons; "Saturday Soap-box," a biweekly open mike taped at a shopping center, where citizens can voice their opinions on matters of concern, and "In Your Own Backyard," which showcases local talent.

The Barton Senior Center in Lakewood, Ohio, produces a monthly show that is shown six times during a given month over local cable. "Senior Showcase" is typical of what can be done with senior volunteers assisted by central staff and cable system technicians. Using a magazine format, with a host and roving reporter, the show highlights entertainment and information of interest to older viewers.

The Area Agency on Aging in Manhattan, Kansas takes initiative to produce a series of shows targeting the interests of the rural elderly. "The Autumn Years" is a weekly show that is carried by the three largest cable stations in the eighteen-county area, plus smaller stations in the more rural areas where there are not many services offered for the elderly. It is issue oriented and ranges in subject presentation from health and wellness through consumer issues, entertainment, and employment for older people.

Berks Community Television in Reading, Pennsylvania is probably one of the best known of the active community programming operations in the country. Originally funded by a number of grants, with the National Science Foundation as a major participant, it now originates a large amount of programming and is well integrated into the community. It specializes in interactive television, using split screens, by means of which people in different locations can see and talk with each other while the rest of the community listens and watches the exchange. Programs are offered throughout the day and range from talent showcase productions to discussions on health issues and on bridging the generation gap.

In Fairfax County, Virginia, Media General Cable Television—in consultation with the American Association of Retired Persons (AARP)—cosponsors a unique weekly talk variety show entitled "Pathways." A national finalist for the prestigious Hometown U.S.A. Award, "Pathways" airs interviews with gerontological experts, national personalities, local specialists, political figures, and local senior leaders. The show also features pretaped informational segments on such topics as health, crime, and local services and demonstrations providing tips for everyday living including exercise, nutritional facts, local talent, and arts and crafts. A local retired teacher and a young gerontologist join as co-hosts of this well-received local origination program.

Equally well known is the PACE program in San Diego, California. PACE is an acronym for Public Access Cabletelevision by and for Elders. It is operated by a crew of about twenty-five retired enthusiasts who create their own productions and work in the diverse aspects of the PACE program. A local cable television company, Southwestern Cable TV, is actively involved in assisting in the production of numbers of television shows targeting interests of older viewers.

Finally, examples may be given of two other nontraditional television operations that offer information both for and about older persons. The first is the Hospital Satellite Network, which is a unique national satellite television network designed to serve the hospital community exclusively. Original programming is presented that is designed for key audiences of the health care executives. Hospital patients and their families are included in the intended audience. The Hospital Satellite Network is an example of *narrowcasting* rather than *broadcasting*. (Signals are sent along certain specified frequencies that differ from broadcasting frequencies.) With the addition of satellite dishes at subscribing hospitals, the program signal can be received and staff can avail themselves of in-service educational experiences, while patients can view either entertainment programs in their rooms, or tune in those programs that explore various aspects of the hospital stay or health-related subjects.

Among the several advisory boards for the Hospital Satellite Network is a gerontology panel, which encourages the development of programming related to the concerns of those who treat the elderly as well as to older patients and their families.

The second example of very specialized programming is also a health issues programing operation. Cable Health Network is a commercial venture offering information on science, on fitness, on life-styles leading to health, on nutrition in general, and on aging. A percentage of the 24 hours daily programming would be devoted to aging issues. This service is cable delivered and is nationwide. The network sells advertising that, following the company spirit, is "part of the overall philosophy of the network—to inform the audience about good health and how to prevent sickness."

These several examples of programming serve to illustrate that television has discovered the older market. Advertising is beginning to reflect demographic shifts. Program content now contains references to issues that would not have been considered relevant 10 years ago and would not have appeared on television at all 20 years ago. The medium is no longer young, and the population it serves is growing older too.

References

Allan, C.B. 1981. Over 55: Growth market of the '80's. *Nation's Business* 69:25–32.

Bartos, R. 1980. Over 49: The invisible consumer market. *Harvard Business Review* (January 15):140–48.

Burstein, D. 1983. Exploring new images. *Advertising Age* (August 29):M9–12.

Don't overlook the $200 billion 55-plus market. 1977. *Media Decisions 12* (10):59–61, 116–22.

Dupont, T.D. 1982. Communicating with senior citizens—the fastest growing age group. Paper presented at the 28th annual conference of the Advertising Research Foundation, New York, March 3.

Forbes. 1969. The forgotten generation. (January 15):22–29.

Gage, T.J. 1980. Ads targeted at mature in need of creative hoist. *Advertising Age* (August 25):S1–5.

Kirkeby, M. 1980. The maturity market comes of age. *Advertising Age* (August 25):S1–11.

Kohn, A. 1984. Memo from Department of Health and Human Services, Office of Human Development Services, March 29.

Neiman, J. 1983. New products tiptoe into uncharted territory. *Advertising Age* (August 29):M21–22.

New York Times. 1984. Catering to older age groups. (February 23):1–23.

The power of the aging in the market place. 1971. *Business Week* (November 20): 52–58.

Rand, J. 1978. The consumer is not a moron, she is your grandmother. *Viewpoint* (in-house magazine for employees of Ogilvy and Mather), (Spring):8–11.

Reinecke, J.A. 1964. The "older" market—fact or fiction? *Journal of Marketing* (January):60–64.

Select Committee on Aging. 1982. Pub. No. 97-332. Washington, D.C.: U.S. Government Printing Office.

Soldo, B.J. America's elderly in the 1980s. Population bulletin, vol. 35, no. 14. Population Reference Bureau Inc., Washington, D.C., 1980.

Stephens, N., and R.A. Warrens. 1984. Advertising frequency requirements for older adults. *Journal of Advertising Research* 23(6):23–32.

Televised advertising and the elderly. 1977. A staff review prepared for the House Select Committee on Aging, Washington, D.C., January 26.

5
A Profile of the Older Viewer

The influence of television on society has been a topic for discussion since its early days. It became obvious soon after its introduction that television was to be the dominant channel for mass dissemination of information. It is only since the early 1960s, however, that anyone has given particular attention to the medium's significance in the lives of older persons. We have already considered (in chapter 2) the ways television influences people who are not yet old in their understanding of aging and of the elderly. But what influence has television on the older viewers themselves?

It is important to recognize that the elderly as an audience for the mass media are not dramatically different from any other audience. It is true that people do change in audience behaviors following retirement just as they change some other behaviors. These changes are due probably to a reallocation of time more than anything else. Because the retired person simply has more discretionary time than ever before, some activities are allocated more time than they were given while the individual was employed.

However, broadcast scheduling patterns do not change to accommodate the retired population. Game shows and soap operas are found in daytime programming for the most part, and news is telecast in the evening. The network's prime time assortment of comedy and drama fills out the nighttime program schedule. If the broadcast market warrants it, independent stations as well as network affiliates compete for the viewer's attention. These independent stations will provide even more opportunity to watch reruns of former prime time favorites. But is that what the older viewer chooses?

Viewing Behaviors

A number of social scientists in recent years have investigated the place of television in the lives of the older viewers. There is universal agreement among them regarding the importance of television and its several functions. Early researchers, such as Glick and Levy in 1962, first characterized older viewers as "embracers." This term describes a population with a particularly close identification with the television experience. Further, they tend to be less discriminating than the general population. Their attitude is one of acceptance, even strong appreciation. Finally, embracers tend to make great use of the medium. Very young children are seen as embracers, and many researchers classify older viewers similarly.

Both Schramm (1969) and DeGrazia (1961) found that older people listed watching television as the most frequent "leisure time" activity. The majority of both samples cited viewing television as a daily activity. The 1974 Harris poll found that more persons over 65 spend time watching television than spend time reading newspapers, listening to the radio, or reading books or magazines. In fact, this and other studies indicate that television viewing is the favored pastime of older people in general without regard to socioeconomic status, education, or other variables.

Time Spent Viewing

One dimension of viewing behavior, along with program choice, that all audience measurement is concerned with is time spent viewing. It is easy to quantify such behavior. But the findings may be subject to question. When viewers are asked to report number of hours spent viewing, it is easy for them to underestimate. There is a sort of social restriction on being overinvolved with this passive behavior. Individuals may truly not realize how much time they spend viewing; or if they do, they may be reluctant to report it accurately. Other measures have been taken that rely on mechanical means of recording how many hours the receiver is turned on. This may be a more accurate reporting of only that—the amount of time the set is turned on. It gives no guarantee that anyone other than the family cat may have been in the room all the time the set was on. Nevertheless, there are reportable figures. Numbers of studies show that watching television is a major activity of older people; in fact, viewing time seems to increase with age.

One of the earliest studies of time spent viewing was Ripley and Buell (1954). Two samples of male viewers were compared and it was found that men over age 61 tended to view 3.15 hours per day. This is compared with men aged 19–31 who tended to view 2.35 hours daily. Similar increases were reported for female viewers who, as a rule, tended to watch more hours per day than do males.

In 1962 Cowgill and Baulch interviewed 224 older citizens of Wichita, Kansas, whose daily viewing time averaged more than 5 hours. In 1970 Bower looked at data collected from a national sample of 1,900 adults and found that those aged 60 and over viewed an average of 4 hours on weekday evenings and on weekends. In 1975 Danowski interviewed residents of a retirement community in Michigan, finding the 162 residents to be viewing as much as 6 hours daily. (This is the one exceptional population, viewing more than 5 hours daily.)

The 1976 study of Davis and Edwards utilized Rustrack Event Recorders to collect viewing data in a mechanical fashion rather than relying on self-reported viewing times. The recorders automatically registered the amount of time the set was on and in use by residents of communal facilities throughout Los Angeles. They found that this older population viewed an average of 3.4 hours daily.

In more recent studies, Rubin and Rubin looked at viewing behaviors of 128 hospitalized older patients in 1981, finding that they viewed an average of 5 hours daily. The same research team measured viewing patterns in a Wisconsin sample of 340 people aged 55 + in 1982. This sample viewed nearly 5 hours daily.

Finally, the Nielsen annual surveys substantiate this viewing pattern as they make their annual breakdown of audience behaviors. Their older samples are aged 55 +, which tends to skew this data a bit; however, they consistently show in their sampling that older women view more than any other age group. The 1981 report indicates that women age 55 + average 38.26 hours of viewing per week, or about 5.4 hours daily. The 1982 tabulation reports the older female population as viewing an average of 39.20 hours weekly, or about 5.6 hours daily. The average time in front of the television set appears to increase with age. Nielsen reports males in the same age group as viewing almost 4 hours less per week than their female counterparts.

What we learn is that nearly all studies show that older adults view more television than do adults in younger age groups. Although there may be discrepancies in the way data is collected, and the way viewing is reported, it is evident that the amount of viewing increases with age. This trend is demonstrated from age 30 on before showing a decline around the age of 70.

When Do Older People Watch Television?

Viewing patterns do not differ greatly from the general population. Older viewers tend to tune in earlier in the evening assumedly for the late afternoon and early evening news. They remain to view prime time programs, but phase out of the viewing situation between 9:30 and 10:00 P.M. This is an hour earlier than the younger viewers. Older women tend to spend daytime hours with the soap operas and daytime talk shows.

What Are the Program Choices?

Television fare is varied: news and public affairs, dramatic serials, movies, talk shows, game shows, comedies, musical specials, nature shows, and sports events make up the majority of the television program schedule. Older people are reported as watching a variety of these shows; in fact, most samplings indicate preferences spread across the spectrum of program types. Early studies made some assumptions that older people would not watch game shows because the action would be too fast for them to absorb information easily. There was an assumption that movies were too long to hold attention, that action shows were too violent, and daytime programming the exclusive province of women. None of these generalizations has been proved empirically. Evidence indicates that like most other populations, individual preferences are not necessarily age-related.

Of course, there are exceptions to that statement. Children, for example, have some decided preferences in programming that differ from adult choices. The broad age range of adults demonstrates a variety of choices. Davis used the 1977 Arbitron ratings to make a comparison of viewing patterns of adult men and women from age 35 through 65 + . Program preferences were compared along age dimensions. (Arbitron is an audience survey company providing pertinent demographics to networks and advertising agencies.) There were definite age-related differences in program type preferences. Younger men tended to choose detective and action shows. The older males indicated that seven of the ten programs most favored by them were news and public affairs shows. In contrast, the youngest group viewed only two of this type of programs.

Women demonstrate more consistently across the age span than do men in their choice of programs. At all ages they tend to choose shows with a strong family-centered theme. It is only in the oldest age group that women indicate a significant percentage of programs in which they share an interest with their male age-mates.

The one program type that always appears as first choice on any list of favored programs of the older viewers is news and public affairs. The older viewers have clearly been identified as major consumers of news programming. Samplings taken across age groups show that more time is invested with news programs as age advances. Studies by Bower (1973), Danowski (1975), Davis (1971), Hopf and Bedwell (1959), and a host of others demonstrate this finding.

Doolittle's 1979 study showed that televised news was the preferred medium for news acquisition by older adults. This supports the earlier 1975 Harris findings. There is an assumption made that older people are drawn to this program type because their need to be kept aware of current events is greater than their need for mere diversion.

Doolittle also concluded that there was a correlation between education and news consumption, but little relationship between income and news consumption. Even so, criticizing news presentation by the media was more likely to come from older viewers than younger viewers. Further, the higher the educational and income level, the more likely the television viewer is to be critical. In his sample, news viewing, like general television viewing, tends to peak in the early 70s and drops after age 74.

Although not much has been reported about patterns of viewing by older viewers of daytime programming, both Barton, in 1977, and Elliott in 1981 credit the older viewer as being a major part of the audience for soap operas. In fact, Barton credits soap opera with being the major programming providing positive models of aging and contributing substantially to the lives of the older, mainly female, viewers. Elliott reports that women over age 55 supply a larger number of audience members for many of the popular soaps than any other age group.

Both Davis in 1971 and Rubin and Rubin in 1982 reported variety shows as being a second-place favorite with the elderly. The musical variety show is not presently seen as a series on network television. What is currently popular changes every second or third season, and the musical variety show seems to have disappeared for the time being. The high cost of producing such a show may be one factor in its absence, but the musical as a rerun continues to attract older viewers to independent station offerings. The situation comedy show may be next most popular, although the Rubins' sample indicated the drama to be more popular than the comedy.

The important conclusion regarding program preference is that after news and public affairs, there is a fairly even distribution of choice among several program types enjoyed by the older viewers. Attracting the least number of older viewers seem to be movies, action or adventure shows, and, of course, children's shows.

Why Do They Watch?

What motivates older people to spend a significant part of their day with the television set turned on? What are the reasons for television to be such a valued part of their lives? Several speculations can be made in response to these questions.

Today's elderly, after all, became a television audience perhaps 35 years ago when they were middle-aged. They had grown up in a world quite different from the one future generations of elderly will have known. Television for today's elderly has been something unusual, supplanting radio, which had been the major source of entertainment and current affairs. It has become a convenient, easily available, and assumably free source of pleasure. It is easier to hear the news than to read it when vision begins to fail. And it costs less than the newspaper.

Television supplies role models to the elderly as well as to all viewers. In other seasons there were such people as the fictional Grandma and Grandpa Walton who were admired by older viewers as much as they were admired and looked up to by the young. The very real Walter Cronkite represents stability and wisdom to all ages. He provides a very socially acceptable model of being old. Using television for models of behaviors is as valid for the old as well as for the younger viewers.

Significance and Impact. Television is an environmental plus for most people in today's society. It is especially valued by older people for three reasons: accessibility, convenience, and utility. Television is perceived by most people as a gift; it appears to have no cost associated with its use. Of course there is the cost of electricity to operate it, but who knows what that might be for this one appliance among many in the modern house? Not only is it "free," but it is also close at hand. It is accessible in a way that other media are not. One does not have to pay at the box office—unless one subscribes to a cable service. Television shares with radio the advantage of "coming alive" at the flick of a switch. And, like radio, most receivers do not require much maintenance or costly repair.

Television is convenient to use as a source of information and entertainment, much more convenient than reading. It does not demand as much concentrated attention as the newspaper. Other tasks can be performed with the program tuned in providing a background diversion to be viewed or not viewed as one wishes. Once the various fine-tuning knobs are mastered, the receiver needs little attention. The newer models may not even require periodic attention to the sound, color, and tuners. It is the author's experience that older viewers are sometimes hesitant to adopt the newest television technology. They prefer to deal with a set that is familiar even if it does not have the latest innovations. In the 1970 Davis study, modified color television receivers were distributed to a select group of older viewers. Resistance was found from some subjects because of the need to use a special remote control device. Even though the older population was offered the free use of color receivers, some owners of black and white sets needed convincing and had to be patiently and sensitively instructed in the operation of receivers before they would agree to be a part of the study.

When there are problems with vision, television assumes still more importance because it is easier for many to see what is happening even in a small screen picture than it is to read the print in newspapers or magazines. In fact, for older people, as for many who are not old, the major utility of television is that it provides easily understood information without requiring the recipient to exert much effort. For those elderly with seriously impaired vision, the television picture is not useful; how-

ever, if the hearing is not severely impaired, it is possible to get sufficient information from the soundtrack alone. Since the newscast is the
most valued kind of program, for the elderly the visual is a plus, but not
an absolute necessity. For those who have very poor hearing, it is possible to get an extension speaker to bring the sound closer to the ear.
Some programs and some stations offer captioned television and even an
inset of someone interpreting with sign language.

Television offers all consumers two commodities: entertainment
and information. These are not necessarily two distinct and different
program types. Information programs are designed to be entertaining,
and entertainment programs are either intentionally or unintentionally
informative. We expect television to keep us up to date with local, regional, national, and international affairs. Most of us do not really feel
the need for in-depth information, and therefore the evening news satis-
fies the need to be informed. Those who do want more information
about current topics can find opportunities outside of prime time programming hours.

It is the news program that is universally viewed by older people. In
fact, there is evidence that the older the audience, the greater the amount
of time spent viewing news and public affair programs. For older people,
television is a special window to the world. It allows the housebound or
bedridden to escape the confinement of the apartment, hospital, or nursing home. It allows the isolated individual to feel part of the larger society. The news program enables the individual to know the same facts
and figures, and the same scandals and disasters, that everyone talks of
with varying levels of sophistication and knowledge. The important
thing is being a part of that larger society of the knowledgeable.

The Parasocial Experience. Television's role as companion should not
be overlooked. Many researchers term this the "parasocial" dimension
of the viewing experience. By this is meant the granting of acquaintance-
status to familiar and likable individuals who appear on regular television programming. Program people know the value of charisma in attracting viewers to personalities. The popular talk shows are compara-
tively easy and inexpensive to produce. At the local level they provide a
forum for community opinion and the airing of community concerns.
At the same time they fulfill the station's commitment to operate in the
public interest. Nationally syndicated or network distributed, the late
night talk show attracts millions of viewers, and millions of dollars in
advertising revenue. Here is where the television "personality" is important in attracting viewers.

Networks in former years offered such pleasant personalities as Mike
Douglas and Dinah Shore as host and hostess for their own daytime

shows. As times change and something (and someone) new is needed to revive waning interests, we find talk shows still occupying network daytime, but it is with different personalities such as Phil Donahue and Merv Griffin now presenting material for public interest that Mike and Dinah may not have considered for their shows. Donahue talks about things that as one older woman put it, "shouldn't be talked about in the living room," but in doing so he commands a large audience—and it is not an age-limited audience. Griffin parades celebrities through the living room, adding a little glamour to the day. What is important to note is that these two men become known persons, they are "Phil" and "Merv" to their followers. They are, in fact, friends—fictive friends, but thought of as familiar and trusted. This is very attractive to numbers of people regardless of age who appreciate these substitutes for real relationships.

In other ways as well television enables people to be a part of established groups. It is almost as though there were certain viewing clubs. There is the "Phil Donahue" club, the "All My Children" club, the "Johnny Carson" club, and so forth. Being familiar with a certain show is a social facilitator. One can discuss details of "Dallas" if one views that show with other regular viewers. There are retirement homes that schedule lunch at 11:30 so that the residents can be sure to be in their rooms in time to watch "Days of Our Lives." It is an easy assumption that the intricacies of the plot are discussed at more than one luncheon table.

It is not only in the realm of talk format that the viewer finds relationships that might be labeled parasocial in nature. There have always been certain citizens who populate the world of television who have become part of the extended family. The most obvious illustration of that phenomenon with reference to the older viewer is the cast of "The Lawrence Welk Show." Viewers everywhere knew the personal histories of the singers and dancers of that musical show. This was an intentional strategy of the program decision makers. Welk and company knew that they had a "family" that included (what was presented to the public at least) models of shiny, clean, all-American young people.

Other residents of television land have also become members of viewers' extended families. John Boy of "The Waltons" is a case in point. Older viewers especially responded to the sentimental portrait of a family struggling through the depression in the 1930s. John Boy, the youth who aspired to "be something better" despite the hard times and with strong family support, stood as the reminder for many of life as it might have been and often *is* in the reconstructed reality of memory.

More recently there may be some difficulty in finding people inside of the world of television who can be given friendship status with the older viewers. Daytime viewers may settle for a friendly and exuberant host of a game show. But for all viewers, the population of news programs are very, very real and very familiar personalities who are perceived as "friends."

Those who deliver the news are cast as carefully and as surely as casting is done for the comedy and drama programs that fill out the evening schedule. The panel of newsmen and newswomen usually includes first of all the anchorperson. This is frequently most often an older male. His very age gives him the look of mature wisdom, dignity, and trustworthiness. He is seen most often in the national news segment. The outstanding example of all time is, of course, Walter Cronkite, the dean emeritus of news anchormen. Each network and each local news staff includes the Cronkite-like lead person. There are others: the pretty and sharp young woman, the handsome and alert young man, the athlete (for sports news), and the comedian (for weather news). With some variations, these are the carefully chosen persons on every news program. And in a multichannel television environment, people are as likely to choose the station for news viewing according to their preference of personality as they are for styles in handling the news. After all, some may reason, news is news, but those who deliver it are individually different—and it is that different degree of personal charisma that attracts viewers to the news program.

Passing Time. Television also offers older viewers a way of marking off time. When one is working, there are all sorts of time-related events: the time to leave for work, to check in at work, to have a coffee break, to eat lunch, to attend meetings, to go home. These time-associated events are lost once the individual retires. A day that was once marked off in meaningful segments because of appointments and other work-related events may stretch as one long, meaningless span of time after retirement. If the day, or week, is punctuated by specific television programs, which are always scheduled according to a specified time, then there is a sort of meaningful pattern laid onto the expanse of time. One or two nights a week may acquire significance because those are the nights of favored programs. Certain times of the day can be anticipated with more interest because those are the times for special programs.

Finally, television also offers the opportunity to fill time that may otherwise lie unoccupied. It is a doing something as opposed to doing nothing. Even though there is a certain amount of social stigma associated with excessive viewing, there is a greater stigma connected with being absolutely unoccupied. More than that, there are those who do lack mobility, lack contact with other people, lack resources for creative or intellectual stimulation. Television is accessible and useful for filling these voids.

Television in the Lives of an Older Population: Long Beach Revisited

A Current Audience Study

In 1982 the authors conducted a study on the viewing behaviors of older persons especially for this book. The study, a time-lag survey research, is reported here in full. The intent of this section is to acquaint the reader with some conventional older audience behavior study methods and results. This current information helps to illustrate the place of television in the lives of today's older viewing population.

The study reported here replicates a 1969 study of television viewing behaviors in an older population (R.H. Davis 1971). Its purpose is to compare responses to a similar survey instrument in a comparable population after a 13-year lag. Reflecting the circumstances of the researcher in 1969, the original study was simple in its design. Because its age makes the study less relevant now than it was originally, the contemporary investigation of a similar nature was undertaken. The question asked was: Do viewers in today's 55 + age group perceive television any differently, and do they behave differently as viewers than an earlier generation of television viewers?

It seemed warranted to return to the first research site, administer the study to as similar a population as could be gathered today, and use up-to-date analysis techniques to report on current audience behaviors and, more importantly, to compare today with yesterday by way of time-lag survey research. Do different cohorts report different behaviors, preferences, or attitudes about television? With these questions in mind, this study was conducted during the fall and spring of 1982–83.

The Long Beach Replication

The 1969 Study. A questionnaire was distributed to a population aged 55 and over. The sample, numbering 174, was representative of the norm for their age category in that they lived in private housing rather than in an institutional setting.

All respondents lived in the greater Long Beach, California area and were self-selected in that they were attendees at functions of a then existing adult education program titled "The Institute of Lifetime Learning." This program was sponsored by the American Association of Retired Persons and was held at AARP headquarters in downtown Long Beach. This population was deliberately chosen as representing healthy, autonomous, and actively involved older persons.

The survey was completed in early December 1969 when it was felt that the new viewing season had been sufficiently established for viewing habits to be fairly stabilized. The written self-reported form was administered to those who attended classes by their teachers and other program people. Some used it as a discussion tool after respondents had filled out the forms. Questionnaires were coded for data processing. Punch cards were made and fed into an IBM sorter for numerical analysis.

The questionnaires dealt with four areas: (1) demographics, (2) television use and viewing habits, (3) program preferences, and (4) attitudes and opinions. A total of thirty questions was asked.

Several optional open-ended questions which enabled the respondents to air their feelings about the general subject of television were included. The resulting comments were coded according to the broad classifications into which the answers seemed to array themselves (see Appendix A, questions 10 and 11 of part 4).

The state of the art in computer technology and data analysis being what they were in 1969, coupled with the "pilot study" nature of the investigation, brought us to a decision to report only raw data—frequencies and percentage distributions. The current (1982) study has employed contemporary data analysis techniques. However, even in today's climate of easy access to computers, it is impossible for us to perform a more sophisticated analysis of the 1969 data, as all of the questionnaires were eventually (and purposely) destroyed.

The 1982 Study. The current collection of data was conducted in late November and early December of 1982. As in the previous study, the responses were solicited in a time period prior to the flood of television's Christmas specials. Data were gathered from questionnaires presented to and returned by 274 members of the Long Beach Jewish Community Center and the Long Beach Senior Center. At both sites, self-selection was the vehicle by which participants were incorporated into the study (the biases introduced by self-selection are acknowledged). The sample of 274 individuals comprised 83 elderly Jews and 191 elderly non-Jews.

Again, the written self-report form was administered to those attending various educational programs at the two community centers. The administration was accomplished by staff and program people of these two centers, not university researchers. This was deliberate so as to conform with the methodology employed in the first study; in addition, it was thought that the use of university researchers would bias the respondents. Again, some program people used the instrument as a trigger device for discussions following the completion of the forms.

The research employed a 73-item scale (see Appendix A), which was a modified version of the original 1969 Davis audience survey scale. The scale was designed to tap four specific dimensions: (1) demographic data, (2) television use, (3) program preferences, and (4) audience opinions. In analyzing the data, univariate statistics, *t*-tests, and crosstabs were generated. Correlation and regression analyses were also performed in order to secure a greater wealth of information. These analyses were not useful in making the simple comparisons of frequency distributions for the time-lag research. They are relevant and necessary, however, for the analysis reported in study two and three.

Results and Discussion

Demographic Data. Both the 1969 and 1982 studies contained questions tapping demographic information: gender, age, marital status, living status, and education. Table 5–1 presents the percentage distribu-

Table 5–1
Percentage Distribution of Demographic Data, 1969 versus 1982

Variable	Response Options	1969 Percentage (N = 174)	1982 Percentage (N = 274)
Gender			
	Male	22.4	29.0
	Female	77.6	71.0
Age			
	55 or less	2.9	5.5
	56–65	16.9	26.5
	66–75	51.7	45.2
	Over 75	28.5	22.8
Marital status			
	Married	37.6	37.4
	Single	22.0	8.5
	Other (divorced, widowed, separated)	40.5	54.0
Living status			
	Live alone	54.6	53.5
Education			
	Less than high school graduate	23.7	19.0
	high school grad or more	76.3	81.0

tions for the five retained demographic variables in the 1969 and 1982 studies. There are 6.6 percent more men in the current sample than in the 1969 sample. Still, the ratio of men to women reflects the general older population, where women outnumber men significantly. That there is a larger percentage of older men in the current population than in the original population may reflect some gains in longevity for males over the past 13 years or may reflect the existence of programs at the study sites which are attractive to males.

The population for the 1982 study is slightly younger than that of the first study. The under-66 age group increased by 12.2 percent. However, a clear majority of the population falls into the older half (above 66) of the study group.

Another difference in the two populations is exhibited by the marital status data for both groups. The current cohort shows a 13.5 percent increase in the numbers who list themselves as divorced, widowed, or separated (as opposed to identifying themselves as singles). Those older people who are still in a marriage relationship remain in the minority. The percentage of those who live alone remains about the same.

In the 1969 study 76.3 percent, a majority of the population, had an educational attainment equal to or beyond high school graduation. In 1982 that population had increased by 4.7 percent, to 81.0 percent. This difference between the two populations' educational level is in agreement with the gerontological literature, which indicates that each successive cohort arrives at age 65 possessing more education than previous cohorts.

The present sample is a little younger and contains more males than the 1969 sample. It has about the same ratio of marrieds to nonmarrieds as the earlier one, and about the same percentage of the 1982 sample is higher than that of the 1969 sample.

Viewing Behaviors. Patterns of television viewing, program preferences, and opinions about the programming and the meaning of the viewing experience were explored in this part of the survey.

Television Use. Table 5–2 presents a comparison of the self-reported number of hours spent watching television in the two populations. In 1969, 17 percent of the sample admitted to spending in excess of 5 hours daily with television. By 1982 that percentage had changed to 21 percent reporting they viewed 5 or more hours per day. Although these viewing figures may be questioned as to how accurately they reflect reality, this change is indicative of a shift toward more viewing. This overall increase in the proportion of heavy viewers reflects the reality of television being increasingly interwoven into the fabric of our lives. However, we must

Table 5–2
Percentage Distribution of Amount of Television Watched, 1969 versus 1982

Daily TV Viewing	1969 Percentage (N = 174)	1982 Percentage (N = 274)
Less than 1 hour	7.8	11.9
1–3 hours	44.0	35.8
3–5 hours	31.1	31.0
Over 5 hours	17.1	21.3

also recognize an equal shift in the opposite direction: 4 percent more than was reported by the 1969 population of the present population indicated that they watch less than 1 hour of television daily.

Self-reported viewing times might well be suspected of being somewhat contaminated; a lack of awareness of the actual amount of television watched, and/or a tendency to allow social desirability to color one's responses, are two possible contributors to data that does not entirely reflect reality. Projecting from these figures, only one-fifth of our current population clocks as many as 35 hours of viewing per week. There appears to be a lack of agreement between what our sample self-reports and what is stated in the 1982 Nielsen report on television, which identifies the 55 + audience as those most invested in viewing. Nielsen reports an average of 39.2 hours per week for women 55 + and 35.4 hours per week for men in the same age group.

Daily viewing patterns of our two groups are compared in table 5–3. Such patterns reflect choices from available programs as well as current prevailing life styles. For whatever reasons, there are some shifts from 1969 to 1982 in the times of day during which the older audience is most pronounced.

As reflected in table 5–3, weekday viewers in the 1982 population are inclined to stay up later than their 1969 counterparts. However, that the 1982 group watches less on Saturday and Sunday evenings than does the 1969 age group may mean that the current sample may be more social than the earlier cohort—or is it just that the programs they enjoy are not available on weekend nights?

Program Preferences. The elderly viewers in both samples were asked to choose and rank their three top preferences from a list of program types. In 1969 that list included the following: (1) news and public affairs, (2) educational programs, (3) travelogues, (4) documentaries, (5) comedies, (6) drama, (7) specials entertainment, (8) sports, (9) movies,

Table 5–3
Percentage Distribution of Daily Viewing Patterns, 1969 versus 1982

Variable	1969 Percentage (N = 174)	1982 Percentage (N = 274)
TV viewing: Monday to Friday		
6 A.M.–Noon (morning)	21.3	19.5
Noon–6 P.M. (afternoon)	27.6	22.8
6–9 P.M. (evening)	79.9	77.6
9–12 Midnight (night)	31.6	41.2
12 Midnight–6 A.M. (late night)	3.4	4.0
TV viewing: Saturday		
6 A.M.–Noon (morning)	3.4	8.1
Noon–6 P.M. (afternoon)	7.5	21.3
6–9 P.M. (evening)	56.3	51.8
9–12 Midnight (night)	33.3	31.3
12 Midnight–6 A.M. (late night)	2.3	2.9
TV viewing: Sunday		
6 A.M.–Noon (morning)	12.1	15.1
Noon–6 P.M. (afternoon)	17.8	18.4
6–9 P.M. (evening)	61.5	54.0
9–12 Midnight (night)	25.9	31.3
12 Midnight–6 A.M. (late night)	1.7	2.2

and (10) variety shows. Respondents indicated their three top choices of program types to be (1) news and public affairs, (2) educational programs, and (3) travelogues.

The list offered respondents was modified for the 1982 sampling. It was thought that some of the labels were misleading and that others were no longer valid program offerings. The 1982 list was as follows: (1) feature films, (2) general drama, (3) informative documentaries, (4) news, (5) situation comedy, (6) sports, and (7) suspense, mystery, drama. The three top choices in 1982 were (1) news, (2) informative documentaries, and (3) feature films. These choices probably reflect, in great part, what programs are available in a given season.

In both samples respondents were asked to indicate the specific shows they viewed more or less regularly. Although the 1969 audience said that news and public affairs, educational programs, and travelogues were their favorite program types, the latter two were not among their favorite shows. Music ("The Lawrence Welk Show") and drama ("Bonanza" and "Gunsmoke"), followed by comedies such as "Mayberry, RFD" and "The Red Skelton Show" were the most frequently mentioned favorites. Such shows were distant second and third places, following the overwhelming first choice: news and public affairs programs. Walter Cronkite was the number one choice as favorite personality and his show, the CBS evening news, the favorite program for older viewers in 1969.

By 1982 the situation had changed only slightly. Again, news format programs were on the list of top-rated shows of older viewers. The informative documentary and the comedy were second and third choices, respectively.

In 1969 only four programs on the Nielsen top fifteen programs for the total population were on the list of top-rated shows of older viewers. These were: "Bonanza," "The Red Skelton Show," "Mayberry, RFD," and "Gunsmoke."

In 1982 of the top fifteen regularly scheduled network programs listed by Nielsen, six programs captured more than 30 percent of the older audience. Listed in order of their popularity, they are "Sixty Minutes," "Love Boat," "Archie Bunker's Place," "M*A*S*H," "The Jeffersons," and "Little House on the Prairie." Given our 1982 population's stated preferences in program types, we would expect "60 Minutes" to be first and the news second or third. However, it is interesting that "Love Boat" is *the top* non-news show, and that it is so different in content than "M*A*S*H" or "Archie Bunker's Place."

Greater congruity between program preferences by type and by title is exhibited in the responses of the 1982 audience; their three favorite program types were news, documentary, and comedy. "60 Minutes," which might be classified as either a documentary or a news format show, is viewed by 71 percent of the 1982 sample. The daily evening news shows are also heavily viewed. The 5:00 P.M. news is watched by 44.3 percent, 6:00 P.M. news by 47.6 percent and the 7:00 P.M. news (usually national coverage) is viewed regularly by 34.8 percent of our sample. Apparently, the older viewing population is more interested in and concerned with the local news (5:00 and 6:00 P.M.) than with the national news (7:00 P.M.).

"Love Boat," a comedy/drama, captures 43.2 percent of the audience. This show regularly features older, well-known personalities from films of the 1940s and 1950s. "Archie Bunker's Place" draws 37.0 percent and "M*A*S*H" 35.5 percent of the older viewers. "M*A*S*H," even in reruns continues to be favored by this audience.

In passing, it is interesting to recall the cancelation in the early 1970s of such bucolic favorites as "Gomer Pyle," "Mayberry, RFD," and "Green Acres" because their loyal audience had grown older as it stayed with the durable shows. Could this same awareness have contributed to decisions to cancel "Archie Bunker's Place" and "M*A*S*H"?

Audience Opinion. Respondents in both studies were asked to make subjective evaluations on various aspects of television. Respondents were asked, "On the whole, the entertainment that television offers to you personally is (1) very unsatisfactory, (2) somewhat unsatisfactory, (3) somewhat satisfactory, or (4) very satisfactory." Of the 1969 audience, 42.5 percent felt the entertainment offered was somewhat satisfactory, and 19 percent felt it was very satisfactory. These percentages increased in the 1982 data: 48.6 percent found television entertainment to be somewhat satisfactory (a 6.1 percent increase), while 21.7 percent report it as being very satisfactory (a 2.7 percent increase). It would appear that positive opinion about television's ability to entertain has increased appreciably.

Similarly, the companionship role of television is more positively evaluated by the present sample. In 1969, 60.3 percent of the respondents believed that television served a moderate or strong function in providing companionship. By 1982 that percentage endorsing television's companionship role had increased to 75.8 percent of the respondents. Not only did the percentage of our sample identifying the companionship function of television increase a significant 15.5 percent from 1969 to 1982, but also the percentage identifying the companionship function of television as weak or nonexistent dropped by 8.3 percent. This stands as another testimony to how intricately television has become woven into our lives.

When asked to evaluate the image of aging and the aged as they saw it projected in the dramatic material of television program content, 53.6 percent of the 1969 population reported that they were satisfied with the portrayal of older people. That figure increased to 59.2 percent of the respondents satisfied with the image of aging in 1982. Opinions about television program content held by older viewers have shifted, with a larger percentage holding positive opinions about television in their lives. Approval of the depiction of older people in dramatic program content is more widespread today than in 1969.

In contrast, however, responses to an inquiry about the factual and honest presentation of older people in television commercials did not indicate such positiveness. In 1969, 38.2 percent believed the presentations were honest; in 1982 the figure had increased only slightly to 39.7 percent. When asked if commercials influenced their buying habits, the percentage of 1982 sample saying "yes" was 19.2 percent, compared with 18.9 percent in 1969.

Both sets of respondents were given an opportunity, through open-ended questions, to identify areas of programming they would like more of. The survey item reads: "If there are any subjects of interest and importance to you that are not presented on TV now and you would like to see presented, what are they?" The 1969 audience identified three areas of program need. These areas, categorized from their statements, were

(1) educational, (2) musical, and (3) philosophical (that is, programs dealing with problem-solving techniques and concerns with various aspects of the human condition).

The 1982 sample's responses clustered most easily into similar topic areas, but in a slightly different order: (1) musical/cultural, (2) educational (mainly health and politics), and (3) philosophical issues.

On the one hand 37.4 percent of the early sample thought program content to be lacking, while 37.2 percent of the present sample feel the same lack. On the other hand almost two-thirds of both samples implied satisfaction with program content. This appears to bolster further the labeling of the elderly as satisfied television consumers.

Another open-ended question allowed for the specification of program materials judged to be objectionable by the elderly respondents. In 1969, 48 percent of the sample indicated objections to program content. By 1982 the percentage of respondents indicating objections to program content had dropped to 38.0 percent, although the actual list of objections had changed very little. In 1969 violence, sex, commercials, and "overexposure of minorities" were the prevalent objections. In 1982 sex led the list. Crime and violence placed second (although the mentions of violence numbered only half as many as in 1969). The third area of objection was offensive commercials, and then sensationalism in news reporting. There was no mention of minorities. Either fewer people object to violence in program content, or the viewing population is now conditioned to accept it more easily. Almost in contradiction to their stated objections to sensational news coverage, our sample's program choices indicate that fewer of this population view the 7:00 P.M. news, which tends to be national and perhaps less sensational in nature, while the majority watch the 5:00 and 6:00 P.M. news, which tends to be local and usually more sensational in nature.

West Coast versus East Coast Audience Samples

Assisted by Gerald Jay Westbrook, we also conducted research on how television affected the lives of older persons on the East Coast as compared with the West Coast. The same written self-report form used for the Long Beach sample was administered to older persons in senior centers, clubs, and residences in the Maryland suburbs of the Washington, D.C. metropolitan area. The sample included 288 participants. The results, especially relating to viewing behaviors, program preferences, and selected audience opinion, show interesting similarities to and dissimilarities from the West Coast sample.

Demographic Data

The demographic makeup of the East Coast and West Coast samples (see table 5–4) was quite similar, with two exceptions. A significant percentage of the West Coast sample lived alone, while their East Coast counterparts were far more likely to live with another person. The East Coast participants were also far more likely to be married than were their West Coast counterparts.

Viewing Behaviors: Television Use. The substantial majority of both East and West Coast samples (see table 5–5) acknowledged watching between 1 and 5 hours of television per day, but West Coast viewers indicated they watch more television on the average weekday. All told, 9

Table 5–4
Percentage Distribution of Demographic Data, East Coast Elderly versus West Coast Elderly

Variable	Response Options	East Coast Percentage (N = 288)	West Coast Percentage (N = 274)
Gender			
	Male	29.7	29.0
	Female	70.3	71.0
Age			
	55 or less	5.0	5.5
	56–65	20.9	26.5
	66–75	46.8	45.2
	Over 75	27.3	22.8
Marital status			
	Married	47.9	37.4
	Single	5.3	8.5
	Other (divorced, widowed, separated)	46.9	54.0
Living status			
	Live alone	41.3	53.5
	Live with another	53.0	
	Live in group setting	5.7	
Education			
	Less than high school graduate	15.3	19.0
	High school graduate or more	84.7	81.0

Table 5–5
Percentage Distribution of Amount of Television Watched, East Coast Elderly versus West Coast Elderly

TV Viewing	East Coast Percentage (N = 288)	West Coast Percentage (N = 274)
Average weekday		
Less than 1 hour	6.3	11.7
1–3 hours	50.2	35.8
3–5 hours	31.0	31.0
Over 5 hours	12.5	21.3
Average saturday		
Less than 1 hour	24.7	25.8
1–3 hours	55.6	36.0
3–5 hours	15.8	25.5
Over 5 hours	3.9	12.7
Average Sunday		
Less than 1 hour	13.6	18.7
1–3 hours	60.1	43.4
3–5 hours	19.2	23.6
Over 5 hours	7.0	14.2

percent more of the West Coast than East Coast viewers watched more than 5 or more hours of television a day.

On the weekends both the East and West Coast populations watched less television. Again, however, there was a noticeable amount of difference in the amount of weekend viewing time between the two coasts, the East Coast sample spending far less time involved in this activity. This discrepancy may reflect differences in the entertainment and other activities available in each of the geographic areas.

Daily viewing patterns for both groups (see table 5–6) were almost identical. The heaviest viewing time occurred (as might be expected) during the prime viewing time between 6 and 9 P.M., with around three-fourths of each sample watching during this time slot. A substantial proportion also watched television during the night viewing period from 9 P.M. to 12 midnight. Dispelling a well-accepted myth that older persons are avid viewers during the morning and afternoon hours, only around one-fifth of each group of viewers indicated spending time in front of the television set in the morning (6 A.M. to 12 noon) and afternoon (12 noon to 6 P.M.) time periods.

The weekend viewing patterns, however, indicated a more noticeable difference between the two populations. The East Coast viewers tended to watch less television in the morning and more at night compared to the West Coast viewers. One can speculate that this might reflect the ef-

Table 5–6
Percentage Distribution of Daily Viewing Patterns, East Coast Elderly versus West Coast Elderly

Variable	East Coast Percentage (N = 288)	West Coast Percentage (N = 274)
TV viewing: Monday to Friday		
6 A.M.–Noon (morning)	23.3	19.5
Noon–6 P.M. (afternoon)	19.4	22.8
6–9 P.M. (evening)	74.0	77.6
9–12 Midnight (night)	41.0	41.2
12 Midnight–6 A.M. (late night)	4.9	4.0
TV viewing: Saturday		
6 A.M.–Noon (morning)	2.8	8.1
Noon–6 P.M. (afternoon)	16.3	21.3
6–9 P.M. (evening)	50.7	51.8
9–12 Midnight (night)	39.6	31.3
12 Midnight–6 A.M. (late night)	2.4	2.9
TV viewing: Sunday		
6 A.M.–Noon (morning)	10.8	15.1
Noon–6 P.M. (afternoon)	21.5	18.4
6–9 P.M. (evening)	51.4	54.0
9–12 Midnight (night)	29.2	31.3
12 Midnight–6 A.M. (late night)	3.1	2.2

fects of the 3 hours' time difference in programming, particularly with regards to weekend sports events.

Program Preferences

When asked to list the program "types" they most preferred, both population groups agreed on their first three program preferences; the top choice being news, followed by informative/documentaries and feature films. The groups differed in their preference for situation comedies, sports, and general drama—the East Coast sample showing greater preference for situation comedy and sports and the West Coast sample preferring general drama and situation comedy. There was agreement by both populations that suspense/mystery was the least favorite among the seven choices.

Both samples also were asked to list their three favorite television shows. The results showed complete agreement among the East Coast and West Coast viewers on the first three choices. The news was clearly the first choice, with "60 Minutes," a news/documentary show, a solid second. The popular comedy "M*A*S*H" was rated third by both groups. The real differences appeared in the third through sixth choices.

With East Coast viewers, "Masterpiece Theatre" and "Family Feud" were tied for third, followed by "General Hospital" in fifth place, and "Dallas" and "Nova" tied for sixth. The West Coast viewers chose "Dallas," "Merv Griffin," and "Little House on the Prairie" as their third through sixth choices. Thus, the East Coast viewers placed much stronger emphasis on educational or public television as compared to the West Coast viewers' in their preferences for popular nighttime programming.

When respondents were actually given a list of popular programs, according to the Nielsen ratings, and asked which they viewed "more or less regularly during the past year," viewers on both coasts chose "60 Minutes" and "Love Boat" (which often has big-name stars from the 1940s, 1950s, and 1960s) as their top two favorite non-news programs. However, when news programming was placed on the list, the second and third choices on both coasts became newscasts. Both samples selected the local news at 6 P.M. as their second choice, while the East Coast preferred national news at 7 P.M. and the West Coast local news at 5 P.M. as their third choices.

Selected Audience Opinions

Both populations were asked about the function television played in their lives. More than 70 percent of the senior viewers on both coasts saw television as a "strong" or "moderate" companion. In answer to the question of whether television was an entertainment source, however, there was a marked difference in opinion by the viewers on each coast. Around 70 percent of the West Coast sample perceived television as "somewhat or very *satisfactory*" in entertainment value, while an almost identical percentage on the East Coast felt it to be "somewhat or very *unsatisfactory*" (see table 5–7).

The study also sought to find out whether the older audience was being effectively reached by television (see table 5–8). Asked whether older persons were presented honestly and factually in drama, comedy, and commercials, the viewers on the East and West Coasts were generally split on this question. They tended to believe that dramatic programming portrayed their peers better than comedy and commercials, however.

The study also asked whether television offers adequate programming for the older audience. A majority of the samples on both coasts seemed to think that this was not the case. This particular data can serve as excellent ammunition if you are considering trying to gain access to the airwaves (see chapters 8 and 11).

In addition, the study queried whether older adults differ from other adults in their viewing needs and interests. Most of the older viewers on

Table 5–7
Entertainment and Companionship Provided by Television, East Coast Elderly versus West Coast Elderly

Variable	East Coast Percentage (N = 288)	West Coast Percentage (N = 274)
Entertainment		
Very unsatisfactory	10.4	12.4
Somewhat unsatisfactory	60.0	17.3
Somewhat satisfactory	12.6	48.6
Very satisfactory	17.0	21.7
Companionship		
Strong	15.0	16.9
Moderate	56.9	58.9
Weak	17.3	15.3
Not at all	10.8	8.5

the East and West Coasts—but certainly not an overwhelming majority of the samples (64.7 and 58.3 percent, respectively)—responded that the older audience did not have distinct viewing desires.

Finally, the study asked if commercials influence what older persons buy. Few of the respondents on either the East Coast or the West Coast (16 and 19.2 percent, respectively) acknowledged they were influenced by television commercials. Of course, few of us would admit to being influenced by television commercials, but our buying habits at the local grocery store would seem to indicate differently.

Table 5–8
Selected Audience Opinions, East Coast Elderly versus West Coast Elderly

Variable	East Coast Percentage (N = 288)	West Coast Percentage (N = 274)
Yes, older people are presented honestly and factually in		
Dramatic material	61.8	59.2
Comedy material	47.5	46.5
Commercials	44.4	39.7
Yes, commercials influence what I buy.	16.0	19.2
Yes, TV offers adequate programming for older adults.	41.8	39.6
Yes, older adults differ from other adults in their TV viewing needs and interests.	35.3	41.7

Summary Comparisons

1. The numbers reporting viewing in excess of 5 hours a day have increased since 1969.
2. The numbers reporting viewing less than 1 hour a day have increased.
3. Viewing patterns have remained fairly similar, but with fewer elderly viewing evening and night programs on the weekend.
4. The top program choices remain news and public affairs.
5. Feature films have become a new program preference, replacing travelogues.
6. Specific shows popular with older viewers reflect the available choices.
7. The satisfaction with television as entertainment has increased by a significant percentage since 1969.
8. The perception of television as providing companionship has increased significantly.
9. Satisfaction with the portrayal of older people in commercials increased over time, but only by 1.5 percent.
10. Satisfaction with the portrayal of older people in program content has increased.
11. There was basically no change (+0.03 percent) from 1969 to 1982 in the buying self-reported influence of commercials on our samples' buying habits.
12. Older viewers report that they would still (as in 1969) like more music, culture, and educational experiences presented on television.
13. Older viewers no longer evidence concern about the presence of minorities on television.
14. Newly identified as a needed subject is health information.
15. The 1982 sample indicates concern over what they see as sensationalism in news reporting, whereas our 1969 sample did not report such a concern.
16. East and West Coast audiences report similar viewing patterns, with the West Coast viewers engaging in more television viewing on the weekdays and weekends.
17. While both populations agree that favored shows are the news, "60 Minutes" and "M*A*S*H," respectively, the East Coast sample includes a stronger emphasis than the West Coast sample on educational or public television in their top six choices by including the Public Broadcasting System's "Masterpiece Theatre" and "Nova."
18. Both East and West Coast populations favor news, documentaries, and feature films as preferred program types.
19. The East Coast sample prefers 7 P.M. network evening news, whereas the West Coast viewers prefer the 5 P.M. local news.

20. More than twice the percentage of West Coast as East Coast viewers find television to be "somewhat or very satisfactory" in terms of entertainment value.

This study accomplished a number of goals. The primary intent was to compare and contrast audience behaviors as measured by the same instrument with a 14-year time lag between test 1 and test 2. We have found that there are some changes in these areas since the original survey in 1969. These changes are summarized in the preceding list. They lead us to generalize that today's older population is more strongly an "embracer" of television than was the earlier one. This study has, in many ways, been simplistic in nature. It was not designed to uncover cause and effect relationships. However, it has still yielded useful information. We have found that the older audience continues to be loyal, accepting, and satisfied with television. They would like to see some changes, most significantly in the area of health care, where they request still more programming. The earlier concerns of older people about minorities on television have disappeared. Finally, as every survey of the elderly audience indicates, they are the strongest and most loyal audience for news and information shows.

The older market is a growing one and, contrary to popular opinion, it is one that is economically significant. As its numbers continue to increase, it will become even more important to take this elder population into consideration when planning programming and advertising strategies.

Future Research

As the U.S. population continues to become increasingly older, increasingly heterogenous culturally, and increasingly integrates television into its life, it will be necessary to inspect with great rigor the differences between various elder subpopulations in their television viewing habits, their viewing interests, and their expectations of the role of television in their lives.

What are the viewing behaviors of blacks and other minorities whose numbers of elderly are also increasing? What other regional differences, if any, exist between older viewers in the midwest, the southeast, and the southwest as well as other neglected areas? What more can we uncover about elder viewing behaviors and related spending patterns among the affluent elderly? The list can go on, but it is clear that such information being provided to the broadcast industry can be invaluable in the development of programming and advertising strategies.

How might we learn more about older audiences? Other survey instruments can be created and we can expand our knowledge base thereby.

It is also possible to conduct intensive, in-depth, focused group discussion surveys. These kinds of data can be dealt with in a manner appropriate to the methodology. Results can be discussed qualitatively as well as quantitatively.

Small research projects such as the one reported here can aid programming decisions at local, regional, and national levels. As such research moves into the domain of academic sociology, it will enable us to learn still more about the leisure time pursuits of the elderly, the impact of televised images on the elderly, and the influence of television on spending patterns of an older society.

Television is almost universally accepted as the most influential of the mass media. Further, there is a growing recognition of the increasing importance of television as a channel of information about aging as well as a molder of attitudes about aging. Finally, there is interest in television's potential as a service delivery system for older audiences. Given all of the above, it is clear that there is much room for further investigation of television viewing behaviors and of person–television interactions.

References

Barton, R.L. 1977. Soap operas provide meaningful communication for the elderly. *Feedback* 19:5–8.

Bower, R.T. 1973. *Television and the Public*. New York: Holt, Rinehart, and Winston.

Cowgill, D., and N. Baulch. 1962. The use of leisure time by older people. *The Gerontologist* 2:47–50.

Danowski, J. 1975. Informational aging: interpersonal and mass communication patterns in a retirement community. Paper presented at the meeting of the Gerontological Society, Louisville, Ky.

Davis, R.H. 1971. Television and the older adult. *Journal of Broadcasting 15:* 153–59.

Davis, R.H. 1980. *Television and the Aging Audience*. Lexington, Mass.: Lexington Books.

Davis, R.H., A.E. Edwards, D.J. Bartel, and D. Martin. 1981. The assessment of television viewing behavior of older adults. *Journal of Broadcasting 25* (1):1–13.

DeGrazia, S. 1961. The use of time. In R.R. Kleemeir, ed., *Aging and Leisure*. New York: Oxford University Press.

Doolittle, J.C. 1970. News media use by older adults. *Journalism Quarterly* (Summer):439–41.

Elliott, J.C. 1981. Image of older adult characters on daytime serial drama. Unpublished Ed.D. Dissertation. Teachers' College, Columbia University, New York.

Harris, L., and Associates, Inc. 1975. *The Myth and Reality of Aging in America*. Washington, D.C.: National Council on the Aging.

Glick, I.O., and S.J. Levy. 1962. *Living with Television*. Chicago: Aldine.

Hopf, H.L., and R.T. Bedwell. 1966. Characteristics and program preferences of television listeners in Columbus, Ohio, April 1959. In L.W. Lichty and J.M. Ripley, II, Eds., *American Broadcasting*. Madison, Wis.: College Printing.

Nielsen, A.C. 1981. *Nielsen Estimates: National Audience Demographics Report*. Chicago: A.C. Nielsen.

Ripley, J., and S. Buell. 1954. Characteristics of the television audience of Columbus and Franklin County, Ohio. Unpublished manuscript, Ohio State University.

Rubin, A.M., and R.B. Rubin. 1982. Older persons' TV viewing patterns and motivations. *Communications Research* 9(2):287–313.

Schramm, W. 1969. Aging and mass communication. In M.W. Riley, J.W. Riley, Jr., and M.E. Johnson, Eds., *Aging and Society. Vol. 2: Aging and the Professions*. New York, Russell Sage Foundation.

6
Other Broadcast Technologies and the Older Audience

Conventional television is the most popular of the electronic media, but other means of electronic communication also have impact on the older audience. These are the newer technologies in television communication as well as the established medium of radio. The new technologies, those variations on standard telecommunications, have come along in the last 5 years to prove themselves especially strong contenders for a share of the viewer market. And radio, long considered by many as a low-growth area of communications, is emerging as a new leader for marketing to special audiences. One of the special audiences is now recognized to be the older population. Radio is changing to reflect this new awareness. In addition, the new technologies of cable and satellite system telecasting are making inroads on those shares of the market claimed by standard television operations. The impact of these broadcast technologies is explored in this chapter.

Radio

The 1930s and 1940s are sometimes referred to as the golden age of radio. Television did not become commonplace until after the Second World War. In fact, it was not until the 1950s that home television receivers became commonplace. Prior to that, families would gather in the evening to sit in the living room and *listen* to radio programming. For those born after 1940 it may be difficult, if not impossible, to remember the special thrill of hearing the squeaking door of "Inner Sanctum," or the hollow bell ringing in "I Love a Mystery." Jack Benny's comedy was greatly enhanced by the *sounds* of his Maxwell automobile and of the descent into the basement where his money was kept in a safe. Sound carried the radio listener all around the world and into many situations—all on a much, much smaller budget than the cost of television production.

Radio allowed the listener to participate to a much greater extent than does television. The sound of radio stimulated the imagination of the listener, making it necessary to insert oneself mentally into the action in order to experience the full impact of the program's intent. The result was a much more intimate communication in many ways.

Television's advent brought the visual image into audience experience. The visual gave us reality; it did not allow for many flights of fancy. Now we could *see* the squeaking door and, furthermore, see what was behind it. Perhaps our imagination had supplied more dreadful apparitions, but we became content with what we could actually see. Television was the motion picture brought right into the living room. Now personalities became more real to us. The aspect ratio on television is different from that of theater film. The head of a performer is not 6 feet high as in the theater, but is closer to the size of our own heads. Television allowed for the creation of a new intimacy.

Radio listenership declined as audiences turned away from radio to enjoy the new technology. Radio network operations soon ceased carrying dramatic and comedy series; and eventually the soap operas could no longer be listened to while doing household chores. They were all on television. What filled the time gaps? For one thing, whatever filled the time had to be less costly. National sponsors were making their major investments in television. Lavish radio productions were not worth the investment; significant numbers of listeners simply were not there. People were too busy watching television. So radio air time began to be taken over by low-budget operations such as recorded music and talk shows. With few exceptions, that remains the bulk of programming today.

In the process, radio did not lose its audience completely. On the contrary, the new formats attracted new audiences. They were mainly the young, those who responded to music, which became instantly portable with the advent of small, carry-around radios. The transistorized receiver has increased radio's popularity even more. The young are not the only radio listeners, however, everyone spends some part of the day with radio. Radio's portability has made it useful outside the house.

As prime time in television refers to the time where there are more people available and tuning in (for television the evening hours of 8:00 to 11:00 P.M.), prime time for radio became "drive time," that time when commuters are in their cars moving to and from work. This captive audience spends a considerable percentage of their entertainment hours with radio. Further, radio has become so ubiquitous that we hear it at the beach, in the park, even on the telephone as we are put on hold. Some offices, elevators, stores, and airports have radio piped in to provide a soothing background sound. Young people walk through city streets with stereophonic radio blasting, and joggers are seen with phones clamped tightly on their ears. No, radio has not died.

Radio in the Lives of Older People

Surveys indicate that radio is overwhelmingly the primary source of early morning news and the weather. In fact it is these two types of broadcasts that attract most listeners. A survey conducted by Frank Magid Associates for Blair Radio in 1982 sampled a national audience to monitor trends in radio listening and audience attitudes about radio programming. In answer to the question "What is your primary source of news in the early morning? Is it TV, radio or newspaper?," 60.3 percent of the respondents indicated that radio was the primary choice; 71.2 percent of the respondents indicated also that radio was the primary source of weather information in the early morning.

Responses in the Magid study were broken down by age groups. Not surprisingly, the youngest listeners (18–24) preferred FM programming and the 50–64 age group preferred AM programming. In fact, the reason by this older age group given for listening to AM radio was the availability of complete news programming and current weather information. These pieces of information were least popular with the youngest group. This tends to reinforce the oft-repeated assertions about the importance of news and public affairs programs in general for the older audience whether they be on radio or television.

The survey shows that FM listeners choose these channels for the available music, for the better sound and, in third place, for news and weather. Those who listen to AM give news and weather information as the first reason, more complete news as the second reason, and the available music the third reason.

This choice of radio for news can be compared with the Roper Organization's reports that consistently list radio as a third-place choice for source of news among all audiences. However, remember that the Magid study asks specifically about early morning news broadcasts, while the Roper question is posed quite differently: "First, I'd like to ask you where you actually get most of your news about what's going on in the world today—from the newspapers, or radio or television or magazines or talking to people or where?" This question has elicited answers that consistently place radio in third place. Nor is the data reported with age breakdowns. Were it to be so analyzed, it would not be too surprising to find that the older audiences still indicate radio to be a major source of information.

Other studies show that the addition of cable to a household does not necessarily cut down on the time spent with radio. This is attributed to radio's out-of-home portability. The Radio Information Center surveyed the thirty-six-channel cable areas of Tulsa, Oklahoma in 1983, determining that cable had not had any appreciable impact on radio listening. Listeners appear to spend from 17.7 to 18.1 quarter hours of listening per week. (The quarter-hours report is more useful to radio ratings when the nature of the radio broadcast and of the listener, especially commuter, behavior is considered.) For the 50 + age listener, the time spent is even higher; 91 quarter hours a week is estimated.

An interesting programming phenomenon is becoming more and more apparent; this is the arrival of "Music of Your Life" syndicated programs of recorded music now heard around the country. This is the programming ploy of the once "middle-of-the-road" stations, which have shifted from playing bland, homogenized "beautiful music" to playing records of the 1930s and 1940s, and into the 1950s. These are the big band sounds fondly remembered by today's middle-aged and older generations.

In the 1960s all radio seemed to be programming music for the young. As James Brown reports in *Advertising Age*, the important youth market caused radio programmers to ignore most of the 35- to 49-year-old market and to abandon totally any listener over age 50. Recently, however, there has been an increase in the number of all-news, all-talk stations which have traditionally programmed for the older demographics. Some stations now broadcast the big band sound exclusively. Not only is the day-long schedule complete with such musical choices, there are special personality programs wherein the creation of such music is discussed and the music makers themselves are interviewed and discuss their time and their art. This is not a one- or two-hour-a-day programming decision; this is an entire broadcast day. The market obviously supports such an operation.

There are other evidences of a broadcast renaissance of sorts. Both CBS and Mutual radio networks have at times commissioned the writing and production of original radio drama. Other stations have aired repeats of old radio shows. There is an audience for this. And this audience is composed in great numbers of today's older population. One of the largest of such operations is station KWAO-FM just outside of Phoenix, Arizona. This station takes advantage of being in very close proximity to Sun City, a large and affluent retirement community. The station programs big bands, repeats of old radio shows, and talk and public affairs. This format is successful and is bound to be repeated elsewhere in the nation's sunbelt.

Television/Radio Age reported in August 1983, the creation of a committee calling itself "The 35–64 Committee." Its purpose was to promote this age group as a radio advertising target. Calling it "the new growth market," they make presentations to various advertising agencies in major cities around the country. They seek to correct "misperceptions" about the mature market. Response from some agencies is that a still greater opportunity is in marketing to the 55+ age group. Statistics compiled by the 35–64 committee point to the large amount of discretionary income available in this age bracket. (This market is examined in more detail in chapter 4.) The increasing numbers of "Music of Your Life" format shows and talk-radio shows attest to the recognition of this market by radio.

Finally, there are now numbers of special interest programs targeting the older listener all over the country. These shows come from individual radio stations and are created for local consumption. There are many of such shows and they are difficult to track down and report, but they do exist in numbers. National Public Radio regularly features a syndicated feature titled "Prime Time." This is produced for the National Retired Teachers Association and American Association of Retired Persons, the largest organized body of older people in this country. "Prime Time" offers interviews and commentary on issues affecting older Americans.

Public Radio programs are often broadcast from college radio stations. As examples, Tufts University broadcasts "Across the Ages" to older people living in Boston's northern neighborhoods. "As Young as You Feel" is broadcast by the University of Massachusetts on its FM station. Similar programs are found in local FM programming nationwide.

Development of New Technology

Electronic communication technology has experienced explosive expansion in the last several years. The various methods of transmitting signals, and of receiving signals, has allowed for innovative uses of television. We may now be confronted with new labels surrounding the growth of cable television that puzzle us: instructional television, subscription television. All these new means of transmitting broadcast material pose serious questions for conventional broadcasting organizations, for federal regulators, and for entrepreneurs in the business. At the same time, they open possibilities for communication to special audiences. The elderly, because of their growing numbers, have become an audience that cannot be overlooked as new systems of communication are operationalized.

These communication refinements were forecast in a 1969 article that indicated insight into our future communications environment. The author, Ben Bagdikian, argued that some truths are obvious. He pointed out that new communications are agents of change, whether intentional or not. In addition, Bagdikian believes that new communications technology can be used to meet large-scale social problems and that our new communications technology can be used to support and satisfy aesthetic, intellectual, and emotional needs.

Other writers, such as law professor Monroe Price, of the University of California at Los Angeles, are more pessimistic. Price criticizes the inventive essays on the future of communications, particularly cable. He questions our current expectations about new developments in television and cable and identifies our general lack of understanding about viewers and their relationship to the television set. Furthermore, he points out that we have only a vague notion of how television affects our culture. He seriously doubts that future developments in communications technology will solve public problems.

For the elderly, the introduction and evolution of television has brought mixed reactions and effects. On the one hand it is argued that specialized formats and programs, made available by the new technologies, may result in the further isolation of older adults (Ashmore 1975). Others argue, conversely, that the new technologies, such as interactive cable, provide new opportunities for the elderly to become better integrated into society. Clearly, the developing television technologies will have both positive and negative effects. Still, we must be careful not to assume that technology, no matter what its form, will be an essential agent in social and cultural change and that it will solve all the problems and respond to the many different needs of the elderly. Serious consideration needs to be given to the new capabilities for message transference that the application of new communication technologies will bring about. In addition, it has been proved, with past experiences and previous studies, that the introduction of new communication technologies can have a profound effect upon the behaviors of older adults. Communication researchers need to begin studying the relationships between the introduction of new communication technology (and/or the uses of this technology) with changes in social and communicative behavior. As always with the study of any communication event, multivariate analysis will be needed and easy explanations will probably not be satisfactory.

The National Association of Broadcasters recently published two new titles: *New Technologies Affecting Radio and Television Broadcasting* (1981) and *Radio, New Technology, and You* (1982). Both of these titles reflect the concern that broadcasters have with the impact of technological change on broadcast economics, regulation, and programming content. More specifically, the changes we can expect in such areas as cable TV, multipoint distribution service, subscription TV, direct broadcast satellites, high-resolution TV, and videotext will have a direct effect on individuals and groups within our society, including the elderly.

Although much can be written about each of the communications technologies, emphasis in this chapter is given to cable television. This medium is worthy of attention because of its widespread current use (over 25 percent of the population) and predicted use, because of the numerous services cable can provide, and because of the nontraditional uses that have been made of cable by older populations in recent years.

The Use of Cable

Cable systems have been around for some time. So why has this suddenly become a major concern? Deregulation by the Federal Communications Commission in 1981 allowed cable systems to increase their program offerings. At the same time, cable technology has expanded with the existence of satellites and improved microwave transmission. Cable hookup for as few as a dozen locations is now both possible and profitable. Moreover, several different cable systems can link together to form an expanded and widely diverse network. Adding to the improved future for cable is the waning power of both the film industry and the three major television networks. These industries for creating and distributing program material are now seriously looking at the development of both products and processes for serving the programming needs of cable systems.

Traditionally, the functions of cable have been to provide reception of local and regional broadcast stations in areas where terrain or man-made structures adversely affect reception. In addition, cable has made possible the reception of distant stations not otherwise available. In recent years pay services have become available which provide a selection of nonbroadcast programming such as feature films, religious broadcasts, sports shows, and children's shows. Newer cable systems are capable of high resolution video programming. Cable can also provide non-video services such as security systems, fire alarms, computer access, home shopping, banking, and voter polling. The latter services are the result of cable's two-way, interactive quality. The interactive nature of cable makes it far different from any other mass medium and dramatically changes our understanding and expectation of the basic mass communication paradigm. The new, interactive model is far more capable of handling complex and dynamic symbolic exchanges. For instance, in a major market such as Los Angeles or Chicago a cable system will have the potential for fifty-five channels that operate simultaneously to deliver programming to homes linked by the cable. That is an overwhelming number of hours to fill with subject matter.

Michael O'Daniel, writing in *Emmy*, the magazine of the Academy of Television Arts and Sciences, lists possibilities for easily filling channels with original material. The guideline for such programming is to separate information into areas of specialization. O'Daniel's list actually allows for seventy-seven channels:

6 for general information such as news, sports, weather

14 for specialized information such as legal, financial, medical

10 for general entertainment including performing arts and children's programming

8 for video music

10 for ethnic and religious

6 for politics, local schools, and public access

6 for premium or pay per view

4 for product demonstration and home shopping

7 for interactive services, including education in the home

4 for data transmission

2 to carry the program schedules of all other channels

The sum of all of this is that we are moving into a period of abundant television. In the report of the Sloan Commission on Cable Communications cable is made analogous to the printing press. For decades television has operated as a scarce resource. Gaining access to and using that resource was difficult and expensive. Furthermore, because of its scarcity, television could serve only a few uses. Although cable access and its uses will certainly have limits, a variety of new functions will become apparent which will better meet the varied needs of the public. In the world of publishing, the appearance of one book title, magazine, or newspaper does not prevent the publication of another. In addition, the press makes possible a variety of different mass audiences. Cable presents the same opportunities: access to a variety of audiences and the availability of specialized services.

Cable and the Older Adult

It is known from previous research that the older audience's needs and desires relative to cable programming are extremely varied. Also, the potential of cable for older viewers is like the potential offered to all viewers: the acquisition of specialized information with high utility. It is possible that older audiences have somewhat more to gain from cable than other viewing populations. This gain reflects the unique circumstances of the older person and the unique functions of television in their lives.

The listing of potential cable channels allows us to look at television as a large audiovisual newspaper. Of course, television in its totality has always had a sort of magazine function. Viewers, like readers, can demonstrate choice of subject simply by switching the dial as they would turn the page of the magazine. However, we are aware that even in a multiple channel market, choice has become rather limited. Switching the channel may too often result in turning to more of the same. A cable system that offers as many as fifty-five channels can offer at least eleven choices. Now the system begins to look more like a newspaper of the air with a literature section, advertising, hard news, editorial commentary, comic strips, and so on, all available in one. The choice for the viewer has been greatly expanded. However, preferred program choice surveys only reflect the choices available. Often the most chosen program may really be that one in the time slot which has been voted least objectionable. It makes a difference. Now the viewer can demonstrate choice more finely. Older viewers can let us know how devoted they are to news and public affairs when they are given the option of viewing such shows all around the clock on one of the several general information channels.

Assuming that cable is going to provide a myriad of programming and other services, what influence will these changes have on the older viewer?

Uses of Cable

General Information. It has been suggested that a full diet of news and public affairs programming will be available to keep older viewers informed. Because of there being several channels devoted to general information, it is predictable that different philosophic and stylistic approaches to news will be available. Because of the established preference of the older market for news, there will be competition to gain the larger share of that market through varying presentations. Of course, there will be news channels targeting younger audiences, even children. But it remains likely that there will be a proliferation of gray-haired commentators, each with a different political and social point of view. The older viewer will have a still greater opportunity to link to a news consumer group, sharing common concerns.

Specialized Information. Specialized information channels will recognize the need of older viewers for legal, medical, and social information. It is possible to envision programs designed to clarify social security procedures and to guide older people through the various bureaucratic mazes they confront. Estate planning, preretirement planning, leisure time activities, and so on may all find a place in the broadcast day that is not available in present tightly competitive and expensive television time. The Cable Health Network broadcasts nothing but health-related programming all day. One significant market for this kind of program is the older population, who have an understandable investment in their own health. In setting up programming schedules, specific programs are listed which address geriatric health concerns.

General Entertainment. With several channels offering general entertainment, it is certain (or at least a possibility to be hoped for) that there will be wide diversity in choices of kinds of entertainment. Country and western music devotees may spend the day with such programming if they chose rather than one or two brief programs a week. Those who enjoy the British imports on public television may be able to find a channel devoted exclusively to such fare. Perhaps we might even find Shakespearean repertoire, current stage plays (already available on more than one cable system), and movies in abundance with specialized subjects for plot development designed to attract the older viewer.

Video Music. It is necessary to stretch a little here to imagine programming in this classification that would enhance the lives of older viewers. The present kaleidoscope of images accompanying today's video music may not be attractive to older audiences. However, if the market warrants it, appropriate programming for the older audience could be developed.

Ethnic and Religious Programming. In the literature on the sociology of aging, special attention is paid to ethnicity, and more than one research paper has attested to the place of religion in the lives of many older adults. Having specialized programming developed in both these categories allows for obvious benefits to the older viewer. Aging is a different experience within different subcultures and ethnic divisions. Addressing that difference will provide useful understanding to younger people as well as allowing older persons to find others like themselves on the screen—thus benefiting from the social and cultural validation the video material provides.

We are aware of special religious channels available through both cable and broadcasting today. It is possible to spend the day with religious programming if one is on a system supplying such fare. Should there be more than one such channel available, it is possible that more religious programming, representing a wide spectrum of faiths and denominations, would be made available. This would be especially valued by the older persons who, despite their restricted mobility, would be able to participate in religious practices as at-home members of large congregations.

Politics, Local Schools, and Public Access. Older persons frequently have a greater investment in local politics and community concerns than do younger citizens. Imagine community forums allowing for individual participation such as now available with the interactive system in Reading, Pennsylvania. This system allows for the linkage of four senior centers within the community so that they may talk with one another. Viewers at home can participate in the discussion by calling in on their telephone, or by attending one of the three community centers.

School systems can develop specialized courses for older students. Such course work is presently available in most communities across the country. The advantage here is that several channels will allow for development of specialized offerings for the older student in particular. It is also easy to envision sharing school programs with the community through this channel.

Public access will also permit senior viewers themselves to bring their own concerns before the community. Through direct participation, this segment of society can be proactive rather than reactive. Such a program has been functioning for the last several years in San Diego. Known by its acronym, PACE, for Public Access Cabletelevision by and for Elders, this program allows older people to telecast shows oriented to older viewers. These shows are not only created by older people in cooperation with college students, but are beamed via cable directly into approximately 110,000 homes on the public access channel.

Premium or Pay Per View. Since these channels will serve those who agree to pay a set fee for a specific program, perhaps a first-run motion picture or a sports event, older viewers will be advantaged, only as all viewers are, in being able to experience a special event. Costs will probably determine to a large extent the participation in these channels by older viewers.

Product Demonstration and Home Shopping. Although older viewers have stated that they do not feel they are influenced by television advertising, it is a fairly safe assumption that they do pay attention to commercials and, as everyone else, have those commercials they like better than others. It might be assumed that the nature of the television commercial will change with the development of this channel. No longer must an advertiser think in terms of the 30-second message. An entirely different approach to the marketing of the product can be taken. Pitching attractive and effective product demonstrations toward the older consumer will be to the advantage of the home shopper, who cannot leave home to shop or finds it inconvenient to do so. Perhaps we can even return to what now seems a utopian fantasy: being able to telephone a list of needs to a market or store for pickup or delivery.

Interactive Services. The Reading, Pennsylvania, project is an example of this sort of service. Participation in town meetings and other political group activities is only one example of the utility of interactive television. It seems that a greater possible use, however, is for interactive television channels to set up educational shows and health care delivery. With the decline in the available college age pool, colleges and universities are thinking more these days about the nontraditional student. Already weekend and evening divisions of colleges and universities have been established across the country. With the promise of improved health, greater longevity, and increased interest in quality leisure pursuits, older adults are returning to the classroom. Being able to use an interactive video system for part or all of course content will make taking classes easier. In addition, a greater variety of classes, traditionally limited by the geographic "reach" of colleges and universities, will be made accessible.

In the mid-1970s, a report on the use of interactive television was published by the Alternate Media Center at the School of the Arts, New York University. The report was addressed primarily to those who were interested in planning and implementing the use of interactive television as an alternative means of delivery of services in the health field. Its author, Ben Park, maintains that "telemedicine," which he defines as the use of two-way or interactive television to conduct transactions in the field of health care, will have a dramatic effect upon medical care delivery. He provides several reasons for this belief. First, medical facilities and medical professionals are not distributed evenly throughout the country. Most high technology and medical expertise have gravitated to centralized locations for economic reasons. As a result, many small communities and other scarcely populated areas do not have adequate medical personnel and facilities. Second, most medical school graduates for the last several decades have tended toward specialization; fewer and fewer general practitioners are available to the public. Third, it is difficult for consumers to acquire health care in rural areas, inner-city slums, and fast-growing suburban areas. Fourth, expectations are rising among all segments of the public for better health care and facilities; and fifth, the cost of health care is escalating.

In addition to health care (diagnosis and treatment) interactive television can serve as an excellent way to provide high-quality health care information (health maintenance). The latter service is particularly important to the elderly who are generally in good health, but have a propensity for chronic health problems and other minor health problems that could easily be prevented with proper patient/consumer awareness programs. The interactive nature of cable could make possible a question-and-answer segment in health education programs. Health-related problems could be addressed on such topics as nutrition, mental health, hygiene, safety, and exercise. Programs on these and other topics would be examples of preventive programming. The cable system could provide information on health services available in the community, their costs, and the best ways to use these services. In short, the use of interactive television for health service delivery could foster independence, help promote health maintenance, and provide for more efficient delivery of health care services.

The uses and potentials of television for older adults, given the technological changes that are occurring, are varied and provide opportunities never before possible. It should also be remembered that although cable will provide a variety of new opportunities, other technologies such as direct broadcast satellites, teletext systems, and low-power television will provide numerous other opportunities for the elderly. It is yet uncertain what effects all of the technological changes will have. However, it is important for communications researchers, gerontologists, and other professionals to be sensitive to these changes and to look for new ways of using television meaningfully. We are entering a period when television of abundance and media of abundance will be the norm. How individuals and subgroups in our society will respond and how these changes will affect the interpersonal context of mass communication is still unclear. However, it is clear that we must be creative and risk-taking users of the media. In addition, persons not previously users of the media will need to become active participants.

References

Ashmore, J.S. 1975. Commercial television's calculated indifference to the old. *The Centre Magazine* 8:18–20.

Bagdikian, B.H. 1969. How communications may shape our future environment. *AAUW Journal* 62:123–26.

Brown, J. 1980. Radio encore: Tuning in on the old. *Advertising Age* (August 25):S2.

Cable having little impact on radio: Blair survey. 1983. *Television/Radio Age* (July 18):38, 68.

Davis, R.H., and R.V. Miller. 1983. The acquisition of specialized information by older adults through utilization of new telecommunications technology. *Educational Gerontology* 9:2–3.

De Sonne, M.L. 1982. *Radio, New Technology and You*. Washington, D.C.: National Association of Broadcasters.

Geller, R., and R. Cherow. 1972. The aging: Can cable television help? *Media and Methods* 9:33–35.

Groups in study finds no cable impact on radio listening. 1983. *Television/Radio Age* (April 25):38.

Major presentations to ad community on value of older listeners being planned by 35–64 Committee. 1983. *Television/Radio Age* (August 29):35–36.

Moss, M.L. 1978. *Two-Way Cable Television: An Evaluation of Community Uses in Reading, Pennsylvania (Summary)*. New York: Alternate Media Center, New York University.

National Association of Broadcasters Committee on Science and Technology. 1981. *New Technologies Affecting Media and Television Broadcasting*. Washington, D.C. NAB.

O'Daniel, M. 1981. The great indoors. *Emmy 3* (4):21–25.

Park, B. 1974. *An Introduction to Telemedicine.* New York: Alternate Media Center, New York University.

Price, M.E. 1974. The illusions of cable television. *Journal of Communications* 24:71–76.

Real, N.R., H.L. Anderson, and M.H. Harrington, 1980. Television access for older adults. *Journal of Communication* 30:81–88.

Roper Organization. 1983. *Trends in Attitudes toward Television and Other Media: A Twenty-four-year Review.* New York: Television Information Office.

Sloan Commission on Cable Communications. 1971. *On the Cable: The Television of Abundance.* New York: McGraw-Hill.

Williams, R.W. 1974. *Television: Technology and Cultural Form.* New York: Schocken.

Part II
Helping Shape Television Coverage

7
The Value of Aging-Oriented Programming

This instrument can teach, it can illuminate, yes, it can even inspire.
But it can do so only to the extent that humans are determined to use it
to those ends. Otherwise, it is merely lights and wires in a box.

Edward R. Murrow

So apt an assessment by the late Edward R. Murrow of television's potential to affect our lives! One can only hope it is not also prophetic with regard to the future prospects for senior-oriented television programming.

In the past, as the earlier chapters in this book have outlined, the gatekeepers to this medium clearly have been less than determined to use it to "teach and illuminate" the American public about the process of growing old. The bulk of commercial programming has been aimed at the audience with the bulk of the buying power, the 18 to 49 age group. Popular television shows with an older following, such as "The Red Skelton Show," "Green Acres," "The Virginian," "Beverly Hillbillies," and "Little House on the Prairie," have been canceled to make way for shows that attract a younger audience, and thus pay a bigger bang for the advertising buck.

One could argue that these statistics are more reflective of the senior population's relative small numbers than a deliberate attempt to ignore the needs and desires of this group. Older adults have traditionally made up a small percentage of the overall viewing audience. There is also reason to believe that older viewers just may not be that interested in a senior slant to national television programming. The Davis-Davis-Westbrook study shows that a majority of the older viewers on both the East and West Coasts do not tend to see their television needs and interests as different from that of other adults. On the West Coast only 41.7 percent felt there was a difference, while on the East Coast only 35.3 percent of the older viewers held this perspective.

Perhaps even more significant, it must be remembered that television and even radio mirror the attitudes of the American public. And, let's face it, growing old is not among the most popular "pastimes" for the American people. Most try to avoid it, or at least outward evidence of it, for as long as possible. Even when Americans reach an age at which it is impossible to deny their "elder citizen" status, they are still more likely to try to downplay their age than to proudly proclaim it.

Thus, it is hardly surprising that neither commercial television nor radio—nor, for that matter, public and educational television and radio—have placed any significant emphasis on the older person in their programming. Older characters are rarely the central figures in program plots, if they appear at all. Story lines typically do not incorporate life after retirement. Documentaries on aging are rare. Radio continues to attract a younger audience, as exemplified by the predominance of rock stations.

What's worse, when older Americans are the subject of media attention, the result is often negative. As gerontologist Eric Pfeiffer puts it:

> Quite frankly, and quite literally, aging in the United States has been given bad press. Aging has been presented over and over again as one hopeless, unremitting, downward, drift into despair, deprivation, and desolation. The images of aging that have been presented in the public media have focused on disease, poverty and social isolation.

Unraveling the cause of media inattention, or inaccurate attention, to the elderly is difficult. Do the media portray the elderly in this negative, and cursory, manner because they receive no pressure from the public to do otherwise? Or is the public disinclined to push for increased coverage of the elderly because of the negative perception of aging they have received from the media and other sources?

Both scenarios are probably true to some degree. Clearly, the public has been hesitant to push for widespread coverage of issues that affect the aging—they are not so sure they *want* to hear about it. Equally as clear, the media have shirked their responsibility to use the great power to better publicize a happening that affects all their viewers: the aging process. They take the easy and more lucrative way out by focusing on those issues that appeal to the greatest number of viewers and attract the greatest amount of advertising dollars. And when they do focus on the elderly, they take the quickest route to their goal by utilizing stereotypical characters who require a minimum of character development.

Changing this negative media image of the elderly and focusing more positive attention on their concerns will be no easy task. Commercial programmers will be disinclined to vary their programming significantly until advertising dollar signs so dictate, which will not happen to any great degree until the 1990s or early in the next century when the elderly begin making up a significantly larger share of the viewing audience. Well-organized advocacy efforts may be successful in making some inroads in the interim. These efforts will be discussed in a later chapter.

The most likely and most readily available avenue for instigating a positive change in the media's coverage of the elderly is at the local level and in the public service realm. The remainder of this book will focus largely on how to plan an effective strategy for obtaining aging-oriented public service television programming and how to produce creative programming that will capture the attention and interest of both younger and older viewers, as well as how to make the most of every opportunity to appear on television—whether on your own show or someone else's—and how to organize an advocacy effort that will have the local and national broadcast media responding more adequately to the issue of aging and the older population. But first, a little more about why aging-oriented programming is needed.

Why an Aging-Oriented Program?

If you were a manufacturer of a new product that you wanted to market to the greatest number of people in the shortest possible amount of time, you would probably turn to television as your medium of choice. For the same reason, television is the medium of choice to spread the "truth" about aging in America. Television has the capacity to reach tens of thousands of people with information that can positively, or negatively, affect their daily lives, their perceptions, their opinions, their safety, their jobs, and their relationships. If used properly and effectively, television can provide the opportunity to reach young and old, groups and individuals, government services and community organizations, service providers and service recipients and supporters and adversaries with whatever message you wish to send.

It is true that television is primarily viewed as an entertainment source. It is not true that an entertainment source is all it can be. Television has a tremendous capacity to be an informational and educational tool, and nowhere can this tool be put to better use than in the field of aging.

Educating the Older Population

If any viewer appreciates education and informational electronic media programming, it is the older viewer. As discussed previously, our research shows conclusively that the elderly have a clear preference for news and information/documentary programming. Our study of preference of type of program showed that the elderly on both the West Coast and East Coast ranked news as their first choice, followed by the informational/documentary format—ahead of feature films, comedies, sports, general drama and suspense/mystery. We also found a strong desire to view more programming dealing with elderly affairs, culture, science, and health—issues that directly affect their lives.

Thus, a major objective of any ongoing aging production or limited series is to reach the older population with information especially geared to their lives. Older persons can derive a great deal of benefit from shows that offer suggestions for how to keep physically fit and healthy after age 60, or that provide insight into the dilemmas of retirement, such as dealing with loss of status, changes in relationships and financial difficulties. Television can also be used to issue a call to action on important issues such as those affecting services or taxes.

Specialized programming can also provide the elderly with important information about programs or services available to them. Too often, older persons are unaware of services that could make a significant difference in their lives, whether in the health care area or in housing, legal affairs, nutrition, or recreation.

This type of electronic outreach is particularly helpful for older persons who, for various reasons, have restricted activity or are completely homebound. They often need this information the most, but do not frequent the senior centers, nutrition sites, public gatherings, and locations where it is disbursed.

Wilbur Schramm summed this situation up well:

> The mass media are called upon more and more to build a bridge between older people and the rest of American society. On the one hand, they are challenged to report in depth and breadth, on one of the great societal stories of our time—the emergence of old people as a major segment of the population. On the other hand, because the media have a large and loyal audience among old people, they are in a position to maintain for these people a link to the large society.

Educating the Public

Aging-oriented television and radio shows also can serve as excellent sources of information and enlightenment for younger and middle-aged viewers. Americans tend to view old age as a very unhappy and unhealthy period of the life span. Most would benefit from a more realistic picture of the joys and challenges of the later years. The message for the public? Old age is, more often than not, a rewarding, healthy and interesting time of life, filled with successes, as well as failures.

In other words, informational shows on the elderly should create an awareness of an older population that experiences problems and adjustments related to age, as do most of us, but which is generally productive and fulfilled, with the same personalities and response mechanisms they have had all their lives.

As John Tebbel observed:

> Surely if the media portrayal of the old were to be realistic. . . . they would be shown as people with problems peculiar to their age and to the status society has given them, but otherwise reacting about as they did when they were younger. Old and young alike have behavior patterns appropriate to their ages, but neither has a monopoly on particular characteristics. (p. 7)

A more accurate portrayal of the older years disseminated through local aging-oriented broadcasts may help viewers or listeners to interact with and react more positively to their older loved ones, friends, neighbors, or colleagues. It is difficult to respond appropriately to someone's needs or concerns if you are operating under false assumptions, no matter how honestly held. You can always tell those people who have mistaken impressions of the elderly. They are the ones who "talk down" to older persons; who try to provide far more help than is needed in situations in which elders are quite capable of doing the particular task themselves; who act shocked when Grandma describes a very sophisticated project she is involved in ("Are you sure you can handle that, Grandma?") or who issue other demeaning responses that whittle away at an older person's self-image and confidence.

Having inaccurate or insufficient information about the life situation of an elderly person may also result in inappropriate responses to the depression and loss an older person is feeling over the death of their spouse or to the difficulty he or she is having adjusting to retirement or other adjustments old age brings.

Research indicates that aging-related shows do help create a better understanding of old age among the general public. Initial reactions to the popular PBS series "Over Easy" showed that it markedly improved interest in community senior services in areas where the program was telecast. Another study of 1,104 viewers of the aging-related television series "Getting On" showed vast improvement in their initial impressions (based on a pretest) of the elderly, particularly as related to vitality and efficiency.

Reaching Service and Care Providers

A major objective of aging-oriented local television programming is to reach professionals and paraprofessionals who are in closest contact with the elderly, most notably service and care providers such as outreach workers, senior center personnel, homemakers, home health workers, nutrition site workers, senior program administrators, and nursing home staff. But the thrust of any programming effort also should include those involved in other types of helping relationships with older persons, including the police, hotel or apartment managers, and grocery clerks.

All of these people may find themselves cast in the role of counselor to an older person as he or she faces the many adjustments that old age bring, often one on top of the other: declining health, changes in physical appearance, the death or moving away of loved ones and friends, changes in social and professional roles, alterations in personal life styles, dwindling finances, and strained relationships. Not surprisingly, older persons faced with these challenges may need someone to turn to for comfort and advice.

Mental health services are rarely considered an option by the elderly, who tend to associate this form of assistance with institutionalization or as being designed for the "senile" or "crazy." Instead, they turn for their counseling to the providers of other services, with whom they have ongoing, possibly daily, contact. These providers, however, do not always feel comfortable providing counseling to older persons who are having adjustment problems. They may be unable to recognize problems, or if they do, not quite be sure how to respond to them.

Thus, there is a great need to better educate service and care providers about what is and what is not appropriate behavior for people in their senior years. Even well-meaning providers can have their perception clouded by what they consider to be truths, but which are actually classic stereotypes. Such misunderstandings only serve to impede the relationship between the service/care provider and the older person and further the risk of innappropriate delivery of services.

Television informational programming is the ideal way to head off these problems. Most service providers are unable or unwilling to attend nonrequired training sessions. Some cannot afford it, some cannot work it into their schedules, some have no transportation, and some just are not interested enough to make the extra effort. These individuals, however, might be convinced to watch a television show or series either as part of a group activity within a program or agency or at home on their own time. Discussion and interaction sessions could be scheduled as follow-ups and might provide even more insight than the shows themselves. Educational materials could be developed that correspond to the topic area being covered that particular week.

An Argument for Aging-Oriented Television Programming

Television traditionally has aimed most of its programming efforts at the audience with buying power—the 18 to 49 age group—and has done little to incorporate the process of growing old into characters, story-lines, or documentaries. Of course, older Americans have not complained very loudly simply because a majority of this population do not consider their television needs and interests different from other adults. When you consider that aging is not one of the most popular topics in our youth-oriented society overall, it is not surprising that the result is a very negative media image of the elderly.

There is no simple, one-step solution to creating a more positive image of older people on television. But a good starting point is the development of quality, local aging-oriented public service programming. If produced effectively, such programming can promote a multigenerational reaction in the community.

It can reach older persons, who have a clear preference for informational/documentary programming, with information on issues, and services specifically geared to their lives. It can educate the general public about an old age that can be a rewarding, healthy, and interesting time of life, one filled with successes as well as failures. It can reach the service and care providers in closest contact with the elderly to encourage an increased understanding about the adjustments faced in old age and how they can help their older clients cope better. In sum, it can serve to erase age stereotypes held as truths and positively alter relationships with older family members, friends, neighbors, acquaintances, and clients.

References

Blakely, R.J. 1971. *The People's Instrument*. Washington, D.C.: Public Affairs Press.

Bogart, L. 1972. *The Age of Television*. New York: Frederick Ungar.

Bretz, R., and E. Stasheff. 1968. *The Television Program: Its Direction and Production*. New York: Hill and Wang.

Davis, R.H. 1980. *Television and the Aging Audience*. Lexington, Mass.: Lexington Books.

Macy, J.W., Jr. 1974. *To Irrigate a Wasteland*. Berkeley: University of California Press.

Pfeiffer, Eric. 1975. Successful Aging. In *Quality of Life: The Later Years*. Acton, Mass.: American Medical Association, Publishing Sciences Group, Inc., p. 13.

Powell, J.W. 1962. *Channels of Learning: The Story of Educational Television*. Washington, D.C.: Public Affairs Press.

Schramm, W. 1970. Aging and mass communication. In M. Riley, J.R. Riley, and M. Johnson, eds., *Aging and Society, Volume 2: Aging and the Professions*. New York: Russell Sage Foundation.

Schwartz, T. 1981. *Media: The Second God*. New York: Random House.

Seldes, G. 1970. *The Great Audience*. Westport, Conn.: Greenwood Press.

Tebbel, J. 1978. *The Mass Media*. Washington, D.C.: National Council on Aging.

8
Getting a Show of Your Own

I t is not as difficult as might be thought to secure time for a television or radio public service program. People allow themselves to be unnecessarily intimidated by both television and radio, especially by television. They are more than happy to stand back and point the finger at the media for not responding to the issues surrounding growing old in America. But they are not willing to get directly involved in changing the situation. After all, how can they? A group of seniors or senior advocates cannot take on the establishment, and they certainly cannot run their own show. Right?

Wrong! A senior oriented organization, agency, or group *can* get their own show and they *can* make it a success. All they need is the desire to do so and the patience, stamina, and professionalism to put that desire into action.

That is not to say that getting your own show on television or radio is as easy as wishing it so. There is no guarantee that you or your organization will obtain public service time on television. And if you do, there is no guarantee that you will succeed. If you are willing to put in the necessary time and work that goes into developing, marketing, and producing a high-quality public service show, however, there is good reason to believe you will be successful. The following plan serves as a useful model for strategizing and then organizing a media effort.

Organizing

There can be power in numbers as long as the personalities and egos do not become an issue (or *the* issue). With the right combination of people and organization, a media advisory committee can be quite helpful in developing a proposal for an electronic media series, in approaching the station(s) and in suggesting formats, topics, and guests for future shows. Its formation, however, should involve a very thoughtful process, attempting to integrate the right mix of personalities and appropriate organizations.

You do not want, for example, to have individuals on your committee who will attempt to dominate the proceedings, who are very negative (idea killers), or, still worse, who are unwilling to be farsighted and to work in new, creative directions. You also do not want to have too many people on your committee; too many participants can become unruly, however well-meaning they may be, and the resulting inefficient use of time and energy are certain to lessen the quality of the shows.

The ideal media advisory committee should consist of a relatively small number of people (between eight and twelve), but should represent a broad spectrum of the aging community. Representatives of the local Area Agency on Aging, Gray Panther network, American Association of Retired Persons chapter, your local human rights council, senior service agencies, and the nearest university or college should all be included. So should older persons. The last thing you want is to have a bunch of young gerontologists trying to plan programming for the seniors without any input from the seniors themselves. An intergenerationally balanced committee will be far more effective, especially in convincing a station of the need for an aging-related show.

Strong leadership will be necessary to keep the committee from spinning its wheels. Part of the leadership, whether the individuals hold an official capacity with the committee or not, will need to come from the host(s) and the producer(s). After all, the success of the shows is really in their hands.

In some cases you may not even want an advisory committee. There is no reason you have to. Other equally effective options include forming a planning group consisting of the producer(s), host(s), and other members of the production crew. Weekly meetings could be scheduled to prepare for the next production, plan the topics for future shows, think about potential guests, and plan novel formats and approaches.

Do Your Homework

Whatever support system you set up, preparation is the key to getting public service time. A major part of this preparation is the researching of relevant information that could make the difference between a positive or negative response from the station. Your objective is to make it as easy as possible for the station to judge your proposal's potential.

The value of having the winning edge does not just hold true in sports and politics. The competition for public service time can be fierce; not so much with local cable outlets as with commercial stations, especially now that the FCC has removed all specific public service time requirements. In the past, most commercial or independent stations demonstrated a bias toward nationally syndicated informational programming, such as "Face the Nation," "Meet the Press," and "This Week with David Brinkley," or syndicated variety formats that might have a regional slant such as "P.M. Magazine." Such programs pose fewer complications for the station than does locally initiated programming. Now that these stations are no longer legally bound to air *any* particular amount of public service time, it is a sure bet that local programming will be even harder to sell to many stations (albeit that stations with a good public relations sense will still see the value of locally originated public service shows).

Before you walk into your first meeting with the station, it is imperative that you answer certain basic questions. For example, what viewing audience are you attempting to reach? The older population, the service providers, the general public, or all of the above? Each of these targeted audiences have different interests, different needs, and different expectations from a television program. If you do not take these into account, you will lose your audience.

What subject areas will keep your target audience in front of their television? What impact will this programming have on them? Know the answers to these questions, and others, such as preferred program formats. Hit-and-miss guesswork on programming is a dangerous game.

One good way to increase your information base on your target audience is to take at least a small sample of opinion from your potential viewing audience. It need not be elaborate. Perhaps a short questionnaire distributed at local senior service agencies, senior centers, or well-attended local meetings. Aside from some basic demographic inquiries (sex, age, residence), questions might include the following:

Do you watch local public service programming?

If so, what subject areas are of particular interest to you?

What format makes a public service show interesting to you?

What makes it boring?

A sample of even fifty to seventy-five persons and/or service providers can give you a better feel of the type of programming that will generate excitement among your viewers and reduce the likelihood that they will mark it off as "just another dull public service program."

Such data also could prove beneficial in another way: helping to convince the station of the need for programming of the type you are proposing. Television and radio stations alike are very concerned about local public opinion in the selection of public service programming and, hence, often commission their own surveys to take the pulse of community concerns.

A final key question to answer before you approach the station concerns the existence of other public service programs in your area. You are in a much better position to argue your case if you know what your competition is. Often, there are few, if any, public service programs on the air that older persons can relate to their personal lives—that in itself is a very compeling argument. If other programming does exist, you need to figure out how your recommended programming will complement it.

Don't Slight Radio

The emphasis of this book is on television and the development of television programming, but a quick word to the wise is in order about radio. Although television may have replaced it as the medium of choice for many Americans, radio is no slouch in the communications field. A great many people still turn to radio for news and information; so to ignore this medium is to ignore a potentially powerful outlet for your message.

Admittedly, television is more attractive from a variety of standpoints. It has visual impact. It reaches a much larger audience. And as a result, it creates more community awareness. But radio has its plusses too. There are many who would argue that, because it leaves more to the imagination, radio is actually more desirable than its video counterpart. In addition, there are ten times as many radio as television stations. This undoubtedly improves your chances of getting airtime. But it also calls for more caution in deciding which stations to approach.

Competition in the radio market has forced broadcasters to target their programming to specific audiences and age groups. Thus, you cannot walk into a radio station and assume that it reaches the audience to which you are gearing your programming. Finding out whether it does, however, is relatively easy. Most stations have data available to demonstrate to which audience(s) they appeal.

Deciding between AM and FM frequencies can be sticky. In most areas, FM has become dominant. AM, however, is more likely to be oriented toward talk shows and variety programming. As a result it may be more suited to your needs.

Radio does not, of course, have as many format options as television. It is largely limited to the basic talk or interview format and slight variations on that theme. One of those variations is to have audience call-in interaction, much as you would on television. You may also want to consider some pretaped, on-the-street interviews.

However you try to vary the format, since radio is an audio medium, you are largely at the mercy of the ability of your host and guest(s) to paint a picture with their words. In limited circumstances, you may be able to illustrate the subject matter with taped audio material. For a show on Alzheimer's disease, you might intersperse a tape of a victim of the disease with commentary from your guest. For a radio show on sensory losses in old age, you might play a tape of ordinary sounds muffled in much the way they would be for someone who is hard of hearing. In general, however, you will find radio more limiting than television, and thus, even more dependent on the creativity and verbal skills of your host and guests.

If you do choose to pursue a radio show, and you should at least investigate the possibility, you should undertake a plan of action virtually identical to that outlined for television. You will get no further with a radio station than you would with television if you are inadequately prepared, present your case poorly, and do not know what your audience wants, needs, or already has available.

Format and Topics

As you set about developing your proposal, a great deal of thought should be given to the actual format and direction of your programming. Are you going to propose an ongoing show or a limited series? If your proposal is for an ongoing show, will it be weekly, biweekly, or monthly? If it is to be a limited series, how many parts will the series have? What about the length of the program? Will it be a 30- or 60-minute show? What will the program content be? Are the proposed topics in keeping with the interests of the targeted audience and the original objectives of the program or series? You and your colleagues must have answers to these questions. You should develop those answers with at least two critical points in mind:

1. *Be realistic.* This cannot be stressed enough. Too often, the initial glow of developing a public service program causes its creators to bite off more than they can chew—opting for a weekly show, for instance, without realizing the tremendous time and energy it takes to produce four or five programs a month, or committing to subject areas that reach far beyond the capabilities of local resources. You must also be concerned about what the station can realistically be expected to accept. Hopefully, your research of local programming will have given you a clue to what is and what is not realistic.

2. *Aim to please your audience.* In planning program format or content, always keep your target audience in mind. Meeting their needs and interests is the key to your success. Are you presenting your viewers with issues that really affect their everyday lives? Are you concentrating on national problems when your audience has indicated a desire for a balanced coverage of local and national interests? Remember for whom you are producing the show.

As you make your decision about the frequency of program you would like to have, you must seriously consider who will staff it. How many people have been lined up to work on the productions? Is it a local access cable program where you are expected to provide a full crew? What type of weekly time commitments have been made, especially by the program producers and hosts? The key word here is *commitment.* Electronic media productions, especially on television, do not materialize at the snap of your fingers. They require a major commitment of time, labor, and energy.

It is advisable to move slowly and carefully into the often unpredictable world of electronic media production. Get your feet wet first. You might test the waters with a two- to four-part series on a special topic of interest to your target audience. Once successfully through the first venture, you might seek a more comprehensive series or an ongoing program. If, however, an ongoing program is your goal from the outset, you might consider initially requesting a monthly show with a long-range goal of a weekly or biweekly show once your group has a bit of experience under its belt.

A workable length for individual shows is 30 minutes. This allows time to develop a topic, but not to beat it into the ground. Some topics do, however, need more than 30 minutes to develop adequately. For instance, to try to cover in 30 minutes the topic of mental health care for the elderly would do an injustice to this important area. A better approach might be to put together a series, perhaps in three parts, covering adjustments in retirement, ways to deal with common emotional turmoil, and community mental health care approaches and services.

To produce a 60-minute show successfully—that is, to present a show that will sustain the interest of a typical audience for a full hour—is not an easy task. It takes a unique blend of programming, possibly mixing guest specialists, audience response (whether a live audience or on-the-street interviews), slides, films, and other graphics, a blend that might exceed the commitment of resources the station is willing to make. For that reason, and others, 60-minute local public service time slots are often best reserved for development of local documentaries that can take an in-depth look at important issues of our time and their human consequences. See chapter 9 for more on the potential of local documentaries to provide needed information to and about the aging community.

That is not to say that 60-minute time slots are completely off limits for talk shows or other interview formats. Some national talk shows, such as "Firing Line," with William Buckley, and "This Week with David Brinkley," have used the 60-minute format to great advantage in producing shows that revolve around interviews with nationally and internationally famous people. There is the "Phil Donahue Show," which so skillfully uses a live audience. But it is also interesting to note the long list of successful programs that are only 30 minutes in length, including "Meet the Press," "Face the Nation," "Washington Week in Review," and "Wall Street Week." Especially with a basic talk show format, an audience is usually willing to listen to a stimulating 30-minute exchange and even look forward to a continuation of the theme in an upcoming show. But put that same 60 minutes of programming into one continuous hour-long program, and you will have to really "produce" to keep your audience interested.

Once you have resolved the format question, the next decision to be made is on program content and approach. You might opt for a basic talk show format with a host(s) and guest(s) discussing a prescribed subject. For the most part, this is a sensible, uncomplicated, and time-efficient approach. But a bit of variety and creativity in programming is necessary. A solid 30 minutes of "talking heads" places too much burden on the host and guest(s), and runs the risk of being deadly dull for the viewers.

If you use your creative skills at all, however, there should be no danger of visual narcolepsy. Needed first is a set design that provides a comfortable, homey environment through use of attractive furniture, well-placed plant(s), or even wall-hangings. Complement that with visual support materials (35-millimeter color slides, film, graphs, charts, artwork, or cartoons) or live demonstrations where appropriate. Whether it be an exercise demonstration, a display of artwork from a future exhibit, a graph of property tax increases, or slides showing the CAT scan of the brain of an Alzheimer's disease victim, visual supports will give your program variety and help sustain audience interest.

But you can do still more. If you and the station are willing to put in the extra time and effort, live audience participation (à la Phil Donahue and Dick Cavett) can work wonders for a show. Only 40 to 50 persons are needed. A host might interview the guests for 15 minutes and leave 15 minutes for audience response. (For a show of this nature, however, you might want to consider the hour-long format.) The end result? Your viewing audience will feel more involved in the show and better represented by the live audience. (Refer to chapter 9 for further discussion of possible formats.)

Preparing the Proposal

A well-prepared proposal is the key to gaining acceptance for your desired program. That proposal must be clearly written, visually attractive, professional looking, and need not be more than three to four pages. It should contain the following sections:

Introduction. Describe what has motivated your organization or group to request this program.

Sponsoring Groups. Briefly describe your media committee and organizations and groups that are cosponsoring the effort—their memberships, purposes, and so on.

Community Need. Demonstrate the need for the type of aging-related program you are proposing. Be persuasive! If you cannot make a strong case for this programming, your presentation will go downhill from there. Depending on the approach your particular programming will take, you need to stress the people it will benefit. As discussed in the previous chapter, a general aging show potentially can reach three populations: the elderly, the general public and service providers.

Your argument should be attractive, because local stations are interested in reaching as wide an audience as possible. Strategic use of statistics to support your case can be helpful. It is important, for example, for the station to know if there is a large elderly population in the surrounding area.

The station should also be informed about other ways your program can meet community needs. Discuss the different ways your programming will be utilized in the community. Service providers might use the shows as a part of their training process or as a basis for group discussion. Nursing homes might arrange to have them aired for interested residents to view. They might be replayed at community or organizational meetings with discussions afterward. Again, demonstrating a diverse use for the shows can be an excellent selling point.

Program Format. Outline what you hope to accomplish. If you are asking for a limited series, you should list each show with the formal title (this can always be changed later). Under each title should be a brief outline of topics to be covered, either in the form of questions or as a list of talking points. List potential guests.

For an ongoing program, you should outline the first six to ten shows as you would for a limited series: formal title, brief outline, and possible guests. You should also include a list of potential subjects for shows beyond the six- to ten-show mark.

You also will need to discuss your approach. Are you going to use a talk show format? Are you going to bring in some demonstrations or have community input (e.g., reading letters from viewers)? What other outside resources are you going to use (e.g., visual materials)? How is the set going to be designed?

Promotion of Program. The station will need to know how you plan to promote the programs and build a following within the community. Set forth a realistic, but thorough, promotion strategy that includes notices to local newspapers, contact with community groups, and other public relations techniques.

Commitment of Person-Power. Stress the energy and commitment of your people in the development and production of the shows. The station will be justifiably concerned about the time and energy you and your colleagues plan to dedicate to the program. They need to be assured that you have your bases covered and you are not just another starry-eyed community group with inflated visions of television stardom. Television stations frequently get burned by well-meaning community groups who commit to a certain level of public service programming, which never materializes because they have simply gotten in over their heads.

To alleviate these concerns, outline the role your committee will be playing in such production matters as formulating subject areas, research, development of the introduction, talking points and conclusions, inviting guests, and demonstrations and visual aids. If this is a local access program, you will want to discuss how you will be staffing the show in such crew positions as camera persons, floor director, and control room functions.

Summary. Make one final pitch for why the station should accept your program proposal. Stress the energy and commitment your group is ready to give to this effort and why it will be successful.

Initial Contact with the Station

Your initial contact with the station should be a letter to the program director or the individual in charge of public service programming. It need not be elaborate, but should contain the following information:

An introduction to your organization and its purpose, with, if applicable, a summary of its track record in the community

A short description of the proposed programming, including theme, format, audience, and purpose

A short argument for why the station should adopt this type of programming

A clear timetable for setting up a meeting

A well-structured letter ideally will elicit a positive, though preliminary, response. Do not become discouraged, however, if a reply is not promptly forthcoming. The station may expect you to make the next move. If you have not gotten a reply within two weeks of mailing the letter, you should call and make an appointment to discuss the proposal.

If, by chance, you get the runaround, write to or call the general manager. Going to the top often stimulates quick action. Of course, the need for this step might be avoided altogether by simply indicating at the bottom of your initial correspondence that the general manager is receiving a copy. Remember, though, that station personnel are very busy people. Thus, it is necessary to be patient and flexible.

FCC: A Question of Commitment

The Federal Communications Commission, the federal agency responsible for governing use of the public airwaves as well as licensing radio and television stations and operators, could once be counted on to set out strong guidelines on how stations should respond to the interests of their local communities. Operating with the power to revoke or renew licenses, the FCC was a force to be reckoned with.

By and large, that worked to the benefit of the public. Both television and radio stations were required to provide the public with a specific amount of programming geared to matters of public concern, based on the station's assessment of community needs. Thus, a group seeking time for a local public service television program had a reasonable chance of getting it.

The future, however, is uncertain. In June 1984 the FCC eliminated programming guidelines, ascertainment requirements, advertising rules, and policies and program log requirements. Under the new rules the station no longer is required to assess community needs, chronicle or categorize the type of programming, or, most significantly, provide any specific amount of local programming. In other words, you are on your own. Stations with a good public relations sense—or a genuine social concern—undoubtedly will continue to allocate a fair amount of time to pubic service programming. From now on, however, unless the FCC deregulation decision is reversed, if you want to get a public service program on your local station, you had better be very persuasive.

Given the FCC's ruling, the only real weapon you have to fight unfair treatment by television stations is an effective advocacy effort. That is what inspired the final chapter of our book, where you will learn how to fight back.

Meeting with Station Personnel

Once the initial contact has been made with the station, set up an appointment to discuss your proposal in person. Armed with a small, but effective, negotiations committee, set out for the conquest.

The negotiations committee should consist of a select group of representatives from your media advisory committee. Like the media advisory committee itself, it should have an intergenerational flavor. The station is far less likely to be convinced of the need for a show dealing with issues of concern to the elderly if the group presenting the proposal is made up solely of younger persons. It is critical to have a show of support directly from the senior community and to have articulate members of that community demonstrating the support. Leaders of influential senior organizations, such as the Gray Panthers or the American Association of Retired Persons, often are good choices. You might also want to have a representative from a local senior service organization. A representative of the Area Agency on Aging might be particularly apropos since this organization represents most local aging services.

When you arrive for the interview, get right to the point. The program manager or whomever you will be meeting with is likely pressed for time, and you will only weaken your case by dragging the session out. Cover all your bases, but keep your presentation concise. Remember, the station has your written proposal to refer to. Among the points to emphasize are the following:

1. Targeted audience. Stress that you are targeting for a multigenerational audience: older persons, who are a proven audience of public service and informational shows and who can gain from information that has a direct effect on their lives; service providers, who can put a better understanding of the adjustments older people face to good use in responding more appropriately to their older clientele; and the general public who, by learning some of the realities of growing older, can better relate to their older relatives, friends, and acquaintances, as well as to their own aging process.

2. Format and topics. Discuss with authority the direction the show will take. Map out the format. If it is to be talk or interview, are you proposing a series or an ongoing show? What subject areas will your initial shows undertake? Will it be weekly, biweekly, or monthly?
3. Production effort. Document your commitment to the production of the show. Demonstrate how production responsibilities will be handled. Convince the station management that you have matters under control and that they will not be left holding the bag.
4. Community support. Emphasize the strong support this effort has within the community. The presence of your intergenerational committee should illustrate this point, but it won't hurt to reconfirm the strong commitment within the community. Station personnel need to be convinced that this show is not the idea of a small group of people acting alone, but the desire of a large, diverse body within the community.

Once the station demonstrates an interest in your proposal, you should gently, but firmly, close the deal. Negotiate for a show that does the best possible job of meeting your needs. If you asked for a four-part series and they, instead, give you one show at 2:30 Sunday morning, you must seriously question whether you will accomplish anything by the time and effort involved in producing the show. If the station cannot be persuaded to consider a better time, it probably is best to decline the offer and approach another station. With the experience of the first station under your belt, you will have a better chance of success the second time around.

Even if you succeed in getting your show, you still will have only just begun. Now the real challenge begins: producing creative media programming that will reach a significant portion of your local community with a convincing, positive message about growing old.

Planning an Effective Strategy To Get Your Own Show

Having your own public service television show is not just a far-fetched dream; it is a very real possibility. To be successful, however, you must have an effective and professional plan of action and a well-organized, determined effort. You should involve a broad spectrum of the aging community, including everyone from senior citizens to representatives of senior service agencies, advocacy groups and local colleges and universities. Research your market to determine what shows are on the air and how your idea fits in. Know who your audience is, and what will appeal to it. Identify what format will best present this programming, given the needs of the audience and the commitment level and capabilities of your group.

After you have taken all these steps, you will be ready to combine all you have learned into a top-notch, professional proposal to be presented to the station. If the presentation is a success, you will be on the road to producing a successful public service program—and to helping improve the electronic media's image of the elderly.

References

Belson, W. 1967. *The Impact of Television.* Hamden, Conn.: Arcon Books.

Blakely, R.J. 1971. *The People's Instrument.* Washington, D.C.: Public Affairs Press.

Bluem, A.W., J.F. Cox, and G. McPherson. 1961. *Television in the Public Interest.* New York: Hastings House.

Book, A.C., and N.D. Cary. 1978. *The Radio and Television Commercial.* Chicago: Crain Communication.

Bretz, R. 1976. *Handbook for Producing Educational and Public-Access Programs for Cable Television.* New York: Educational Technology Publications.

Chester, G., G.R. Garrison, and E.E. Willis. 1971. *Television and Radio.* New York: Meredith Corporation.

Dessart, G. 1978. *Television in the Real World.* New York: Hastings House.

Shanks, B. 1976. *The Coolfire: How to Make It in Television.* New York: W.W. Norton.

9
Television Production: How To Produce a Low-Cost, High-Quality Show

The ultimate sign of your show's success is whether your target audience finds it interesting and sufficiently stimulating to stay tuned to the channel and committed to watching the program in the future. Viewers do not care about the time, energy, and various resources that went into the production of the program. They merely expect it to have some intellectual significance, useful information, or entertainment value. If it provides none of these, viewers most likely will switch to a commercial program. Therein lies the real challenge for local productions, especially public affairs programming.

Commercial television has the money and the resources to attempt, for the most part successfully, to provide the viewing public with quality programming. Thus, not only must you hope to be given a time sometime before midnight and after 7 A.M. on Sundays, but you also must successfully compete for an audience against the wide array of programming on network affiliates, independent outlets, and movie stations. Though tough, the competition is not unbeatable. Programming that stimulates discussion and reaction will draw a share of the audience regardless of the competition.

This chapter examines how to produce high-quality local programming. The focus is on less complex formats such as talk/interview, documentaries, demonstrations (cooking, exercise, domestic tips), and entertainment (in-studio musical or comedy performances). A step-by-step look will be taken at how to develop a program that can compete and gain the respect and loyalty of local viewers—including everything from appealing to the viewers' creative side to developing visual appeal to selecting a host and guests that can make things happen.

Although many production steps are identical for all types of programming, to a large extent, production requirements change according to the format. We will spend the first few pages outlining what some of these formats are and how they can best be used.

Talk and Interview Shows

A major part of our discussion of television programming has revolved around talk and interview shows. That may seem tantamount to advocating "talking heads," but it is not. Admittedly, many local talk and interview shows are poorly produced and of marginal value. It need not be that way. There is tremendous potential for developing a creative, sophisticated talk show that is educational, entertaining, stimulating, and interesting. A high-quality product depends upon the thought and energy a production team puts into it. With enough effort, the payoff will be a loyal following and longevity for your show or series.

There also is a question of financing. Most amateur, would-be producers do not have the money to produce a high-budget, multifaceted program. Most will have to depend on the sponsorship and support of public service programming from a local network affiliate or a cable station.

Thus, a less elaborate talk or interview format is a more achievable alternative. The key ingredient to success is to make the show attractively different—to have that special something that will make a niche for you in the public's minds and lives. Ultimately, you want to convince viewers they have something to gain from watching your show, something they can't get from any other. The show should provide information that is stimulating or in some way adds to people's lives.

There are two main interview formats: the expert/informational interview and the personality/celebrity interview. The expert/informational interview, the most frequently used format, provides the audience with information and insight into some area affecting people's lives or their community. It could include such matters as health, politics, religion, business, services, and the arts.

Some of the best talk and interview shows are those featuring noted or much publicized public figures and celebrities in the political, consumer action, entertainment, and literary worlds. A good personality/celebrity interview opportunity is rare and should be aggressively sought. All audiences love famous people.

The right blend of personalities is vital for all talk/interview productions. Captivating personalities, whether national or local, can carry a show with virtually no content (heaven forbid that possibility!) or can hold the interest of viewers who might otherwise tune out an important, but less-than-enthralling topic. The more unique the show and the more unique its guests, the more endearing it will become to the public.

Local Documentaries

It may seem presumptuous if not foolish to include documentaries as a simple format that can be produced at the local level. Not so. Even in the absence of a strong financial commitment, a locally produced documentary can make a significant impression on an audience and, depending on its message, promote changes in attitudes, generate support, or serve as a call to action on important issues. A strong message combined with carefully chosen visual images will go far to compensate for dearth of funds.

Documentary television was really born with the CBS series "See It Now," produced by the late Edward R. Murrow and Fred Friendly. This series, produced in documentary format, boldly investigated the events of the day, the most powerful episode being an exposé of the cruel tactics of Senator Joseph McCarthy in his probe of communist infiltration of the federal government. As the legendary "See It Now," demonstrated, documentaries can provide a persuasive vehicle for social concern and reform. A local documentary can sensitize an audience to certain issues or concerns to which they may have given little thought. If a show strikes a responsive chord, it may even prompt viewers to take some action on the matter by joining an advocacy group or writing letters to public officials.

There are any number of possibilities for documentaries that carry a strong and dramatic social message. You might produce an in-depth review (requiring, of course, hours of research) of the controversial issue of the artificial extension of life by modern medicine. Is life extension worth the billions of health care dollars expended each year? What if the patients and their families do not want heroic measures to be taken? Is life extension being done mainly to satisfy the physicians? A historical summary of the issue could be followed by interviews with patients, family members, doctors, and public officials, interspersed with relevant data. Undoubtedly, sparks will fly.

Another intriguing possibility for a health care documentary would be an investigation of the growing hospice movement for care of the terminally ill. Do hospices really provide a more humane way to die? Do they help patients face death more comfortably? And what about the family and friends? You might follow the lives of certain individuals and families from the time a terminally ill person enters the hospice until his or her death or for a prescribed amount of time. Record how the patient and their family reacts to the impending death, and show the role of the hospice staff. Examine how hospice care compares with traditional ways of dealing with the dying in this country and in other countries. You may also want to examine briefly your subject(s)' life history. Are the terminally ill patients content with what they have accomplished in life, and how does that attitude affect how they deal with dying?

Still another local documentary might look at how different ethnic cultures in our society treat their elders. Do some cultures treat older persons with more respect and reverence? What effect does that have on family dynamics? Has the profit-oriented, fast-paced American way of life adversely affected cultural traditions carried down through the centuries? You might center on four intergenerational families: one black, one Jewish, one white Protestant, and one Hispanic. The different attitudes toward the elderly in these diverse cultures could provide an interesting commentary on growing old in the American melting pot.

At a time when equal rights for women is the subject of great discussion, another particularly compelling local documentary could focus on local older women who have risen through the ranks in traditionally male-dominated professions at a time when the sex barrier was much harder to leap than it is today. How much discrimination did they face? How much harder did they have to work to move up through the ranks? What effect did their professional career have on their personal/family lives? Their reminiscences about their hopes, dreams, and accomplishments, and their thoughts about women's rights issues today could be spellbinding. To add to the visual appeal, a biographical slide presentation of old family photographs could take the viewers on a chronological journey through these individuals' lives up to the present, accompanied by music and/or voice-over.

Local documentaries need not be limited to discussing global issues from a local perspective. Successful documentaries can be produced which focus on local service programs. One good example is a documentary on the efforts of the young to serve the old and the old to serve the young. What kind of helping relationships exist between people separated in age by a generation or two? You might look at some of the special links that form between school-age volunteers and aged nursing-home patients, elderly tutors and elementary school pupils, retired professional advisors and their college-age advisees, and retired business executives and young apprentices. Each side could talk about what made their relationship special, and these discussions could be interspersed with commentary from program coordinators regarding the success of that type of service approach.

Local documentaries can be produced in a number of different formats. A key variable is the role of the narrator, if you choose to have one. The narrator can be visible during the introduction of the show and then provide commentary off-screen for the remainder of the program. He or she also might be off-screen during the entire program, providing voice-overs throughout. With regard to the subject of the documentary, you could consider a modified interview approach, with individuals giving their own first-hand interpretation. If done effectively, this will add a great deal of impact to your production.

Make strategic use of visuals (slides, film, photographs) to provide a historical backdrop and to depict the situations or circumstances surrounding what you are trying to get across to your audience. You might use photographs (which should be converted into slides) or already prepared slides for an emotional 5-minute presentation with voice-over and music or just music without any narration. Keep each slide up on the screen just long enough (maybe 5 seconds) for the audience to get a feel for the scene. Pull on a viewers' emotions, give them a sense of the story that is being told, make them feel a part of what's going on.

Film or video sequences should tell a compelling story. They, too, can be a fully edited sequence or a film clip, and should be kept to no more than 5 minutes. Voice-overs or music can be used effectively, depending on the footage. Consider having your narrator give a stirring introduction to the film footage, perhaps with music in the background to add to the emotional impact.

Whether you have 30 or 60 minutes, use the time carefully. Look at what you have available—the interviews, the slide or film presentations, and the narration possibilities. Take the route that will have the greatest impact on the audience and that will do the best job of selling a message.

Don't ignore the importance of a good narrator; he or she can make or break your program. Much of the criteria outlined for selection of a top-notch talk show or interview host holds true here. The narrator must be articulate, sincere, have style and personality and, if seen and not just heard, an appealing appearance. Don't pass up a chance to get a noted personality that fits this bill. It isn't crucial that the narrator be well known, however. Anyone who will fill the role effectively is fine. If necessary, hold interviews and auditions where the candidates simulate a narration role while being videotaped. When you review the tapes, the right individual should stand out (see the subsequent section, Selecting the Ideal Host(s)).

Other Approaches and Formats

There are a variety of other relatively simple production formats, some of which can serve as free-standing programs, some of which are really just new twists to work into your talk or interview show for variety's sake, and some of which can be utilized in either fashion.

The Demonstration Format. Demonstrations can form the basis for an effective free-standing show. Typical examples are exercise, household hint, and cooking shows. Demonstrations can also be used to liven up a talk or interview show. For example, if a guest on your talk show is discussing the problem of sensory losses in old age, you might want to stage a demonstration or play a soundtrack of ordinary sounds that have been muffled to better illustrate your guest's points. Likewise, an exercise instructor who works with older people might want to bring a few older people with her and stage a very brief exercise session during the course of the interview.

Variety/Entertainment Programs. Another example of a format that either can stand alone or function as part of another show is the entertainment program. For example, you could set up an entire show that would revolve around showcasing older talent in the local area, such as stand-up comedians, dancers, singers, and musicians. During each program, entertainment segments could be interspersed with an interview with the entertainer of the day. On the other hand, variety or entertainment segments can add excitement to a talk or interview show. Whichever structure you opt for, remember that the variety/entertainment format will require an enormous time commitment. Auditions will have to be held with an adequate screening process, or you could find yourself with an out-of-control circus on your hands.

Variations on the Talk/Interview Theme. The Phil Donahue-style audience interaction show is a variation in which the host interviews the guest for a prescribed amount of time at the beginning of the show and then allows the audience to join in. Such a show can be fit into a 30-minute time slot (with the first 10 minutes allocated to interview and the remaining time to audience interaction), but a 60-minute time frame is more realistic.

The beauty of the audience-interaction format is that it can bring a show alive for the viewers as no other format can. Viewers at home often feel more involved because their peers are participating in the show. And the discussion is usually livelier because of the increased number of participants and the different views they represent.

The disadvantage of this approach is that, as with variety/entertainment shows, a massive amount of time and work is required to put each show together. Between forty and sixty audience members are needed for each show, and to make sure you get them, you will have to be in frequent contact with local organizations, schools, and the general community. Do not rely on filling your entire quota just by gathering random volunteers from a shopping center or the college commons. To ensure a lively and pointed discussion within the audience, include individuals who have some kind of personal experience or involvement in the subject. Thus, you will need to focus your recruitment efforts on specific groups within the community who fit that bill.

Another interesting twist might be to adopt a "Dear Abby/Ann Landers" format, in which your host(s) or a specialist responds to questions sent in by your viewing audience. Seek out questions from senior centers, nutrition sites or group meetings (also a good way to publicize the show). The questions should be selected well before the show, and they should be properly researched to avoid off-the-cuff remarks that are ill-advised or not factually based. Selected questions also should reflect concerns that affect the everyday lives of the viewers, including inquiries about relationships, finances, sexuality, nutrition, exercise, or politics.

A final suggestion for livening up a program, if you are lucky enough to have access to remote equipment, is to add an on-the-street interview feature. Either come up with a new topic each week, or use the theme of the interview/talk segment for that particular program. For example, on a show on the public's image of aging, you might ask young people what they think of growing old. For a show on sex, you might ask older persons at a local senior center their thoughts on their peers seeking out a new love life after they have been widowed. During a political season, you could ask both young and old whether age is a factor when they go to the ballot box. The possibilities for subjects are endless and the variety and intensity of responses can be both fascinating and priceless.

The point is, do not produce the same old local programming (more often than not lifeless talking heads) that viewers have been snoozing through since local television productions began. Be bold. Be creative. Try new twists. Use your unique style to create your own niche. If one approach does not work, keep trying others until you find that perfect combination that is a winner with local viewers.

Public Service Announcements

Because of their effectiveness in reaching older persons or the general public with thought-provoking messages, a brief discussion of Public Service Announcements (PSAs) is in order before going on to the nitty-gritty details of producing your own show.

PSAs can and should go beyond simply announcing forthcoming meetings and events. They should inform older citizens of services and issues that affect their everyday lives and provide younger citizens with a more balanced perspective on aging which can help them better understand the life adjustments faced by their loved ones, friends, and acquaintances.

It is much easier to gain access to radio than television PSAs, simply because radio stations outnumber television stations. Radio also allocates more airtime to PSAs than does television.

Radio spots are easier to develop than television spots since they only have to appeal to the ear. Of course, for variety, it doesn't hurt to produce more elaborate radio spots incorporating short skits or involving a personality in the presentation, rather than the traditional individual reading by a disc jockey.

Television PSAs, on the other hand, must appeal to both the eye and the ear. They require a good deal more time and energy to produce, and, unless the station is cooperative, they may not be worth the trouble. On the other hand, if the station you contact is willing to be helpful, television PSAs can be dynamite. In such a situation, there are a number of possible approaches to choose from.

Group Representative Announcement. You may be given 10 seconds (or, if you are lucky, up to 30 seconds or more) to have a representative of your organization deliver an announcement. This individual must be articulate, sincere, and persuasive. It might be helpful to try a format with visuals, possibly using slides, graphs, artwork, or pictures behind the person similar to what you would see on the nightly news.

Testimonial Announcement. This approach typically features a person who has benefitted in some fairly significant way from the services of your organization. The individual tells a penetrating story of how he or she was helped, drawing the audience to this real-life situation and enlightening them about your group's purpose. Again, the individual you select must be articulate and convincing. Be wary of melodrama, but don't hesitate to be hard-hitting.

Personality Announcement. Using well-known personalities can greatly enhance the impact of a PSA. The individual might be locally or nationally known in such areas as sports, entertainment, or politics. The key factor is that he or she present well, be respected and not be too controversial, or you will lose more than you gain. The announcer can simply make the statement to the audience with or without background visuals or can be used for a voice-over accompanying a primarily visual presentation. The latter might be more accommodating to the busy schedule of such individuals, since they would not have to come into the studio, but instead could tape their presentation at their convenience.

Slide/Film/Voice-Over/Music. It is also very effective to use a combination of slides or film with a voice-over describing the organization, service, or issue, with carefully selected music played throughout. With good visuals, a commanding, persuasive voice, and appropriate music, you can grab an audience's emotions. But if the voice is not convincing or the slides look like they were taken in 1956 with an old Brownie camera, the impact of the message will suffer. In a more complex public service announcement, lobby for at least 30 seconds or, better still, 60 seconds, in order to have adequate time to develop the central theme.

Cable TV Bulletin Boards. Many cable television outlets do not program all of their airtime and will run community announcements between programming. This can be a gold mine for announcing meetings or other group events.

Whatever format you choose, you must plan a strategy for developing PSAs that will make the most of a short period of time and deliver a message with the greatest possible impact. Emphasize the most important points and avoid unnecessary details. Remember, viewers cannot retain a large amount of information in such a short period of time. Choose your words carefully. An effective PSA grabs the attention of the audience and keeps it with persuasive techniques and attractive visuals.

Selecting the Right Producer and Crew

The most critical position in any production effort is that of the producer. He or she provides the central leadership, develops the program ideas and makes sure they are translated into action. In other words, he or she is the one who makes things happen.

Great care must be taken in the selection of the producer. The most important questions to be asked are these:

1. Does this person have experience in television production?
2. Is he or she knowledgeable about aging issues and concerns?
3. Does he or she have leadership skills necessary to handle a diverse group of people?

The producer generally selects the crew, and is involved in selecting the host. The number of crew members to be brought in depends on the type of production. For example, local cable *access* programming requires that you provide your own crew to staff the cameras and control room equipment and the floor director position. Do not panic! There are usually many well-trained persons in the community eager to have the opportunity to help staff a television production. Ask the cable station personnel where you can post a help-wanted announcement or find out if anyone has already expressed interest; typically a bulletin board is set aside for this purpose. Also, try the local community college or university television, broadcast, or communications department (it could be under any number of different names). Such departments often have a number of willing students with experience in the different aspects of television production.

If you are convinced you want your "own" people as the production staff, make sure everyone is well-trained and *ready*. Almost all local cable companies offer the community a comprehensive training package, with the greatest emphasis on use of the camera, but with some training in using control room equipment. As a matter of fact, most cable companies will not allow anyone to use their equipment unless they have received this training.

If you want a good-quality local access product, however, don't assume that sending someone through the cable training program is enough. Just as you audition for a host, do the same for all production staff members. Make sure that they have more than just a certificate of completion. Make sure that they also have the skills and creativity to be able to do the level of work that will help guarantee a production you can be proud of.

Selecting the Ideal Host(s)

An ongoing show or a series will fly or flop depending on the effectiveness of your host(s). An exciting host can make a dead topic or dull guests come alive. By the same token, a dull host can kill even the liveliest of shows. The ideal host has just the right mixture of conversational ability, nerve, sincerity, style and personality, sense of humor, knowledge and, needless to say, an appealing appearance. Whatever you do, don't select someone who is inappropriate to host your program, merely for convenience or political reasons. The host is essential to the success of your program, and you will never regret having taken the time and effort to select the right person for it.

Conversational Ability. A host should be an excellent conversationalist, not to be confused with a talker. Good conversationalists are interested in what people feel and how they perceive the important issues of the day. They are good listeners. They know when to react—and when to hold their counsel. By contrast, a talker listens poorly and responds inappropriately. The conversationalist puts guests at ease, enabling them to express their feelings and opinions more freely and openly. The talker tends to make guests uncomfortable and, as a result, inhibits conversation.

In a talk or interview or even a variety format, the host needs to carry on a conversation with the guests as though they were visiting in his or her living room. The conversation needs to flow naturally. It should not consist of one staccato question and answer after another. The host will undoubtedly need a list of the major points to be covered, but he or she should not be tied to them. The host must let the conversation take its natural course but, at the same time, have that special ability to control and redirect the conversation, taking hold of key words and phrases to move the discussion from one point to the next or to put it back on course. He or she needs to be able to pick up the slack in the conversation or to fill in a potentially uncomfortable silence. Above all, the host needs to ensure that there is a three-way conversation taking place: between the host, the guest(s), and the *audience*. The viewers should feel part of this intriguing discussion taking place in their home. They should feel as though they are eavesdropping on a discourse they would not have wanted to miss.

Nerve. A host needs to be gentle, but tough—never backing off, yet not coming on too strong. If a guest is avoiding a critical question, the host should not let up until the issue has been addressed. Getting to the heart of an issue may take some aggressive pursual by the host. Barbara Walters and Phil Donahue are excellent examples of hosts who will hammer at their guests until they get to the point. It makes little difference whether the guest is a nationally known political figure or a little-known specialist. And so it should be with your host. He or she should never be awed by a guest. The guest who senses the host's awe may assume the upper hand. This does not mean that the host should be overly aggressive. Too much aggression can backfire, making the host seem abusive. The audience will miss the point of the discussion and focus on the conflict. Aggressive pursual should be used strategically for optimum effect.

Coolness under Fire. A host must remain in control even when the going gets tough. And there are bound to be some moments that could get the best of any host. Two guests might get into a heated exchange. A guest might make one of the most irrational, irresponsible statements ever uttered, one that could push anybody's buttons. Another guest might try to turn a point around and use it to corner the host. No matter what the situation, the host must remain calm and in control throughout, at least in terms of outward appearance and response. He or she must demonstrate the ability to handle tough situations, whatever they might be, and keep the show on track. A good host can take advantage of a difficult encounter to enliven a serious or dull show.

Sincerity. A host must be sincerely interested in the major thrust of the program or series—in this case, aging issues. If he or she is not, the viewing public will sense it and become bored. By contrast, a sincere excitement and involvement by the host will prove contagious, sparking viewer interest.

Style/Personality. Your host must have a personality and style that your audience can respect and like. If viewers do not care for him or her, they will change the channel even if the subject matter is important.

Hosts like Johnny Carson and Phil Donahue have captivating personalities and unique styles that have created loyal followings nationwide. The same is true of Merv Griffin and Dick Cavett. Each rose to prominence because he was able to develop a close, personal relationship with his audience.

Sense of Humor. It also is important to have a host with a sense of humor. Not only should he or she be able to laugh at the right moments during the show, but, if possible, to add a little bit of humor of his or her own. The audience generally appreciates a tasteful sense of humor at appropriate times. So do guests, who tend to be relaxed and comforted by it. "Cornball" humor can be quite disastrous, however, causing great embarrassment to all involved.

Knowledge. At least one of your hosts should have a sound knowledge of aging or a related field, as well as a working knowledge of current local, state, and national events. A possible exception would be someone who is willing to do in-depth research before each show to be able to converse with ease on the subject at hand. But even then, if the person has not actually worked with older persons or those in the aging field or is not in the senior age bracket, he or she will be at a great disadvantage in responding intelligently to the remarks of experts and other guests on each show. Much of the natural flow of conversation depends on the host's comfort with what is being discussed. Someone who has had little or no contact with older persons or the aging field or is not an older person, may not have a believable level of empathy and understanding, even with extensive research. The host need not be an expert, but he or she should have had some contact with the elderly. It is highly recommended that at least one of the hosts for a show or series be an older person who has actually experienced what is being discussed.

Appearance. Let's face it, a host needs to have an appealing appearance. This does not mean that perspective hosts must look like Paul Newman or Jane Fonda. As a matter of fact, hosts who are too perfect can be a turn-off. What is important is that your host(s) have a pleasant, attractive appearance, a look to which your audience will respond positively.

It may appear that selecting a host(s) that fit all these criteria is a mission impossible. It really is not. Furthermore, you will not regret the effort. Selecting hosts who are significantly lacking in any of the above areas could put the production team in a messy situation and adversely affect the progress and effectiveness of your program or series. With a careful selection process, however, you can avoid some very unnecessary problems.

The most effective selection process for your future host(s) consists of an interview of prospective candidates by a selection committee, whose membership should include the producer(s), selected members of the production team, and selected members of your media committee, and an audition in front of the camera—the result of which would be reviewed by the selection committee.

Applicants from the local community should be sought through local electronic and print media and announcements at meetings of senior organizations and related groups. There should also be direct solicitation by selection committee members of those individuals who they feel are potential hosts. Such invitations might be extended to community leaders who are known for their communication skills or appealing personalities, or to persons in professions that require an ability to communicate and relate well to people. Examples are broadcasters, teachers, consumer advocates, or government employees. Be sure to emphasize that invitations are not guarantees of preferred status. These people must go through the established selection process like everyone else.

The initial interview will give you a feel for an individual's personality, communication abilities, appearance, and knowledge of aging and current events. It should also facilitate narrowing the list of candidates to a reasonable number, say, four to six.

The next step is to film a simulated version of your show in the studio, with selection committee members serving as guests. The candidates should be given an introduction and a set of questions and asked to start the show and interview the guests as if they were the host of the show. Stress that prospective hosts need to use their own style and approach, making alterations where they feel appropriate. If you are planning a two-host format, try out different combinations. If you find a likely choice right away, test other candidates with that individual to find the winning combination.

Upon reviewing the tapes of the simulated interview, try to zero in on the top candidate(s) very quickly. Certain people will stand out on camera. Other elements, both positive and negative, will be evident that would not be apparent in a face-to-face interview. If, by chance, someone does not stand out as the ideal host, retest certain candidates or reopen auditions to others. Be convinced before you make a final decision.

One final recommendation: Attempt to have an older host if at all possible. The best combination is intergenerational, with either an older female and younger male or an older male and younger female. Which combination is more desirable generally will depend on the individuals and personalities involved.

Picking Attention-Grabbing Topics

No matter how good the host(s), the success of a show hinges on the strength of the topics. Creativity is the key. Put yourself in the role of your audience. Most people will not watch a talk or interview show unless the topic piques their interest. When considering topics for a show or series, you need to ask yourself certain questions about them vis-à-vis the audience you are trying to reach.

> First of all, whom are you trying to reach? Primarily an older audience or both old and young?
>
> Will the program have a positive influence on some facet of their lives?
>
> Does the information fill a particular need for the viewers, their families, or their friends?
>
> Will the topic sustain viewer interest?
>
> Does the topic have any entertainment value?

To keep an audience's interest and generate a following, a balance must be found between meeting the needs of the viewing audience and sustaining their interest. There are myriad aging-related subjects to choose from, including economic influences, emotional difficulties, widowhood, nutrition, physical fitness, employment, long-term care, self-help, religion, senior sexuality, consumer fraud, health concerns, politics, and prescription drug abuse. There are literally hundreds of potential topics. A content analysis of twenty-eight actual productions in the mid to late 1970s resulted in the following list of aging topics: roles of older people in society, health, the impact of a changing society, retirement transitions, income, service programs, employment, education, housing, transportation, and crime. From these subject areas alone, you could have dozens of spin-offs for individual shows or series. (See Appendix C for a list of over 100 possible topics.)

In planning topic areas for a series or an ongoing show, it is always wise to gather input from the individuals you are trying to reach. A poll of older persons, service providers and the general community, will enable you to better ascertain the topic areas and approaches to which an audience would best respond. In selecting a topic area, do not be afraid to be unique, daring, or controversial. Try new angles. Attempt the unexpected. So many issues affect the everyday lives of older viewers or could open the eyes of younger viewers with regard to aging that there is no excuse for being boring.

One intriguing idea for a series is a three-part production on "Feeling and Looking Your Best," which skillfully mixes interesting discussion from experts and local seniors with entertaining practical demonstrations. The first show could deal with one of the most serious health problems among the elderly: obesity. The first half of the show could feature a specialist, such as a doctor or a nutritionist, and possibly an older woman or man who successfully shed 30 or more pounds after retirement. The last half of the show might include a demonstration of how to prepare a good-tasting, low-calorie meal.

The second part of the series might look at physical fitness and exercise. Again, the show would begin with an interview of a local fitness specialist, who would discuss how older persons can become involved in an exercise program that would fit their particular needs, and follow with an actual demonstration of exercises by local aerobic dancers (preferably older). The hosts might add to the fun of both shows by participating in the demonstration. The final show in the series can take a look at fashion, hair-dos, and makeup for older persons. Guests could include local fashion designers, buyers, and cosmetics representatives. The potential for demonstrations on such a show are outstanding! You could have a fashion show with older male and female models wearing the newest fashions and demonstrating the most effective use of makeup.

There also are interesting ways of taking advantage of the seasons. You might have a Christmas special featuring a number of older residents of the local area, each originating from a different region of the country, who would reminisce about Christmas as it was during the Depression, the World Wars, or the prosperity of the 1950s. During an election year—or any year for that matter—you might consider hosting a debate on the pertinent issues between representatives of the Democratic and Republican parties.

Pathways, a weekly senior-oriented talk and interview show on the Fairfax County Virginia cable system, presented a two-part series on the lives of the gay elderly. Needless to say, many were shocked by the frank discussion of this life-style. But the gay elders on the shows were able to give the viewers a glimpse into the lives and feelings of a group that is estimated to account for 10 percent of the senior population. The series later was a national finalist for a prestigious national cable award. The message? Be bold, and it will likely pay dividends. And if you look around at what is happening in your local area, there are undoubtedly numerous opportunities to be bold.

A note of caution, however, against an overdose of controversy, especially if it elicits anger and protest from the community. No station minds receiving both supportive and angry letters from viewers, or even demands for equal time. In fact, such an outpouring may work in your favor, as it shows that the community is watching and responding to your show. But if the reaction takes the form of sustained ill feelings toward the station, management may begin to take a dim view of your program. And that is the last thing you want if you hope to remain on the air.

The secret to a successful show, controversial or not, is to have your topics reach into the lives of your viewers and capture them for 30 minutes (or however long your program is). Give them information, personalities, and entertainment that they typically do not receive elsewhere. Each of the successful national talk shows gets to the heart of what their viewers are looking for. Phil Donahue provides a stage for problem-sharing and problem-solving on topics ranging from sex to drugs to politics. Johnny Carson is a master showman featuring creative monologues and skits and light banter with noted celebrities. Merv Griffin and Mike Douglas offer a close-up look at the private lives of their celebrity guests.

Don't forget that a major purpose of your local talk or interview show is to serve as an informational and educational source for the elderly, their service providers, and the general public. Don't get so carried away with being clever and entertaining that you neglect this very important role. Take particular care to diversify the themes of your shows to provide a balance of informational, issue-oriented, practical, stimulating, uplifting, and entertaining programming. Admittedly, that is a tall order, but so is producing a high-quality television show.

To find out whether you are achieving the necessary balance in subject area, it might be useful to take an occasional random survey of viewers to see how they are responding to the topics being covered on the show, as well as to other facets of the show. Since viewer samples are not always easy to come by, you might present a selected show or two to different senior, service provider, or public gatherings, and solicit their input after the viewing. The best way, however, is to gather the opinions of viewers who have seen a number of shows.

Proper Planning

It can't be stressed enough that proper planning is essential to the effectiveness of any television program. You may be able to get away with inadequate planning once or twice, especially in those cases where you are very familiar with the topic area. But a continual lack of organization will catch up with you. The bottom line is that the viewing public will not stick around to watch a poorly produced program. And once a dissatisfied viewer has changed the channel, you probably will never recapture that viewer's attention.

Organize and produce each show as if you have a gun at your head—the viewers'. Always try to plan the best show you possibly can. Do not just try to get by. Obviously, some shows will have to be put together in a short time for reasons beyond your control. But try always to be conscious of those viewers who might be tuning in to your show for the first time. Will they see a show that makes them want to tune in again? Be sure they do.

To ensure proper planning, the key players in production of the show should meet periodically to discuss upcoming shows, review completed programs, and analyze problems. If, for instance, your season runs from September to June (often ongoing local shows will run new productions for nine months and play repeats in the summer), you will want to have a production meeting in late July or early August to formulate the direction your show will take for the next year. Included in that meeting should be planning for subject areas (obviously leaving leeway for creative inspirations during the year), discussion of possible changes in format or emphasis (maybe adding audience participation, more demonstrations, or a consumer section), and a reiteration of everyone's roles in the productions. Following that meeting, the production team should reconvene at least once a month (if not weekly or biweekly) to review recent show tapes and assess where the show is and where it should be going.

Without production meetings and ongoing evaluation, the show will not progress as quickly as it might and the quality of your show will suffer, for months may have passed by the time you recognize problem areas.

It also is important that there be adequate and comprehensive preparation for each taping session, whether you will be taping one or three shows. Producers and hosts need to get together, separately from the team meetings, before each taping session. They need to review the questions prepared for the interview, who the guests will be, the intended flow of the program, any demonstrations or special sections, and timing. A short summary on the subject matter to be featured on the show or series should be prepared in advance of the meeting and everyone, particularly the host(s), should have reviewed it before coming to the meeting.

A separate process of preparation should be followed for guests. Sometimes with veteran television guests, a telephone conversation and pretaping briefing will suffice. It is advisable, however, to have a face-to-face meeting with guests at least a few days before the taping, plus a brief review directly before the taping. The earlier the involvement of the guests the better, since they may have a special sense for the subject and can help make adjustments in the handling of the topic on the show. Adequate planning before each taping will ensure that all involved will be better prepared and more comfortable. The end result will be a higher quality show.

Selecting Appropriate Guests

The selection of guests for each show should be done *very* carefully because they will make the difference between the success and failure of that particular show. And selecting the right guest(s) does not mean just picking those who are most knowledgeable about the subject area. It means picking those who possess the right mix of expertise, personality, and entertainment value. Not every expert speaks well, is interesting, or is personable.

To avoid the potentially fatal mistake of judging a prospective guest *solely* by his or her expertise, producers should ask themselves the following questions:

What is the prospective guest's professional background? The person does not have to be a nationally recognized expert but should have credentials that would be respected by your audience and should be able to respond intelligently to questions.

How good are the guest's communication skills? Your candidate need not be a great orator, but he or she should be articulate. If there is no way to avoid having a questionable communicator because his or her expertise is crucial to the show, invite another guest who speaks well, to provide the necessary balance.

What about his or her personality? A major factor determining whether the audience will respond positively or negatively is the guest's personality. If a potential guest tends to be too dull, either provide another, balancing personality or try to find someone else who will be more stimulating. *Type* of personality is also an important consideration. Some personalities do not mix well—often, because they are too much alike. For instance, two guests who are both very aggressive and outgoing talkers could spend the whole show competing for the floor and making life very difficult for the host. Thus, a balance in personalities is essential.

Is the prospective guest entertaining? This is not critical, but guests who are entertaining to your viewers will help make your show a success.

Your guests may not be able to fill these criteria for every show. Authoritative and stimulating guests are not always readily available, and sometimes political or other factors will force you to select some-one who is less than the optimal choice.

But if you are always on the lookout for guests who are unique and stimulating, you can generally keep your show hopping. A "name" per-sonality is always a good catch, whether it be an author, actor, activist, or politician. Celebrities often are more willing to appear on television than you might imagine. After all, if offers free publicity as well as being a public service. Check published calendars of events to see who is com-ing to town, and then move quickly. Maggie Kuhn, Claude Pepper, Elisabeth Kübler-Ross, or Helen Hayes may be scheduled to appear in your area in the near future. Call the sponsoring group and see if some-thing can be arranged. You could very well pull off a coup.

Of course, a unique and stimulating personality for your show need not to be a household name. You might be able to snag the mile record-holder in the national Senior Olympics, the man who broke the Guiness Book of World Records for hang-gliding across the Grand Canyon at age 70, a husband-and-wife team that played with George Burns in vaude-ville, or a former congressman who served during the Eisenhower and Kennedy years. Search your own local area for people with intriguing pasts; they might well be pleased to appear on your show to talk about the good (or bad) old days.

The ideal number of guests for an interview is one or two, and on rare occasion three, at any one time. If you want to bring four guests on a particular show, have two interviewed during the first half and the other two during the second half. This is especially effective in a situa-tion where you are interviewing experts and participants or victims. For instance, for a show on Alzheimer's disease, a doctor and group coun-selor could be interviewed during the first half of the show and family members of victims in the latter half.

Always choose guests with care. A talk show will go nowhere with-out the right balance of interesting, stimulating, and knowledgeable guests.

Appealing to the Logical and Creative Sides of the Brain

No matter what type of production you develop, there is a secret ingre-dient that will make the difference in whether you capture the viewers' interest and imagination. That secret is knowing how to reach into their minds in a way most local television shows fail to do, by programming to both sides of the brain: the logical, practical, left hemisphere and the creative, intuitive, right hemisphere. The result of this type of approach could have some very interesting implications for not only your local efforts, but for television programming in general.

The brain consists of two halves or hemispheres, resembling half a walnut. Each half is rounded and convoluted in a similar pattern. The functions of the two halves are very different, however. The left hemisphere is logical, verbal, abstract, temporal, analytical, sequential, and symbolic. It is this side of the brain that controls language and language-related capabilities, processes information and verbal stimuli, logically solves problems, analyzes data for details, responds to logical verbal and written appeals, deals with problems sequentially, keeps track of time, and deciphers symbols. The left side also controls the right side of the body.

The right hemisphere, on the other hand, is conceptual, nonverbal, intuitive, nontemporal, nonrational, holistic, and pattern-seeking. This side of the brain controls emotion and feeling, is creative, is responsive to emotional appeals, is intuitive in problem solving, recognizes faces, interprets body language, produces humor, uses images, has no sense of time, perceives over-all patterns and structures, improvises, and makes extensive use of metaphors and analogies. In addition, the right brain controls the left side of the body.

The left and right hemispheres are connected by a small band of neural fibers called the corpus collosum. This band carries messages back and forth to each side, creating an interesting and effective partnership. The right brain will see a picture, slide, or demonstration and the left brain will take in this data and test its validity. The left brain absorbs the logical facts, ideas, and meaning of a particular situation, while the right brain, through metaphors or anecdotes, analogies and examples, perceives the relation among the different parts of the problem and applies this to other similar problem-solving situations. Since the right brain perceives holistically, intuitively, and creatively, it needs to be stimulated in this manner or the mind as a whole will have more difficulty understanding. Neither hemisphere provides the answers by itself, but instead the two work in concert.

This is where television programming often fails, especially the talk or interview format. It orients itself toward the left brain, sending verbal, factual, rational, and analytical signals, and virtually ignoring the right brain's ability to be creative, intuitive, and insightful and to see how the different parts go together to make a whole. Talk and interview producers generally leave the viewer's right brain alone to take care of itself, to imagine, perceive, and create, without giving it proper visual tools. Producers of documentaries tend to provide more visual images as well as more anecdotes and examples to link concept to imagination and insight.

The implications for local television productions of taking advantage of left-versus-right brain function are exciting. Your programming efforts can reach out to the right brain of the viewers, combining logic with imagery to create greater interest and stimulate creativity and new insight into aging topics, issues, and services and their implications for the present and the future. With thoughtful use of visual metaphor, many complicated and diverse aspects of aging and other topics can be simplified for the viewers. The right brain will be able to provide an image or metaphoric perception to the left brain, which can then provide a logical, detailed, verbal analysis of the situation. The result should be enhanced understanding and enjoyment for the viewing audience. Throughout the remainder of the chapter, attempts will be made to incorporate the notion of left–right brain thinking.

Effective Writing

The primary objective in writing for local television is to grasp and hold the attention and interest of the audience. This must be done immediately because, unlike feature films, where the audience has paid and is somewhat captive, television viewers can instantly change a channel (and will) if their interest is not stirred from the outset. An effectively written show can capture your viewer's attention and keep them involved throughout.

In a talk or interview segment, you have three chances to capture the viewer's interest and attention: the introduction of the topic, the introduction of the guest(s), and the first question asked by the host. The goal is to keep the show flowing smoothly and the interest level high, covering the subject area as thoroughly as possible, with a wide range of hard-hitting questions or discussion points that build to a climax and are resolved by the end of the show.

Introduction of the Topic. In introducing the theme or topic area for a program, it is best to whet the viewers' appetite with an intriguing or startling fact. Raising a thought-provoking rhetorical question or two that can be answered only by watching the interview arouses the viewer's curiosity and instills a sense of expectancy. Don't get so caught up in being provocative, however, that you forget to orient your viewers adequately to the focus of the interview. For example, you might begin your show by saying:

> Recent research indicates that abuse of the elderly by family members is as widespread and underreported as are spouse abuse and child abuse.

Elder abuse can take the form of physical and sexual assault, deprivation of life necessities, or verbal and emotional cruelty. Why is this shocking abuse of older persons occurring, and what can be done about it? We hope to find some answers today in our interview with . . .

Introduction of Guest(s). The introduction of a guest must establish him or her as the expert or personality he or she is. A subtler approach can be taken with someone more well known to your viewers. In either case, the introduction need not be lengthy or overdone. Center on the points that will make this individual most interesting and appealing to your audience. For instance, you might say:

> We are honored to have as our guest today one of the most outspoken advocates and leaders of older and younger Americans, Maggie Kuhn. In 1970 Maggie founded the Gray Panthers as a national network of young and old that would work together on such vital concerns as peace, health care and consumer protection. Today, some 14 years later, the Gray Panthers are one of America's most effective advocacy groups and Maggie Kuhn is speaking out as loudly and effectively as ever. Welcome to . . .

Discussion Points. In developing the questions for your guests, strive for attention-grabbing talk or conversational points. The interaction between the host and guests should resemble a smooth, engrossing, and natural conversation, not a boring process of asking a question, getting an answer, and then asking another question. To totally script out a show is to tie the hands of the host and sap the show's creativity. An informal, albeit directed, exchange will be far more interesting and believable than a discussion that is bound by a set format or list of questions. The host must always have the freedom to develop new angles or take the show in a different direction on the spur of the moment, if the points being discussed so dictate.

Like the introduction, your first question or discussion point should be provocative. But if you want to keep the audience's attention, you'll have to keep the discussion lively throughout. Don't forget, however, the importance of covering the subject area adequately. Don't just focus on the "sexy" details. Give the total picture, permitting viewers to gain a better understanding and perspective on the topic at hand. Your outline should reflect this and allow for natural transitions from one point to the next. Structure these points so as to avoid short "yes" or "no" answers or long-winded monologues. Try to encourage 2 or 3 minutes of comment or analysis, as well as frequent give and take between the host and guest(s). A 30-minute show will usually allow for around ten to twelve questions. The host should invite guests to supplement their discussion with interesting stories, anecdotes, and examples. A sample question and discussion point might read as follows:

QUESTION. Masters and Johnson concluded that social-psychological factors were more powerful inhibitors of sexual activity than was biological aging. Among these factors were preoccupation with work, physical and mental fatigue, overindulgence in food and drink, and reactions to societal taboos about sex in old age. How much *do* these factors affect the sex lives of older persons?

DISCUSSION POINT. Loss of role and status:

–What it means to be stripped of your professional identity.

–How loss of social and economic power lessens the ability to reflect American values of achievement, productivity, and independence.

–Why white collar workers have a much tougher time adjusting than blue collar workers.

–Why there is a high suicide rate among white collar retirees.

Whereas the talk or interview format should only be partially scripted, the local documentary should be almost totally scripted. The approach can vary. For instance, you may pick a series of slides, photographs, or film to introduce the theme of the show. A scripted voice-over is needed to accompany them. An off-screen narrator can do the introductions, transitions, or voice-overs for the visuals. Or the narrator can alternate between being on and off screen. Either way, the narrator's presentations must be skillfully crafted in advance. If your documentary is to include a series of interviews, planning is equally important. Although these interviews cannot always be fully scripted, introductions and questions should be written out beforehand. Each part of the documentary must be shaped in order to get at the heart of the subject—the joy, the anguish, the pain, the triumphs, and the defeats—so that the viewing audience feels a part of the action and can gain a better understanding of it.

Whether you are writing for a talk or interview show for a documentary, there are certain additional factors you must keep in mind if you are to have an effective production—namely research, objectivity, and timing.

Research. Each production needs extensive research to be successful. This is particularly true of documentaries. Shows that are inadequately researched all too often miss the mark; major points are left out, recent research findings are omitted, or pertinent experts, proponents, or opponents are overlooked. Avoid this embarrassing predicament by following this two-step approach.

1. Always contact those individuals who are most involved with the subject or issue—the academic experts, the advocates, the victims. They will, in turn, provide you with more contacts. These interviews and contacts will give you the inside scoop on the newest research, the best examples, the advocacy or legal efforts, and future implications. Make sure that you adequately research both sides of the issues. For example, if you are doing a documentary on depression in old age, it will be at best dry and at worst incomplete if you do not properly research the constantly updated research findings and conduct extensive interviews with depressed individuals and family members to better understand the effects on the lives of the victims and their families. Likewise, if you are developing questions or discussion points for a talk or interview show, do not forget to consult the scheduled guests; they are often the best sounding board.
2. Follow up on *all* the leads you receive. Do not rely totally on them, however. Do your own library research of relevant periodicals, books, and newspapers to ensure production of a show that addresses all sides of the subject.

Objectivity. Although you will undoubtedly have your own biases, your audience has the right to an objective presentation of the facts. This applies not only to the selection of guests, namely guests with different perspectives, but also to the manner in which the show is written and scripted. Both talk or interview shows and local documentary productions should strive for objectivity.

Objectivity doesn't mean a host cannot express his or her own opinion. During an interview, it is perfectly acceptable for the host to make his or her own position clear; David Frost, Dick Cavett, and William Buckley certainly do not hesitate to do so. However, the guests on both sides of the issue should be given the opportunity to argue their respective cases without being subjected to unfair attacks, loaded questions, or ridicule. A healthy debate should be welcomed. Always allow for enough objectivity in the program for a fair airing of all sides of a particular issue or concern.

The same reasoning holds true for a documentary. No documentary is entirely objective. Each has an underlying thesis or hypothesis, as it should. If your presentation is too one-sided, however, it will raise serious questions among those in the audience. The goal of an informational production is to present a subject area thoroughly from all sides and to allow the audience to come to their own conclusions. If the presentation is done correctly and skillfully, the viewers will usually come to the correct conclusion.

Timing. All programs must be scripted with time limitations in mind. Timing is essential. With documentaries, you must figure out how much time to allot to each of the major components: narrative, visuals, and interviews. For talk or interview shows the challenge is to adequately cover the subject area in 26 to 27 minutes of actual program time and still allow adequate time for the introduction, conclusion, and intermission(s). For both formats, there is the additional question of how well you have used the allotted time. Did you cover the subject area as well as you could have? Or did you leave out important aspects while giving an unnecessarily long time to areas of less importance? That is why pacing is so important. Stay on one point long enough for the audience to understand, but don't remain there so long that boredom sets in or you forego the opportunity to make an even more important point. In addition, make sure any narration moves along at a pace that is neither too fast nor too slow. If it is too fast, your viewers may miss your point altogether; if it is too slow, they may fall asleep. In either case, you have blown your chance to have an impact on their lives.

Creative Visual Materials

The visual element of television production is where you really capture the interest and the attention of the viewer, where you trigger creative right brain. Visual materials enhance both the audience's enjoyment and their understanding of the subject being discussed. With careful planning, these materials can become a powerful weapon in the successful production of a particular program.

Visuals include slides, charts, maps, photographs, camera cards, artwork, and lettering. Some visuals are picked up by cameras live in the studio, and others are processed into slides for use during a given program. There are certain factors to consider in the development of visuals:

Aspect Ratio. Your viewers' television set will actually show less of the outer edge of the original graphic. Thus, your graphic needs to have an "aspect ratio" of three units high and four units across, similar to the proportions of a television screen. In other words, on an 11- by 14-inch card (which is a standard size), you will have an area of 7 inches by 10 inches that is framed and critical to your message.

Size. The size of the visual also is important. If a guest or host is handling the graphic, it should not be too large or awkward. A larger graphic that is to stand on its own should have firm backing so that it stays in place and does not flop around. Also, make sure that your visual is not so small that its contents are not legible on screen.

Glare. Some pictures can cause glare. Avoid shiny or glossy photos. If the only photos you have are glossy, shading can help.

Technique for On-Camera Display. Always plan well before the show how and when visuals will be used, whether they be photographs, illustrations, or lists of names or words. Slides, for instance, must be numbered and the necessary crew members must be notified as to when they will be used during the show. You must plan whether you are going to set up graphics off stage or have the guests hold and display them. It is usually preferable to set up graphics off the set to avoid the possibility of awkward handling by guests. A studio easel will help. At the appropriate time, it can be moved closer to the guest so that he or she can indicate (with a pointer, if desired) pertinent illustrations. Wall charts, posters, or flip cards (which can be mounted on a small easel and flipped over by the guest as he or she discusses them) can also be used. It is most desirable, however, to have visuals made into slides, which can then be handled from the projection room. This also frees the cameras from having to deal with graphics.

Simplicity. Graphics should be kept as simple and concise as possible. Graphs and charts should be easy to read and understand. Words and pictures should not be crowded or cluttered, and the typeface of lettering should be easy to read. The message should be one that can be comprehended quickly. Again, never risk losing your audience. You might not get them back.

Timing. Never spend a lot of time on a particular visual. More than 15 seconds is probably too much and will cause your audience's attention to wander.

Slides. Color slides (35 millimeter) are possibly the most effective way to illustrate your points. If you had a show on the lives of older people in mainland China, what better way to illustrate that fascinating story than through a series of slides that nicely supplements your expert's discussion? Slides can show beautiful scenery and historic buildings. They can mirror people's joys and sorrows. They can be used to display graphs, charts, or artwork. What is more, they can be easily incorporated into a show. No cameras or special lighting is necessary. Once slides have been numbered and mounted in the projector, only one member of the production crew needs to be responsible for them. Do determine exactly when slides are to be brought into the show to allow for maximum impact. Work closely with crew members to ensure they know the plan. For the greatest visual impact, always bear in mind the aspect ratio, and that the slide you use should be horizontal, not vertical.

Thus, have the desired image concentrated toward the middle to compensate for peripheral loss when projected on television. Whether in an interview or documentaries, strategically placed slides can do wonders.

It is vital that you incorporate visual support materials into your productions. There will be a noticeable result in terms of the impact your show will have on your audience. They will enjoy the program more and will assimilate more information.

On-Camera Demonstrations

Another effective visual tool is the demonstration. You can discuss the value of exercise and physical fitness to your older viewers until you are blue in the face, but you will have a much greater impact if you illustrate the topic with an actual demonstration of in-home or group exercise techniques. A story about a senior acting troupe, likewise, would be greatly enhanced by having the actors and actresses perform a short skit. It is one thing to talk about the necessity of proper nutritional habits for those who live alone, and quite another to actually demonstrate how to prepare a nutritional meal for one. In all three cases, the audience is instructed visually and their interest is piqued.

In an on-camera demonstration use two cameras to allow for more action. Get a close-up of some aspect of the food preparation, then go back to the interaction between the host and your chef. Or focus exclusively on the chef in action. Much of this can be done with one camera, but two or more cameras allows even more freedom of movement.

The success of demonstrations, like most other parts of the production, depends on adequate preparation. Inform your production team of plans for demonstrations well ahead of time. You might also want to do some dry runs before the taping to ensure efficiency and smooth sailing. The last thing you want is to overdo a good thing or eat into needed time for interviews or other activities.

Designing the Set

The design of your set should accomplish two purposes. First, it should be attractive and comforting to the eye of the viewers, and second, it should be devoid of visual distractions.

Two key factors must be taken into account: the actual physical space and the decor. Does the set fit visually with the theme of your show? Does it add to or detract from the overall impression you are trying to make on the audience? Attempts to produce a high-quality show can be seriously jeopardized by a shoddy set. The set should use interior decoration, architecture, and a touch of realism, taking into account available space, color, and lighting. Seek the evidence of knowledgeable individuals at the station or within your group. Remember, if your set is not visually appealing, the creative side of your viewers' brains will be sounding an alarm throughout the show. Even if they continue to watch, the show's impact will be lessened. The following factors should be taken into account if you are to design an effective, visually appealing set:

A Set Plan. It is always wise to sketch a rough plan of your set to visualize how the set will look with your desired layout of furniture and other props. Are you making the best use of available space? Are you allowing for the best camera, sound, and lighting opportunities?

The Size and Shape of the Physical Area of the Studio. Most local studios have a relatively small, confined space. Inherent limitations usually necessitate a simple set design.

Budget. Dreams of elaborate sets are often shot down by a lack of money, a fairly typical problem for local, public service productions. Creativity and ingenuity will pay off. By borrowing furniture and props from the studio's stockpile and from the attics and basements of your group's membership, an attractive, workable set can be pieced together. Another alternative is to seek donations of chairs, couches, tables, and artificial plants from local furniture or department stores. In return, you can agree to run their company name in the credits as donors. A word of caution, however: Make arrangements to select and agree upon the items that are being donated or you may end up with some useless items that have been sitting in their warehouse for months waiting to be discarded.

The Audience. The set must appeal to the tastes of the audience that you are trying to reach. Since you are most likely going to be attempting to appeal to a wide spectrum of ages, you might want a living room or den setting that would be aesthetically pleasing to most age groups.

Furniture. There are a number of factors to consider in selecting furniture for the set. First, you must decide what pieces you want to have on the set. Are you just going to use chairs or are you going to have a couch? There are plusses and minuses with both set-ups. The addition of a couch can help create more interaction among guests. With a co-host situation, you can put one host on the couch with the guests, but turning to speak to others from a couch can be awkward or uncomfortable, creating more problems than it solves. Thus, you may want to give serious consideration to having only chairs. With chairs, the space is more flexible and the interaction tends to work out a bit better. A coffee table can be quite useful for laying down notes and cups, and can be an attractive addition. Plants are another small addition that can contribute to a pleasant-looking set.

If selected properly, furniture can help create a visually appealing set. Another critical factor, however, is the color combination used in designing the set. Brown, tan, navy blue, and some rust colors are generally the best colors for chairs and couches—no loud colors. You can add brighter colors such as yellow or red to the set as accents in accessories such as lamps or throw rugs.

Floor. The audience does not see a lot of the floor. What they do see, however, should blend well with the rest of the set. Unless there is a wood floor, it is advisable to carpet the set with a neutral color such as tan.

Background. Most public affairs shows tend to use a neutral background. This might include drapes or cycloramas (cycs), both of which consist of large expanses of light or dark cloth (typically beige or blue) suspended from tracks. The difference between the two types of backdrop are that cycs are smooth and a more fitting background for set pieces and flats. Set pieces are small units of background scenery such as columns, screens, strategically placed large pictures or paintings, carvings, or sculpture. Flats are large or small backdrops of plywood or canvas, as in theatrical productions. A flat pictorial background or a large painted scene can be used effectively, especially if seen through an artificial window in the background scene.

Realism. In selecting the appropriate props and background for your particular production, consider whether they realistically portray the image you want your audience to perceive. For instance, a show delving into the concerns and issues of the older population would not be taken as seriously with a backdrop of wilderness and mountains. A better backdrop for such a show would be a plain or picture-hung wall that looks like a sitting room or den.

Avoiding Extremes. Make sure not to overdo in the design of your set. Excessive use of props, set pieces, or scenic detail can detract from the visual appeal of your show. Solicit a variety of opinions about the appearance of the set as you develop it.

Flexibility. It is likely that all or part of your set will be used for other purposes by the station. At the very least, they will need to be able to set it up and tear it down quickly to use the area for other programming. Flexibility is also needed so the set can be altered easily to incorporate various forms of programming. You may need to accommodate demonstrations of anything from food preparation to aerobic exercise or a scene from an upcoming community play—all on the same set where you conduct your interviews. Thus, your set should be easy to assemble and disassemble.

The set that you use will be as good as the effort that you put into designing it. Do it justice! The visual image that you present to the viewing audience is very important, regardless of whether it involves how the host is dressed or how the set is decorated.

Strategic Use of the Camera

No matter how well developed a program may be, the audience will not know it unless one essential factor is working as it should—the camera. Imaginative use of the camera can make all the difference in television production. With good camera work, the show becomes more appealing to the eye. Hosts and guests look their best. Visual images and materials are brought out just the way you want.

The camera plays a *very* major role in how the viewer will perceive your show. Is the picture clear? Is it pleasing to look at? Are the eyes of the viewers directed at the important elements of the picture? The ability of producers and camera operators to enhance your show through creative use of the camera is limited only by their willingness to take full advantage of the tools at their fingertips, including framing, compositional balance, and camera angles.

Planning Camera Shots. Creative use of the camera requires careful planning. The traditional method of production is to have two or three cameras in use for studio work. These are controlled by a switching system in the control room made up of a set of buttons and fading handles. The buttons allow "cutting" from one picture to another, while the fading handles allow the image to dissolve into another (by overlapping) or to fade in and fade out. The switching system also gives you the capability of a split screen, in which two images are presented on the screen simultaneously, each fed by a different camera.

Planning for the best use of the camera during a show is not unlike painting a picture, except this picture is captured on the television screen by the camera. To capture this picture in just the right way, many different factors must be taken into account. The goal is always the same, however: to hold the attention of your audience by providing some visual variety.

Length of Camera Shots. There are many options available to vary the size of individuals and objects in the on-screen picture. One is the *close-up*, which focuses on the face of one of the program participants, with some headroom and part of the shoulders in view. The *big close-up* brings the viewer in so close that the top of the head is excluded from the picture. The *medium close-up* includes the chest from about the breast pocket of the subject's suit. The *mid-shot*, or *waist-shot*, is a more traditional shot in an interview situation, from the waist to the head and allowing for greater headroom. A similar shot with two in the picture is sometimes called a *tight two shot*. Another variation, which takes in two or more participants, is the *medium long shot*, or *three-quarter shot*, which covers an area from about the knees on up and adds more headroom. Finally, there is the *long shot*, which takes in all the participants and most of the set, with more headroom than footroom. Of course, these terms may be used in a somewhat different manner in any given production, so always clarify their meaning with your producers and crew.

Good shot selection is vital to a top-quality production. Poor decision-making on the shots used during a show can make memorable performances look forgettable and a well-produced show look mediocre. Much of shot selection is dependent on the type and emphasis of the production, as well as on the experience and instincts of those individuals staffing the camera and switching system.

Framing. How well the camerapersons and crew utilize the framing technique also determines the quality of the visual message your audience receives. Framing involves a decision as to what will be included in and excluded from the picture. The goal is to focus on a certain part of the picture and to avoid distractions, thus, influencing the audience's perception of what they are seeing.

Having just the right amount of headroom at the top of the frame is an important aspect of framing. It is worth mentioning that what you see on the control room monitor shows a larger picture than the one that reaches the home screen. In other words, if your host's head touches the top of the studio monitor, it will be cut off on the home screen. It is always advisable to leave ample space around the subjects and objects in the frame, especially on the top of the frame where more is cut off in transmission. Be particularly on guard for such cropping in close-ups. In the framing of subjects, use the position of the eyes as a guide. The eyes are about halfway up the head; thus, for a close-up, the eyes should be positioned about two-thirds up the frame from the bottom. It is also important for a cameraperson to be consistent in framing.

Camera Angles. The variety of camera angles used during a show can significantly affect the overall visual impact of the program. For example, going through an entire interview with the host and guest center-framed would result in a balanced but boring picture. If ever the adage "variety is the spice of life" were true, it is in television camera work. To add some visual spice to an interview format, you might want to employ an over-the-shoulder shot from each side, integrating close-ups to capture revealing facial expressions. By "crossing" cameras, you get a much more interactive picture than you would with the standard profile or "half-face" shots. Likewise, shots taken from a lower angle shooting upward (called *low angle* shots) and from above shooting down (called *high angle* shots) can add some variety and interest.

Camera Movement. The movement of the camera also can play an important role in the effect you want to achieve. Cameras are mounted on conventional dolly or pedestal stands that allow for horizontal or vertical movement. They can move freely on a wide horizontal or vertical axis. Thus, you can follow the action of a group of aerobic exercisers with a *pan shot.* You also might pan from a guest discussing a recently completed sculpture to the actual artwork standing close by on the set. If the sculpture is quite large, however, you may want to utilize a *tilt shot*, in which the camera moves up and down the object, rather than from side to side. Pan and tilt shots can be used interchangeably or in the same movement, depending on which is more effective for that particular shot.

Compositional Balance. Visual equilibrium will make a show far more attractive and interesting to the eyes of the viewers. If the elements of the picture that should be attracting the most visual attention—individuals saying or doing something, objects being focused on, or other factors of considerable size or contrast—are predominantly placed to one side of the picture, then your picture will be lopsided, unbalanced. The result? A distracted viewer. Color is also a key factor in the balance or imbalance of a picture. For instance, dark-toned subjects look heavier and smaller than their light-toned counterparts. Cooler colors, such as blue and green, look lighter than brighter colors, such as red or orange. Thus, darker colors should be positioned at the bottom of the frame to offer a more stable, solid look. If placed at the top of the frame, these colors tend to give the picture a top-heavy look.

This does not mean that all persons and objects must be perfectly centered in the picture for it to be balanced. If the host is introducing the show and looking straight into the camera, he or she should be centered. If the host is shown alone in the picture looking at something or someone off-screen, however, you would want him or her framed with less space behind the head and more space in the direction he or she is looking. This compensates for the off-screen interest. Likewise, if a guest is showing an object to the viewers, holding it away from the body, the picture will appear better balanced if the guest is not centered, but is off to one side of the screen. Much of the balance depends on where the center of attention is in the picture.

One of the first things an amateur photographer must learn is that what he or she sees through the view finder of the camera is exactly what is going to be visible on the printed photograph. Likewise, what the audience sees on the television screen at home will be no more or no less than what the camera "saw" on the set. Fortunately, in the studio setting you have a distinct advantage over the lone photographer: you are not dealing with just one set of eyes and one view finder, but a number of views, angles, and possibilities that, with the right amount of creativity, you can mix and match to make your show come alive.

Lighting for Results

Lighting is an area that most amateur producers will not have to worry a lot about unless they are producing a cable local access program where they supply the entire crew. Station personnel usually take care of this facet of production. Nevertheless, proper and creative use of lighting *is* important to the overall visual appeal of your show. Thus, it is helpful to have a working knowledge of how lighting should be handled.

The basic function of television lighting is to ensure that the area and people being filmed are well enough illuminated so that the audience can see what they are supposed to see. But good television lighting shouldn't stop there. It should help achieve the producer's aesthetic and artistic objectives by establishing a certain mood, time, location, and, most important, atmosphere.

To accomplish that goal, lighting must create the right shadows and dimensions of a person, object, structure, or scene. For instance, trying to light a typical interview situation effectively is not always as easy as one might think. The human face and body has planes, curves, shadows, and sometimes even hair (particularly red) that can be quite difficult to light. Add to that an array of types and colors of clothing, and you have a very difficult task. The goal in this kind of a situation is to control the focus and intensity of the light to make all involved in the show look as good as possible. Proper use of lighting can go a long way toward bringing out the good and playing down the bad in people's on-screen appearance.

Light can also be used to create more of an illusion of reality or to lend the right atmosphere or mood to a particular scene or situation. If, for example, you were filming a dramatic reading by an older poet, you might want to have the lights subdued or softened and then place your poet by a realistic-looking fireplace in which lighting is used to create the illusion of a fire. Through use of creative lighting, you will have evoked images of spending a quiet winter evening in front of the fireplace reading poetry.

Lighting can and should be used to make the most of the color, texture, and depth of the people and objects in your production. As such, it is one of the many key ingredients to a visually appealing television production.

Going on Location

The invention of lightweight equipment revolutionized television. With it, this electronic medium's range and power increased almost overnight. Now the camera can go where the news and the events of our time are taking place. Now it can interact with people in their own environment, instead of in a sterile studio.

Remote broadcast, from outside the studio, are not limited to just "big time" television productions. Most stations that have the appropriate remote equipment will allow public service programs to avail themselves of the mobile production unit to do some interesting production work on location. The ideal situation is a station that has a van, a lightweight truck, or a small van unit that can carry one or two studio-type, lightweight cameras. The programming that is videotaped can then be taken back to the studio for editing at a later date.

With remote equipment, you have access to a whole new production world. You can interview people in their everyday worlds, rather than in an impersonal studio. Interviewees generally feel more at ease and comfortable in their own milieu; thus, the quality of the interaction with them improves. In addition, you are in a position to allow your audience to become more a part of the interviewee's life. For instance, an interview with an older artist in his or her studio (if it is large enough), would provide you with the opportunity to "paint" a much more vivid picture of an artist's creative world. In a sense, "remotes" allow you to become an artist who can paint electronic images of fascinating events that might otherwise go unrecorded.

On-location production is virtually a must for documentaries and specials. Whatever the subject area, the camera should capture that world, taping the people, events, and situations that will bring it alive for the audience. For a documentary or special on younger people's attitudes toward the elderly, for example, you could take your cameras into the local elementary and secondary schools and tape some intriguing footage. You could capture spontaneous interactions between elderly persons and the youngsters or film planned class or group interactions. You might interview children before and after their interaction with the older persons. You could then interview their parents and teachers and draw comparisons between their perspectives.

Another example of an on-location "shoot" might involve an investigation into the lives of institutionalized patients. You might spend many hours following the lives of two or more individuals in local nursing homes. What kind of life do they lead from morning until night? You could capture on tape their activities, their relationships, their frustrations, and their joys. You could interview them, their families, their friends, and the facility staff.

With remote equipment, endless possibilities open up to you. Don't abuse them. Make wise use of the remote equipment and the station personnel working with you. Use of remote equipment is a luxury representing a major financial commitment on the part of your sponsoring station. Make it worthwhile. Plan carefully so that wasted time and tape footage is kept to a minimum.

Not everyone will be so lucky as to have access to sophisticated remote equipment. A good alternative is a battery-powered, complete mobile system that can be carried and operated by one person—commonly called a portable video system, or a portapak. With their training series under your belt, most cable systems will lend out a portapak. Although picture quality is not as good as with higher level remote equipment, there are still some creative possibilities with the use of a portapak. For example, if you have an on-the-street interview section in your show, you could take the portapak out each week and interview both young and old on a variety of topics from politics to sex.

Seeking Guidance

In this chapter, we have attempted to give you a few helpful hints about creative production work. It is by no means intended as an exhaustive overview, however. In the production of your programs, you still will need to rely heavily on those who are experienced in television production and the use of the camera and switching room equipment. Whether you are developing programming as a part of the public service efforts of your local commercial, independent, or educational station, or as part of the local orgination programming at a local cable outlet, the station in question will likely provide you with experienced staff to help in this effort.

Ensuring Your Show's Success

The goal of local public service television programming is to capture the interest and attention of your targeted audience, to stimulate discussion and reaction, to meet the needs of your audience and, hopefully, to entertain. What is more, you must do it all with such a flair that your viewers will forsake the programming alternatives to watch your show.

Local programming formats—whether they be local documentaries or talk or interview shows with various creative approaches like audience participation, use of local talent, the "Dear Abby/Dear Ann Landers" format and on-the-street interviews—can be developed that compete quite favorably with other local productions and gain the respect and following of a loyal audience. But a "winning" show doesn't happen by accident; it requires a winning formula—and that means building a talented, energetic production team and selecting a host who has conversational ability, nerve, coolness under fire, sincerity, style, personality, a sense of humor, knowledge, and the right appearance. It also means deciding on topics that provide your viewers with interesting content, needed information, and entertainment value.

Even the most intriguing topic will fall flat, however, unless you are willing to put tremendous energy into planning: into researching the subject area, considering format changes, reinforcing production team roles, and preparing hosts and guests. The selection of guests is also a pivotal factor in the success of a show. Each show's guests must be balanced according to personality, expertise, communication skills, and the unique skills and contributions they can provide to the show.

In the long run the success of your show will depend on your ability to pique and sustain the viewers' interest. To do that you must write creatively and make imaginative use of the camera to make the set come alive by carefully planning your shots, trying different angles and length of shots, and paying close attention to camera movement and compositional balance. You must also use lighting to set the mood. On occasion, you may even want to go on location to add a little spice to your program.

In other words, do what television historically has done a very poor job of: appeal to the intuitive, creative right side of the brain, instead of just to the logical, analytical left hemisphere. This can be accomplished by placing strong emphasis on the visual aspect of the show. Design your set so that it is attractive and comfortable to the eye. Fit in relevant visual materials—slides, camera cards, charts, graphs, maps, artwork, and photographs—whenever possible. Consider featuring demonstrations, whether they be exercise, acting skits, or cooking how-tos.

Remember, you are out to sell a product: your show. Anything you can do to make that product more appealing, from creative writing to eye-catching visuals, will help you close the deal, and make your show a success.

References

Bay, H. 1974. *Stage Design*. New York: Drama Book Publishers.

Bensinger, C. 1982. *The Video Guide*. (3d ed.) New York: Scribners.

Bluem, A.W., J.F. Cox, and G. McPherson. 1961. *Television in the Public Interest*. New York: Hastings House.

Bretz, R. 1976. *Handbook for Producing Educational and Public Access Programs for Cable Television*. New York: Educational Technology Publications.

Bretz, R., and E. Strasheff. 1968. *The Television Program: Its Direction and Production*. New York: Hill and Wang.

Chester, G., G.R. Garrison, and E.E. Willis. 1971. *Television and Radio*. New York: Meredith Corporation.

Conrad, P. 1982. *Television: The Medium and Its Manners*. Boston, Mass.: Routledge and Kegan Paul.

Field, S. 1974. *Professional Broadcast Writer's Handbook*. Blue Ridge Summit, Pa.: TAB Books.

Hilliard, R. 1964. Writings. In R. Hilliard, ed., *Understanding Television*. New York: Hastings House.

Hilliard, R. 1976. *Writing for Television and Radio*. New York: Hastings House.

Jones, P. 1971. *Television Cameramen*. New York: Hastings House.

Kingson, W.K., and R. Cogwill. 1965. *Television Acting and Directing*. Indianapolis, Ind.: Bobbs-Merrill.

Lewis, C. 1968. *The T.V. Director/Interpreter*. New York: Hastings House.

Macy, J.W. 1974. *To Irrigate a Wasteland*. Berkeley: University of California Press.

Madsen, R.P. 1973. *The Impact of Film*. New York: Macmillan.

Millerson, G. 1979. *The Technique of Television Production*. London: Focal Press.

Nash, C., and V. Oakey. 1978. *The Television Writer's Handbook*. New York: Barnes and Noble Books.

Parker, N.S. 1968. *Audiovisual Script Writing.* New Brunswick, N.J.: Rutgers University Press.

Shanks, B. 1976. *The Coolfire: How to Make It in Television.* New York: W.W. Norton.

Tuchman, G. 1974. *The T.V. Establishment.* Englewood Cliffs, N.J.

Weber, V.W. 1964. Staging. In R. Hilliard, ed., *Understanding Television.* New York: Hastings House.

10
Guest Appearances: Strategies and Opportunities

A goal of any organization of the elderly or citizens' group should be to make optimum use of electronic media, particularly television. It could make the difference between the ultimate success or failure of your major projects or issues. What has made groups such as the Gray Panthers so effective, often without the membership or financing of other, more established organizations, is their strategic and timely use of television and radio. It is impossible to avoid electronic media if you expect to reach the public and move forward on vital issues and projects. Especially with the onslaught of cable television, there are more and more possibilities for exposure over the airwaves.

The ideal situation may be to have your own television or radio show, but that is not always possible. Thus, you should strive to maximize your coverage in your city's or region's electronic media, especially on local talk shows or in-studio interview segments (often attached to the noon or early evening news).

And don't expect local stations to come running after you or your group to be interviewed, however. They will not necessarily appreciate the importance of what you are doing. The burden of proof is on you to demonstrate to them why it is important to give you coverage. Do not hesitate to call stations and suggest that they devote more airtime to the concerns of the elderly. Make sure you have a specific suggestion in mind. You may be able to set up airtime with a "cold call." If you have a local media committee organized, put them on the phones. Your contacts with stations will be especially effective if they have an intergenerational flavor.

When you are pursuing airtime, be aggressive but not antagonistic. Take whatever time is offered you and make the best of it. If you are persuasive and come across well, other invitations will be forthcoming. In other words, get your foot in the door and make sure your performance guarantees you will be asked back.

But how can you be sure your group is up to the task? Some people take to television or radio like a fish to water, but most must work at it. Whatever you do, don't make the mistake of taking electronic media appearances for granted. They are too great an opportunity to waste. Work at coming across as effectively as possible and at creating a good image. Make the media work for you and you will never regret it.

The remainder of the chapter is dedicated to a step-by-step formula that should help you make the best of every media opportunity you or your group might get. Using electronic media effectively can help you reach thousands more individuals than you ever thought possible.

Preparation

Practice makes perfect. This statement may be an overused cliché, but nothing could better state the need for careful preparation for a television show, whether you are the host or a guest. No athlete would approach an important athletic event without a conscientious program of practice. Actors spend hours rehearsing their parts. So why should an appearance on television be any different?

The results of preparation will be evident in your appearance. You will look more polished. You will sound more knowledgeable and cover the critical points more convincingly. You will have less chance of getting caught off-guard. Most important, you will feel—and be—more in control!

The first step is to take some time to think of the questions you suspect will be asked and those you hope will not be. Although the chances are good that you will not be asked a sensationalistic or "tacky" question, you never want to be caught unprepared. The results can be devastating. One tragic case in point was the 1979 Roger Mudd interview with Edward Kennedy in which the Senator was asked whether anyone really believed his previous explanation of the Chappaquiddick incident. Senator Kennedy apparently was inadequately prepared for the possibility that such a question would be asked, and, as a result, came off sounding defensive and implausible. His image was hurt badly, and some political observers believe the incident may have cost him the Democratic presidential nomination the next year. Remember, a difficult question is only damaging when you are unable to answer it adequately and positively.

The most important reason for thorough preparation and research of potential questions is so that you will be in control of the flow of the show, both in the preparation stage and on camera. A good host is likely to involve guests in the preparation of questions and/or discussion points for the interview. If you are prepared to promote the areas you think should be covered, you can help direct the course the interview will take. The host or producer will probably be relieved to have the assistance. You will have saved him or her time and a certain amount of research and, as a result, will have enhanced your chances for a successful interview.

If the host or producer does not call you for suggestions, it is quite appropriate for you to offer your assistance in the preparation of the show. Simply outline the areas you think should be covered in the interview. You may also want to supply show personnel with a packet of background materials, including a description of your organization, group, or project, short biographies of the guests, a statement about your cause or issue, press clippings, or other materials you think will be helpful. Make sure the amount of support materials is not overwhelming. The less you provide, the better the chance that a harried host will take time to review them. Supply these materials and suggestions a week before the interview so there is ample time for the producers to incorporate them into the show. If you wait until right before your appearance, your points may get lost in the pretaping chaos.

Do not allow yourself to become overly confident, however. No matter how much involvement you have had in the production of the show, you still need to give ample time for research and preparation. First of all, it is doubtful the program's producers will follow your suggestions exactly. They will have their own ideas of what should be covered and their own approaches. Furthermore, a sensitive question could still crop up. Your best defense is preparation and practice. Prepare notes on each of the areas you think will be covered. Do not overdo statistics or long descriptions of activities and programs. Always think about what the viewers will want to hear and what they can understand. It helps to be prepared for the detailed questions, but it is unlikely they will be asked unless there is particular public interest. And even then, the more succinctly and simply you can respond, the more likely that the public will understand your message.

Once you have adequately researched information that could be covered in the show, practice aloud and to yourself how you might respond to each point. Have a relative or friend act as the host, or practice by yourself in the car or even in the shower.

An even better alternative, if available, is to use video equipment to practice. Many agencies or universities have videotape equipment (as do some lucky individuals) and most have a tape recorder on hand. If you are one of the privileged few who have access to this equipment, make good use of it. It will make a difference! With a willing friend or associate acting as the "host" and another covering the camera, the videotape allows you to make "test runs." More important, you will have the opportunity to see how you look before a camera and make necessary corrections in voice, gestures, posture, and the content of your presentation. Are you consistently leaving out important points that should have been covered? Do you repeatedly say "uh" or "you know"? Does your voice sound muffled or unnatural? Are there long pauses between thoughts? Do you have distracting gestures? Are you slouching in your chair? What about nervous habits such as hair-twirling or beard-pulling or foot-wiggling? It is better to recognize and attempt to correct such tics in practice tapings than to see them on television after the actual taping.

For radio appearances, practice with a tape recorder so you can hear how you sound and correct both voice and content. The tape recorder can also be useful for television appearances if videotape equipment is not available.

One other major step in preparing for your television or radio appearance is to familiarize yourself with the show and its host. Watch or listen to the show several times if possible before you appear on it. Get to know the host's style and approach. Is he or she "laid back"? Aggressive? Liberal? Conservative? Knowledgeable? Well-researched? It also helps to find out about the host's background. Is it in journalism, academia, politics, or business? Get a feel for the format of the show. Is there a break in the middle? Approximately how long is the interview? It is important to get an idea of how long you will be on the air. That way, you can better determine when and how to fit in your critical points.

What To Wear

How you dress for an appearance on television will make a significant difference in how you are perceived by the viewing audience, the host, and guests, and, of course, the camera. The key ingredient is to look professional and moderately conservative. Suits are appropriate mode of dress for most interviews. A sport coat and tie also are acceptable for men. Women can wear a simple, tailored dress, but should avoid a pants suit. Medium tones such as navy blue, brown, and beige are most appropriate for suits and slacks. Light blue and yellow shirts are good choices. The camera can handle a white shirt under a suit, but too much white can cause glare under the bright lights, as can other very light colors. Black is another color that should be avoided if you want to remain on good terms with the cameraperson. It has the opposite reaction to white, absorbing too much light.

Keep your clothing relatively simple. Flashy, loud clothing should be avoided at all costs. Stay away from wild colors, stripes, checks, contrasting or loud patterns, or hats. Make sure any pattern is subtle and does not clash with the set. Hats should be worn only if there is some compeling reason for doing so, which is unlikely. Wear dark shoes (especially men), since light-colored shoes make the feet appear larger and can be distracting. The focus of attention should be on you and the points you are making, not on the clothes you are wearing. Clothing should add to your appearance and not detract from it.

Also avoid large or sparkling jewelry. Polished gold and silver or rhinestones can reflect studio lights and distort the picture. Necklaces or bracelets may create noise that can be picked up by the microphone. Too much jewelry can be distracting no matter how good you think it looks. Mr. T might be able to get away with it, but you must be cautious. Stick with simple rings, a watch, and maybe a gold necklace.

Your safest bet is to wear clothing that you feel comfortable in and that you know you look best in. This is not the time to try a new style. Think about how your outfit will look on television, particularly with the program's set (another good reason to watch the show before appearing on it). Remember, too, that color television adds 10 to 15 pounds. Unless you are so thin that you could use some extra padding, avoid bulky fabrics or patterns that make you look heavier. If you have any doubts about the clothing you have selected, sit in front of a mirror, or, better yet, take a small opinion poll, asking members of your family or friends who will be honest and frank.

Makeup can be used strategically to improve your appearance on television, but be careful not to overuse it. The purpose for using makeup is to prevent the lights in the studio from reflecting off your face in an unbecoming way and, for certain individuals, to absorb unsightly perspiration.

Most women can benefit from the use of some makeup on television. Natural tones lightly applied with sparing use of eye shadow and flesh-colored powder on exposed skin areas to prevent shine, are best. Blend makeup evenly so no demarcation line is visible. Lipstick can help delineate the mouth, but keep to a subdued color, not too bright; the best choice is often a muted color of red, applied lightly. Every face has different needs, however. If you are not skillful with makeup, find someone who is and practice. And remember, don't overdo! Inappropriate use of makeup can harm your television appearance as much as effective use can improve it.

It is not mandatory for men to wear makeup, but there are some individuals who could benefit from its use, particularly those who are bald or balding or have very pale skin. Makeup can also be helpful in covering up oily skin, blemishes, or a heavy beard. Pancake makeup that matches the skin coloring is the best choice. It should be applied lightly and thoroughly to cover all exposed skin areas, including the hands.

It is especially important that men not overuse makeup. Visible and inappropriately used makeup adds little to a man's appearance or credibility with the viewing audience.

Even a brilliant "performance" can be overshadowed by ill-advised or distracting clothing or makeup. Following these simple guidelines should help ensure that your "look" won't cancel out your message.

Speaking Convincingly and Concisely

The greatest weapon you can have on television or radio is the effective use of language. Choose your words carefully; ill-chosen remarks can be turned against you, damaging your credibility very quickly.

Take, for instance, the much-publicized quote of Colorado Governor Richard D. Lamm in an address to the Colorado Health Lawyers Association. Governor Lamm was quoted as saying that the terminally ill "have a duty to die. It's like if leaves fell off a tree forming the humus for other plants to grow out. We've got a duty to die and get out of the way, with all our machines and artificial hearts and everything else like that, and let the other society, our kids, build a reasonable life."

Few quotes in recent memory have caused more controversy. The reaction was quick and, for the most part, hostile. Some viewed the statement as tantamount to supporting mercy killing or possibly even extermination of the sick and aged. Senior advocacy groups said it was an insult to the elderly. Individual older citizens were furious.

Judging from what Lamm said later, however, the only "sin" the governor was guilty of was discussing a very sensitive subject in a very callous, offensive, and politically intolerable manner. He has explained that he meant to raise the issue of whether we are acting in the best interest of the patient or society when we pump huge amounts of money into extending the life of terminally ill patients even when their life depends on an array of respirators, tubes, and medical machinery. What if the patient in such a situation prefers to die naturally? There are important, thought-provoking questions on this subject that need to be addressed. Unfortunately, Governor Lamm's choice of words clouded his message and raised a national uproar instead of promoting the kind of thoughtful discussion he had envisioned.

Governor Lamm's experience illustrates just how important it is to choose your words carefully. Don't become paranoid, but always be on guard. Steer away from glib statements and unsupportable facts. Do not allow yourself to become so relaxed and "informal" that you end up ad libbing—Making impromptu comments more appropriate for a cocktail hour than a television interview.

The safest way to guard against an embarrassing remark is to be prepared for the questions, to have specifics on hand to back up your arguments, and to speak confidently and enthusiastically. The more sure of yourself you seem, the less likely your information will be questioned and the more believable you will sound.

It goes without saying that the information you give out had better be correct! When you speak off the cuff, you run the risk of finding yourself out on a limb with the host holding the saw. If the information you so confidently express contradicts facts and statistics well known to the host, he or she most likely will call you on it, jeopardizing your credibility from that point on. If you do not know the answer to some question, it is much better to admit it and go on. No one expects you to know everything, but you *are* expected to be honest.

Caution extends beyond the words you choose to speak, however. A substantial majority of communication is nonverbal. Be very careful not to communicate one thing with your mouth and something very different with your eyes, facial expressions, gestures, and even voice level. Radio allows you far more flexibility with your nonverbals. But on television you can find yourself trapped if you give conflicting messages verbally and nonverbally. Such a contradiction will raise suspicions and conflicting impressions, both consciously and unconsciously, in the minds of your host and the viewing audience.

Even a gesture as innocent as a polite nod to your host or other guests may result in conflicting verbal and nonverbal signals. Maybe you are just trying to be polite, or maybe you are trying to appear as if you are tuned in to the conversation when your mind is really miles away preparing for your next blockbuster comment. But the viewers and the host and other guests are probably going to interpret your nod as agreement with the comments being aired. If you *don't* agree, you've just gotten yourself in a pickle! The best rule is to nod only when you have clearly heard the comments and actually *agree* with them.

It is also important to avoid jargon and professionalese. Whether you are the only guest or among two or three guests, your time is limited. On a 30-minute talk show, you have between 8 and 15 minutes to get your message across. The worst way to utilize this valuable television time and the best way to turn off your audience (and their television sets) is to use professional jargon or complicated language that nobody but a select few understands. It is just as easy, and much more understandable, to talk about "recent changes in the telephone system and how they will affect elderly persons' phone bills" than to talk about "the divestiture of AT&T and the implications for telecommunications rate structures for end users." Likewise, don't say a certain practice is "medically contraindicated" when what you really mean is that it is "unhealthful."

Do not fool yourself into believing that the use of complicated professional terminology will make you appear more impressive. This might be true at a professional conference (although this point is arguable as well), but it certainly does not work on television. If you must use language or terms not commonly known outside certain professional circles, be careful to illustrate them in lay language. Remember, a substantial majority of your audience will have little, if any, previous knowledge of in the particular area you are discussing. Only a few will have expertise or training in the area. Thus, you must walk the delicate line in your presentation between trying to reach viewers who are involved and interested in such issues and those who have never given the issue much thought.

You also should avoid the presentation of material in too much detail or depth. The audience is not likely to have deep enough interest to warrant detail nor are you likely to have the time. A simple, direct explanation is going to make a far greater impression on the viewers than concentrating on details that will have little effect and will be soon forgotten.

This does not mean that you should speak down to your audience. One can make excellent use of vocabulary and available information and data in a way that is interesting and understandable to the average viewer without insulting their intelligence or one's own. And it is critical that you do so if you are to maintain audience interest in the topic that you are discussing. Once you lose your audience or your host, you may not get them back again. Likewise, every minute you waste speaking in a way that is incomprehensible or uninteresting is a minute that you cannot retrieve, a minute that you cannot use to make other valuable points.

One effective means of getting your message across is to use mental imagery—to "draw a picture" with examples, anecdotes, stories, and other visualizations. This metaphoric technique helps the viewer retain the views and information you are expressing by giving him or her a picture to associate with the ideas. Recall that one of the keys to success in reaching the television or radio audience is to exercise the creative, intuitive, right side of the brain as well as the logical, left side of the brain. Often, too strong an emphasis is put on presenting the logical arguments, and not enough effort is put into drawing a clear picture for the viewer. You must build a bridge in the mind of viewers that allows them to cross from vague understanding to total conceptualization.

For instance, to aid the viewer in understanding sensory loss, you could describe a family dinner scene as perceived by an older person with hearing and sight losses:

> Grandmother sits there wanting to be part of what's going on, but feeling somehow separated from it. It's almost as though a soundproof screen has been placed in front of her: a screen that lets through lights and colors but blurs the shapes and obscures the features on the faces of her family; a screen that lets through sounds but so muffled and indistinct as to make it impossible to understand what is being said.

By stratetgic use of the metaphoric technique, you have helped unlock the part of the viewer's mind, namely the creative right hemisphere, that is left untapped by a presentation based totally on logic. In other words, you have stimulated your audience's imagination! You also can do so by using visuals and graphics such as slides, charts, graphs, pictures, and placards. Remember, however: your time is limited. Make your narratives short and use them to your best advantage.

A final point to remember about on-air presentations is to keep your responses succinct and to the point. Not only are there time limitations, but your audience's attention span is very short. A long, complicated response will only lose the viewers and frustrate a host who is trying to cover a number of points in a relatively short period of time. Your answers should conform to good journalistic style. The important points should come first and be followed, where appropriate, by concise, thought-provoking supporting material. Avoid the embarrassing situation of being cut off, especially before you have made the necessary points.

Meeting Tough Situations Head-on

The greatest desire of any talk show guest is to have the show flow exactly as he or she planned, with no difficult questions, no disagreements. And chances are, that is more or less what will happen. You are not likely to be placed in any tough situations that you can't handle unless you tend to be controversial or have a skeleton or two in the closet. Even so, your dreams may turn into nightmares if you do not prepare for the outside chance that the questions you dread most will be asked. It can't be stressed enough: Always be prepared for the worst.

A difficult question is only damaging if you are unable to respond adequately. Actually, as crazy as it may sound, you should become confident enough to welcome the tough questions so that you can have the opportunity to turn them around to your favor. To do this, however, you must be well prepared. Do not limit yourself to figuring out how to respond to difficult inquiries; think, too, about the counterarguments that can be made to your responses. The absolutely worst thing you can do is to evade tough questions or refuse to answer. This is an open invitation for an aggressive host to pursue the point with a passion. The result: You look bad and your credibility takes a beating.

Always answer the difficult questions and act as if you are glad to have the opportunity. Use your response to restructure both the question and the answer in such a way as to make you and your organization look as good as possible. Tell it like it is, but do so in a strategic manner that allows you to provide only that information you believe is necessary. Never stretch the truth, and do not make the mistake of fabricating some "juicy" statistics to make your answer sound a bit more knowledgeable and informed. Some speakers believe that if they do not have a statistic to back up a particular point, there is no harm in making one up, that after all, no one will know the difference. This is wrong. Someone may, and then you will really be in a mess! Reckless responses can trap you in a corner that may be impossible to get out of. There is no substitute for adequate research and review of a topic before appearing on television or radio.

When dealing with a potentially hostile situation, it is important to move quickly, but smoothly, to defuse it. Stress the positive. Move the conversation gently, but firmly, in the direction you want it to go and, most likely, the host will follow suit. Whatever you do, do not dwell on the negative or point the finger of blame. However correct you might be, if you emphasize the negative, you will look negative and gain little support from the viewing audience. No one has this technique mastered better than President Ronald Reagan, who is widely regarded as one of the best communicators ever to occupy the White House. Political opponents constantly grumble about Mr. Reagan's ability to deflect criticism and turn hostile interviews to his advantage. Often he accomplishes this by being an unremitting "nice guy." After all, how long can you stay angry at someone who is smiling pleasantly and reminds you of your favorite uncle?

If a question is raised on a very delicate situation that you have not taken a stand on or would prefer not to make a public statement about, discuss the pros and cons of each side of the issue, strategically placing emphasis where you want it put and praying that it will not be pursued any further. The host, however, may not be satisfied and may continue to press you. If he or she does, remain calm. Do not become defensive or feel that you must "spill your guts" on the issue. As in a good game of poker, do not reveal your hand until you have to. Simply reiterate the points you feel are most important in as pleasant a manner as possible. Think about how the viewing audience will respond. Am I providing enough information to be credible? Am I being confusing? Do I need to make a stronger statement? Most important, do not let the host wear you down into making comments that you will later regret.

Another danger is the "loaded" question. Often, the question itself is not so bad, but the way it is worded turns it into a lighted stick of dynamite. The host might ask, "Given that an enormous proportion of all Medicare benefits are awarded to people in the last year of their lives, how can we begin to get the cost of the program under control?", instead of asking, "What steps can be taken to control rising Medicare costs without denying benefits to older Americans who desperately need them?" Both questions get at the enormous escalation of health care costs under Medicare, but the first one raises another very sticky question in arriving there: namely the very controversial "health care rationing" issue of whether we should be spending as large a percentage of the Medicare budget on people who will likely die within the next year. As many red-faced politicians (including Colorado's Governor Lamm) have found out, there is no easy way of answering this question.

Often the best way to respond to the loaded part of a question is to acknowledge that it is a delicate area that needs further study and evaluation, and then to move the conversation back to the area you are prepared and willing to respond to. In some situations it is also possible to avoid entirely the loaded part of the question if you are skillful enough. Do not feel any obligation to acknowledge fully the loaded part of a question unless you are prepared to do so. To jump in unprepared could yield some damaging results. It is always safest to concentrate on the meat of the question. In the Medicare example, you could focus your response on the various alternatives being discussed for reducing escalating health care costs, particularly in the Medicare program.

In addition to maneuvering skillfully around loaded questions, a clever guest learns how to use to his or her advantage opportunities that can arise during interviews. If you want a particular point to be brought up or want to move away from an area with which you are unfamiliar, learn the art of transition. Answer the question that has been put to you, but do so in such a way as to pave the way for raising some point you would rather have discussed.

For example, if your host insists on pushing for the gory details of specific cases of elder abuse instead of allowing you to discuss the victims' assistance program that you have established and that you came on the show to discuss, you might gracefully deflect the line of questioning and provide an opening for discussion of your program by saying:

> There are as many manifestations of elder abuse as there are people with emotional problems to perpetrate them. And certainly society must be concerned about discovering the causes so as to eliminate them. But many experts believe that society in general has focused too much attention on the perpetrators of crime and too little on their victims. That is why my organization has set up the County Elder Abuse Victims Assistance Program and why we are so excited about its potential.

Having opened the door, you can then proceed to discuss the program you were invited to discuss and prevent the show from focusing only on the sensationalistic aspect of the problem and not the solutions.

With this technique you can take control of an interview. In the process you can be assured of achieving the mission, whether it is reaching the public with some message or issuing a call to action.

Whatever you do, do not let yourself be intimidated! Not by the television studio. Not by the cameras. Not by the television audience. Not by other guests. And particularly not by the host. Once you are intimidated, you have forfeited control of the situation. Never forget that an interview is an exchange between equals. If the host or other guests make a statement with which you do not agree, feel free to challenge or correct them, albeit in a polite manner. Don't wait for someone else to take up the banner. If you do not respond, you will kick yourself later, and so will those you represent. Never leave the viewing audience with the wrong impression just because you are afraid to speak up.

Generally, you will find your host pleasant and easy to talk to. Occasionally, however, you may run into an individual who thinks he or she is William Buckley and Phil Donahue all rolled into one. Such a host may try to load every question, corner you whenever possible, and rarely allow you to finish an answer before resuming attack. The best response to this type of host is be polite but firm. If the rude behavior persists, there is nothing wrong with challenging the person politely to allow you to finish your remarks. ("Mr. Jones, I will be happy to respond to all your questions, but I would appreciate being permitted to finish what I'm saying.") It also does not hurt to remark gently about his or her editorializing. ("Although you seem to have made up your mind on this issue, Mr. Jones, there is strong evidence that suggests the opposite.") A calm, firm response will establish that you are not willing to be pushed around and that you are in control of the situation. You must never let an overly aggressive host or guest take control of the show. Also, never lower yourself to your aggressor's level by getting angry or aggressive in return. The viewing audience wants to see strength in an individual, but will tend to side with those whom they perceive as being friendly and positive as well as strong.

Another tricky situation that must be handled gracefully is the ignorant question asked by the host who has not adequately researched the subject at hand, such as "Is there a biological reason why almost all elderly persons become senile?" No matter how ageist or totally absurd the question might be, you must control your natural impulse to tell the host how stupid and bigoted his or her question is. Remain calm and polite. Patiently explain that only 5 percent of the older population ever become senile and that there are environmental as well as biological reasons why these people are so afflicted. Then proceed to discuss the vast majority of older people who are active and alert, still learning and contributing to society in very positive ways. Probably the host will get the point, but if he or she does not, your best strategy is to gently take as much control of the interview as you can and lead it in the direction that will best showcase your issue, cause, or project.

Remember, an interview is meant to be a free and open exchange. There does not always have to be total agreement. In fact, if there is, it can make a show downright boring. Lively discussions or friendly (even not-so-friendly) arguments can add a little flavor to an otherwise dull talk show. Even a bit of disagreement among guests can stir things up for the better.

Most interviews will go smoothly, but never take them for granted. If the unimaginable does occur, these steps will help put you in the position to turn the circumstances around to your advantage.

Facing the Camera

To make the most of a television appearance, you must also respond effectively to that much-feared contraption: the camera. Typically three cameras will be used: one focused on the guest(s), one focused on the host(s), and one used for a "wide" shot of the whole set. The camera can catch you from all angles; from a distance either straight on or from a left or right angle; from the waist up only, from close-up to your face, or in any number of other ways. Thus, you must always be on guard and aware of everything you are doing if you want to present yourself to advantage.

The cardinal rule of camera strategy is not to look directly at the camera except in rare and very calculated instances. Instead, maintain eye contact with whomever you are speaking to or whomever is speaking to you, whether it be the host or fellow guests. Only on those rare moments when you are speaking to the audience, should you look into the "live" camera (usually indicated by a red light). If you *do* look into the camera to make an important point, pretend that the camera is an associate you are having a serious conversation with in your own living room. Never think or respond as though you are talking to thousands of people, even though you most likely are. In other words, act natural. Do not raise your voice or gesture in a way that is not natural for you. Move your gaze from the camera at a natural transition point (most likely at the end of your important point) so that you do not appear insincere.

The host can get away with looking into the camera more often to appeal to the audience. But, aside from introductions, conclusions, and the like, even the host must be select as to when he or she looks into the camera. Playing to the camera is an art that few have mastered, but that many more believe they have.

From the moment you take your seat on the set, always act as though the camera is trained on you, even if you think it is not. All of us have watched some unsuspecting guest caught off-guard in a compromising pose; wiping his nose, playing with her hair, scratching his ear, or sitting ungracefully. Embarrassing? It could easily happen to you.

Never do anything on the set that you don't want the camera to catch you doing. No sooner will you open your mouth to yawn than the camera will capture the full view of your dentistry for an audience of thousands.

Having a good camera presence goes beyond avoiding obviously embarrassing behavior, however. All of us have distracting habits that we do without even thinking. Among the most common are nervous mannerisms such as continual foot movement, twirling of hair around the fingers, unnecessary gestures or hand movements, and body swaying. These mannerisms only serve to distract the audience from what you have to say and to lessen your visual image. By remaining conscious of how you are sitting and what your hands and feet are doing, you can usually stop yourself from indulging these habits and increase the impact of your message.

Last, but not least, do not let the camera catch you watching yourself on the monitor. It is the crew's job to watch, not yours, and you can always see the tape later if you want to know how you looked. You also do not want to be caught looking off the set at something that's happening in the studio. In both instances you will appear disinterested. Try to look involved and interested even if you are not a part of a particular conversation or even if you *are* bored. It is also good to remain attentive so that you are ready when the conversation shifts back to you.

The camera is not something to fear. If used correctly, it can be a very powerful friend that can aid immeasurably in spreading your message. Whether it is a friend or a foe, however, depends on you and your willingness to play by these few simple rules.

Getting Along with the Host and the Audience

The camera is not the only friend you must win over in the studio. To be successful, you need to get along with the audience and the host(s), in that order. Your ultimate goal, however, should be to win the favor of both.

This is true no matter what your opinion of the host might be. Before the show and on-camera, be courteous, listen intently, show warmth, maintain a pleasant facial expression, never belittle your host's lack of knowledge, massage his or her ego where necessary, and, above all, do not get into an argument unless absolutely necessary to defend an important issue or to save face.

Humor is always a good ice-breaker unless your brand of humor is somewhat off-beat or sarcastic, in which case you may want to use it selectively. What you want to avoid, if possible, is alienating the host. After all, the host can make life very miserable for you. You are on the host's turf, where, with a negative question or two, he or she can put you on the hotseat. The host can also close you out, paying attention to the other guests and leaving you with little time or opportunity to express your point of view. He or she also can turn other unfriendly guests loose to attack you. Thus, there is more than one reason for staying on the good side of your host(s).

It may not always be possible to please every host, however. He or she may not like you or your organization, or may have a strong bias against the issue you are discussing on the show. Whatever the reason, if you sense the host is antagonistic, move cautiously and remain calm, polite, and rational. In some cases it may be necessary to take a slightly more aggressive stance. Try not to get rattled, or to respond harshly, because in almost all situations, you will come out ahead with the audience if you behave with class and dignity. By being a Mr. (or Ms.) Nice Guy, you will even win points with those who disagree with your point of view.

And winning points with the audience is more important than winning them with the host in any event. After all, that is whom you are aiming your message at—not the host. Chances are, the audience will not retain most of what was brought out in the discussion. You can count on the fact, however, that they will come to some conclusion, either positive or negative, about you, and that that conclusion will color how receptive they are to your message. If you handle yourself well in both normal and stressful situations, if you are warm and pleasant, if you appear very knowledgeable about your subject matter, and if you seem interested in what others have to say, a surprising number of those in the audience will be inclined to give far more credence to what you have to say.

How you look is also very important in whether you will win acceptance among the public viewers. President Ronald Reagan is a classic example of a person whose warmth, style, and appearance can so captivate an audience that what he says is almost secondary. Many experts felt that President Jimmy Carter won the 1980 presidential debates on the merits of his arguments, but it was Mr. Reagan who won the hearts of the television viewers—President Reagan has been doing so ever since, most notably in the crucial second round of the 1984 presidential debates with Democratic nominee, former vice president Walter Mondale. In the 1960 presidential debates, the first to be telecast nationally, Richard Nixon, an articulate speaker, did not have a chance against the composed, warm, "telegenic," and equally articulate John Kennedy.

Never forget that the success of your message hangs on the whim of your host, and particularly, your audience. If the audience doesn't like you, they may reject your message, no matter how compeling. Likewise, if you keep them eating out of your hand, you may convince even the doubting Thomases to give your idea or program a fighting chance.

Dealing with Other Guests

In your effort to maintain the goodwill of the host and audience, don't make the mistake of ignoring your fellow guests. They can nicely supplement your presentation or they can be a thorn in your side. If at all possible, you want to avoid having another guest make a surprise attack on you or your organization during the show. Some hosts relish the thought of two or more guests fighting it out on the air. A disagreement can add excitement to an otherwise dull discussion.

There are times when a show is set up for the very purpose of debate. Two guests representing opposing viewpoints are asked to appear to provide a forum for both sides of the issue. In this situation presumably you will have some warning so that you can prepare, and prepare you should! Having a rival appear on a show with you is an excellent opportunity to display your point of view through skillful debate. Nevertheless, this welcomed opportunity could turn into an unwelcomed disaster if you are not well prepared.

No matter how much you dislike or disrespect a fellow guest, however, you should not show it. Be cordial. Bite your tongue when he or she makes a pointed remark, misstatement, or ridiculous comment. Hold your temper. Let the speaker finish. Collect your thoughts. Then proceed calmly, and strongly, to respond to each point with articulate, effective arguments that are factually supported. Be assertive, but not pushy. Be polite, but not a pushover. Always remain positive. Personal attacks or negative remarks will only make you look bad. Remember, the viewing audience tends to support the individual who is positive, and emphasizes constructive alternatives, not the one who is negative and critical. To make the most of joint appearances with friend and foe, it is wise to be cautious to avoid being sideswiped or dominated.

Body Language

As alluded to in the camera section, your body can be your best friend or your worst enemy in your television appearance. Your verbal language may be very positive, but if your body language says the opposite, or distracts from, what you're saying, your message will be diluted. Thus, it is important to be completely conscious at all times of what you are doing with your hands, your feet, and your body. If the camera catches you yawning, the audience will assume you are bored. If your eyes dart from side to side, or you twist your ring around and around on your finger, no amount of measured speech will convince the audience that you are calm and collected.

Probably the most difficult appendages to deal with on television are your hands, mainly because you often are not quite sure what to do with them. Some people are blessed with instinctive, attractive gestures that flow naturally as they talk. Most of us, however, are not so lucky and need to be conscious of where our hands are and what they are doing (without *appearing* to be thinking about where they are or what they are doing). You do not, for example, want to indulge habits such as pulling on your ear, playing with your beard, tapping your fingers, or twisting your rings. Practice keeping your hands in your lap or folded, unless you are planning to use them to make a point or create an impression.

Even then, you must use your hands strategically. A limited use of hand motions can help you make a point more powerfully or lend to a thoughtful appearance. Frequent, indiscriminate waving, pointing, or gesturing, will only distract and annoy the audience. And keeping your hand on or near your mouth when you are talking will add the problem of making you harder to understand. In sum, use hand gestures as a complement to what you are saying or doing, but don't let them become a hindrance.

That is true as well of other body movements. Sit firmly in your chair and try not to squirm unless shifting position helps to make a point more strongly or to make your presence felt. For instance, you might lean forward to show strong interest in a subject area being discussed or to place increased emphasis on a point you are making (if you can do so in a way that appears natural and is not awkward). Be careful not to rock your body back and forth or otherwise engage in constant motion while you are speaking, however. If you do, the viewers will end up watching your torso sway back and forth and lose track of what you are saying. This also will happen if you are unconsciously moving or rocking in a movable chair, or if you are rotating your foot around and around. Whatever body part it affects, any unnatural bodily movements will distract the audience and detract from your presentation.

Most people can remember their mothers lecturing them about the importance of proper posture. This advice is well taken for any appearance on television. The posture and position of your body, as well as any movements you make with it, give the audience a very strong message about you, your confidence level, and your credibility. Slouching will make you look bored or lacking in confidence. Sit up straight, with your feet planted squarely on the floor. Be wary of overstuffed chairs; one can get lost in them easily. Sometimes crossing your legs can help you to look and be more relaxed while still maintaining good posture.

It is not only your mouth that speaks to your audience, but the rest of your body as well. To make the most of your appearance on television, it is critical that you use your body language to enhance your message, not to nullify it.

Creating a Positive Image

If you had to place a title on this process of watching your hand movements, sitting up straight, avoiding nervous habits, and getting along with your host, the audience and other guests, you would call it "Creating an Image."

Television is one of the greatest image-makers and image-breakers of all time. And though you are unlikely to become a household name even after appearing on several local talk shows, the success of your message will be inextricably intertwined with the kind of image you leave in the viewers' minds. And that image will have as much to do with your nonverbal as your verbal communications.

One of the quickest ways to ensure that the impression you leave will be a negative one is to act like something or someone that you are not. If you are not an intellectual, a statesman, or a humorist, do yourself and your audience a favor and don't pretend you are. Unless you are an exceptional actor, the audience will likely see through any act or phony role you try to put over on them. It is always best to play your most natural role: yourself. Put your best foot forward, but don't shed your personality in the process. If you do, you will have done a disservice to yourself and everyone else, and your screen image undoubtedly will have suffered in the process. After all, if you've got friends, they must see something interesting and likable in you. If you just act natural, it is likely that the audience will as well.

Although much of being personable comes naturally, there are certain factors that are guaranteed to work against a positive audience response, including looking confused, bored, angry, hateful, superior, or defeated. If being yourself means displaying these attributes, maybe a bit of acting would not hurt. The audience nearly always responds better to someone who is confident, calm, enthusiastic yet warm, concerned, and caring.

Again, your facial expressions and head movements will play a role. As noted earlier, if you nod your head, the audience is going to think you agree with what has just been said; they will not know that nodding is just a habit you have. If you smile pleasantly to mask the anger you feel over a particular statement, the audience is likely to think you are pleased with it. Your face and head are a major part of your communication vehicle. Use them to your advantage. Although you do not want to show anger, irritation, or disgust in response to a statement with which you disagree, you can politely show your disapproval through a look of concern or surprise. Conversely, if you heartily agree with a remark, don't sit there like a marble statue—express your feelings with a smile or an approving nod.

Unless you are planning to be the next Dick Cavett, your on-screen image is highly unlikely to make or break your career. But it can do a lot to solidify or weaken your message, and so it is an important factor to consider.

Being a Good Listener

The final ingredient to a successful interview is to be a good listener. An interview does not usually follow a set script verbatim. The host may decide on the spur of the moment to take the interview in another direction. The host or another guest may make a misstatement or may unexpectedly accuse you or your group of something. If you are not listening or are only concentrating on part of what is being said, you may leave a misleading or false statement unchallenged, and your viewers may accept it as fact. This may cause you a great deal of embarrassment, not to mention the anger it may generate among your associates.

There can be other embarrassing consequences for not listening properly. The host might decide to ask you to respond to the remarks of one of the other guests on the show. If you are caught off guard, you may jeopardize your whole presentation with one foolish mistake.

Thus, it is critical that you listen carefully to everything that is being said. Your over-all effectiveness depends on how you respond to all the proceedings and conversations taking place during the show as well as on how you respond to those questions that are directed specifically at you. If need be, you might even want to consider taking some notes during the show so you can be prepared to make a timely, knowledgeable response to the points being raised.

The Key to Selling Your Message

A key factor in the success of any project or issue your organization may undertake is the coverage you get by the local electronic media, especially television. Special attempts should be made to get on talk shows or interview segments. Once these opportunities become available to you, it is incumbent upon you and your group to make the best of them. If you do not, you can be sure that invitations will be few and far between.

Making the best of your media opportunities means being well-prepared and appropriately dressed. It means knowing your material and having answers for all the possible questions—even those you hope will not be asked. It means talking to your audience in a language they can understand, without being condescending. It means speaking confidently and enthusiastically, and backing your verbal comments up with consistent nonverbal signals. It means getting along with your host, the audience, and other guests by being polite, considerate, and attentive, but knowing how to stand your ground if necessary. It means, in sum, creating a positive image that will make your audience like you and help you sell your message.

References

A duty to die? 1984. *Boston Globe* (April 8):A26.

Bluem, A.W., J.F. Cox, and G. McPherson. 1961. *Television in the Public Interest.* New York: Hasting House.

Hilton, J., and M. Knoblauch. 1980. *On Television.* New York: Amacon.

Johnson, H. 1984. Furor over 'Duty to die' remark obscures serious question. *Washington Post* (April 1):A2.

Lamm angers elderly with remark on death. 1984. *Washington Post* (March 24): A3.

National Association of Broadcasters. 1973. *So You're Going on T.V.* Washington, D.C.: NAB.

National Clearinghouse on Aging. 1978. *Public Information Activities for State and Area Agencies on Aging.* Washington, D.C.: Administration on Aging, U.S. Department of Health and Human Services.

Pfeiffer, Eric. 1975. Successful Aging. In *Quality of Life: The Later Years.* Acton, Mass.: American Medical Association, Publishing Sciences Group, Inc., p. 13.

Question: Who will play God? 1984. *Time* (April 9):68.

Talburt, L. 1975. How to be effective in a TV interview. *Association Management:*30–34.

11

Advocating Your Rights
to the Airwaves

The 1960s marked a time of great social organizing and protest. The 1970s were the "me" generation, where people turned from social interests to a greater emphasis on self-interest. The verdict on the 1980s is still out. But there could be no greater time for standing up for our rights than now.

Our liberties are being challenged all around us. The past few years have witnessed a gradual erosion of our individual freedoms as the Supreme Court decided in favor of government nearly every time its interests ran up against those of the individual. Our rights to the airwaves also have been pushed to the limit as they never have before. Yet, most people seem to think there is little they can do to challenge what is going on in the broadcast industry. If you or your organization has been lulled into this type of thinking, how wrong you are!

In theory and, supposedly, in practice, the airwaves belong to the public. The government, through the Federal Communications Commission, provides television stations with a license to operate provided they follow certain laws and regulations. Private industry, under these laws and regulations, is allowed to take part in this enterprise, provided its participation is "for the good of the public." Television stations must serve the needs and interests of the diverse populations of a local community.

However, in recent years the public has been slowly and quite silently losing its grip on the conduct of the broadcast industry. It has lost its grip on what important issues and concerns will be discussed on the air. It is losing its grip on how much of "its" airtime will be handed over to commercial, profit-making interests. To listen to those perpetrating these changes, you would think they were being done in the public interest. Unfortunately, all indications point to a broadcast industry that is moving further and further away from what the public wants and needs.

As our country moves into this new communications era, the public must make sure it does not end up being disconnected. Citizens must make sure their rights to the airwaves are not usurped in the rush by large corporations for profit and control. The answer? Organize! As citizens' advocate Ralph Nader so appropriately noted:

> What information and ideas people receive and when they receive them is the nourishment for the enlightened and participatory societies. Citizens need no longer be passive recipients of what a few large corporations choose to beam to them. Rather, they can become part of the communications process. (Ianacone, 1979, p. 5)

Ralph Nader is right. Too much is happening in the telecommunications industry for us to remain silent any longer. Local communities must begin organizing media advocacy coalitions to concentrate on the important issues affecting older people and the media.

Why Organize?

Before we start our discussion on how to organize, we should answer more specifically one very important question: *Why* do we need to organize? There are four compelling reasons: a tradition of television discrimination against the elderly, the need to access the television media, the deregulation efforts of the FCC, and the importance of maintaining the Fairness Doctrine.

A Tradition of Discrimination

Although there has been improvement in recent years, television is still predominately youth-oriented. It is still rare to see an elderly character within the fictional television population. When older characters make their way onto a program, more often than not they will be treated with disrespect, have little or no romantic involvement, be in a lower income category, show signs of disorientation, suffer from some physical or emotional ailment, or act in a foolish manner. Rarely does a documentary, feature, or news special focus on the lives of older persons. When one does, it will more than likely deal with a crisis situation, whether relating to some major adjustment in the lives of the elderly or the actual or potential negative circumstances caused by cuts in or possible bankruptcy of aging programs such as social security and Medicare.

The bulk of television advertising treats the elderly at least as badly as do regular programming segments. If the elderly appear at all in commercials, they are often the snowy-haired grandmother cookie-baking her way placidly through old age, or the older gent extolling the merits of some hemorrhoid salve or denture cream. To watch how television deals with growing old, you would think that the elderly either spent their days rocking down serenity lane or were sickly individuals whose every waking moment was occupied by concern over an endless stream of ailments and encroaching "senility."

Americans spend a tremendous amount of time in front of their television sets. Thus, it should come as no shock that the attitudes of the American public are adversely affected by constant exposure to this kind of ageist programming. How can anyone reasonably expect a teenager to sit week after week and watch the grandfather on *Gimme A Break* forget his own son's name, forget where he lives, be unable to understand normal conversation, and otherwise be set up to ridicule without assuming that all elderly persons are "senile"? How can anyone expect a young adult who already holds negative images about aging, to watch reruns of the popular nighttime serial, "Soap," in which Arthur Peterson portrays a disoriented, shellshocked, elderly Major, without having these stereotypes reinforced? How can anyone expect a 5-year-old to watch the nearly blind cartoon character, Mr. Magoo, precipitate crisis after crisis for himself because of his inability to complete life's easiest tasks, without applying this negative image to the elderly persons he or she comes in contact with?

The stereotypical programming and advertising we see on television is ageism in its worst form. The term *ageism* was coined by noted gerontologist and psychiatrist Robert Butler to connote discrimination by reason of age. As Butler defines it: "Ageism allows the younger generation to see older people as different from themselves; thus they subtly cease to identify with their elders as human beings" (p. 7). How appropriate this definition is to our discussion of television programming and advertising, where so often the younger people see the elderly portrayed as so "different from themselves," a little less than human.

The negative emphasis placed on aging and the older population by the television medium and its advertisers, underlines the importance of a strong grassroot effort to "watchdog" television programming and raise the voice of protest against this constant onslaught of ageism. Local stations and the networks need to get the message that aging should be portrayed in a more realistic, positive manner. More specifically, they need to understand that older persons should be portrayed on television as the majority of them are in real life: healthy, energetic, intelligent, and full of life. When they are not so portrayed, we must make our disapproval known!

The Need to Gain Access to Television

It is one thing to talk about the airwaves being public domain, but a very different one for the public actually to gain access to them. There are two different levels of access to the television airwaves, however. The first involves access to commercial television stations; the second, to cable broadcast outlets. Cable television is far more accessible to the public and provides many public affairs programming opportunities. A local "public" access channel is open to any group that is interested in producing programming (on a first come, first served basis), as long as you are willing to supply the crew and do most of the production work. Another level of cable access that is more exclusive is "local origination" programming, which is selected and produced by the local cable system and its staff. Of course, there also are "leased channels" that can be reserved for community-based, advertiser-sponsored, or commercial programming.

Access to commercial television is a completely different issue. Money talks here. Although local commercial stations are to operate "in the public interest," they are businesses that derive their profits primarily from two sources. One source is, of course, advertising time purchased. Another source, for network affiliates, are the payments received for each network show broadcast. Thus, of the 18 hours of airtime a local station needs to fill, the networks (ABC, NBC, and CBS) account for 14 hours. Local stations have leeway in using what programming they wish, but are paid for each show used. As a part of this agreement, a station is required to do only 4 hours of its own programming per day. During the weekdays and even on Saturdays, this is easily filled by local news broadcasts and possibly a variety program like "P.M. Magazine." That usually leaves free Sunday mornings or afternoons (except for sporting events) or the wee hours of the morning for public service or other community-oriented programming.

There is a good reason for the consignment of public interest programming to these less-than-attractive time slots: It is not profitable. Public service announcements run up against the same problem. That is why you rarely see PSAs for nonprofit groups and their causes on before midnight. It is important to add, however, that stations do vary in their commitment to public service programming. Some are quite dedicated to airing the public interest message. Others, unfortunately, are not.

Other local television stations, including the independents and Public Broadcasting System outlets, provide additional public service opportunities. Independent stations typically use syndicated programs, independently produced programs, serial reruns, old movies, and local sports. PBS stations, funded by public funds and private donations, offer a wide range of educational programs.

Access to the television airwaves is a basic right of the people, despite messages and actions to the contrary by certain local stations and the FCC. There is every reason to exercise this right. People need a format to debate important issues affecting their local communities or to express new ideas. People need to know how they can get more actively involved in their communities. People need to have the concerns that affect their lives addressed from a local perspective. People need access to the airwaves!

The door to access, however, remains essentially closed in many areas. Community and nonprofit groups too often are cut off from the opportunity to reach thousands with their very important messages unless they are able to be involved in a newsworthy event that attracts coverage on the local news.

In many cases the failure to gain access to the television airwaves is reflective of a lack of organization and mobilization of your resources. You can change this, however, and make your dream of television time a reality by building a broad-based grass roots coalition that can persuade local stations of their responsibility to respond to the public's need.

The Deregulation Efforts of the FCC

Acting under authority of the Communications Act of 1934, the FCC requires that local stations operate "in the public interest, convenience, and necessity." This requirement not only sets the guideline for the station's use of the airwaves, but also serves as a "basis" for renewal of their licenses (although in reality, renewal is almost automatic). The initial purpose of this law and the regulating power of the FCC was to ensure that the airwaves were treated as a resource of the American public—not of private industry or the government. Today, however, it appears that the public is quickly losing its hold on the television airwaves. For all the public uproar (or lack thereof), however, you would think nothing had changed.

When the Reagan administration took office, it made very clear its strong commitment to deregulation. Television broadcasting was no exception. Led by Chairman Mark Fowler, the FCC's agenda became clear soon after President Reagan's inauguration: to deregulate the industry by getting rid of requirements for public affairs and news programming, limitations on advertising, ascertainment of needs within the community, requirements to maintain logs of programming, equal time provisions for candidates, and the Fairness Doctrine. The FCC believed that the pressures of the marketplace, not the protection of the government, should govern programming decisions, that if viewers do not like what is aired, they can change the channel. If they continue to do so, the station will lose advertising revenue and will make changes accordingly. According to Fowler, the FCC is the last "of the New Deal dinosaurs. And we are going to change that. Today we strike a blow for freedom."

One might dispute whether Fowler's efforts have struck "a blow for freedom," but they undeniably have been successful. Already the FCC has succeeded in wiping out most the regulations that pertained to informational programming and logging of program content. There are no longer any requirements for cable operators to allocate channels for educational, governmental, and community access. Key regulations on advertising on both cable and public television have been removed. Licence renewals for television stations have been changed from three to five years. And in the most startling move of all, in the summer of 1984, the FCC announced that it had taken the following actions.

1. Eliminated the requirement that at least 10 percent of a station's programming be in the "nonentertainment" area—half of which should be "informational" (news or public affairs)—and that, in addition, 5 percent of a station's programming, whether informational or entertainment, be locally produced.
2. Eliminated the requirement that stations submit a report on how the station has ascertained the needs of the community (usually through meetings and other contacts with community leaders) and how they met those needs and concerns.
3. Eliminated the requirement for a 16-minute ceiling on the amount of advertisements telecast each hour.
4. Eliminated the requirement for logs chronicling programming and categorizing the type of programming open to public view. Now any logs kept will not be open to the public, but only to advertisers to prove that a commercial has actually run. The only information in the public inspection files will be a quarterly list of five to ten issues to which the station gave particular attention. This list is to be accompanied with an explanation as to how these issues were treated.

Chairman Fowler backed up this FCC action by saying: "Our decision to deregulate T.V. removes these unnecessary intrusions. It recognizes that quality entertainment, news, and other programs that genuinely serve the public are not produced by artificial rules and regulations." The FCC chairman also stated his belief that a quota on public service television simply required many stations to "run a half-hour of talking-heads at sunrise." In Fowler's opinion, under the new guidelines, television stations would still provide programming that addressed important community issues, but they could do so without the paperwork. The thrust behind the FCC chairman's argument was that the viewers should have a choice of the programming they watch; that commercial television should be produced because it "appeals to the viewer, not because a Washington bureaucrat orders it."

Admittedly, broadcasters are still required by the Communications Act of 1934 to program in the public interest. Nevertheless, older persons, program administrators, service and care providers, and community advocates should be more than a little concerned about the ramifications of the FCC's deregulation efforts.

Did these rule changes really give the public more freedom of choice in the programming they watch, or did they just give the networks, who have a stranglehold on television programming already, a blank check to program as they wish? Only time will tell. But the fact remains that these rule changes have seriously threatened the public's access and role in television programming. No longer is a station required to provide an acceptable level of public service and informational programming. No longer are local stations accountable to the public for the programming they provide. Stations do not have to survey the community as to their interests or concerns. How are stations going to program in the public interest without knowing what that interest is? The public will not even have access to programming logs, though this information will be made available to advertisers. And then there is the issue of blanket approval to televise as many commercials as the station deems appropriate. The previous rule already allowed stations to sell advertising time during 26 percent of each hour of programming time. Although stations currently average less than 13 minutes per hour of commercials, what is to stop this percentage from going up considerably in the future?

With no requirements on programming, no limitations on advertising, no public input, and no records available to the public, what kind of criteria is the FCC going to use to judge whether a station should be relicensed? Of course, the FCC has rarely slapped the hand of a station not meeting its public obligation in the past. But deregulation makes the possibility of censure even more remote.

The public is not without fault in this situation. Americans have been far too quiet in the face of the onslaught against access to and involvement in local television broadcasting. If they continue to keep mum, the onslaught will continue. If they begin to organize, it probably will not. The ticket is for local community organizations, agencies, and groups to join together to let local stations know they want to have a say in programming. The public still possesses powerful weapons: the ability to influence TV audiences regarding what channels they turn to and the ability to file complaints that can influence licensing. Never feel that there is nothing you can do. But don't make the mistake of standing on the sidelines until it is too late.

Maintaining the Fairness Doctrine

Without public and congressional intervention, the FCC may succeed in abolishing its next targeted victim: the Fairness Doctrine. If it does, your right to hear fair and equal coverage of controversial issues of public importance will be seriously threatened. The Fairness Doctrine protects two very essential public broadcast rights: the right to programming that addresses controversial issues and the right to programming that is balanced and provides a "reasonable opportunity for the presentation of contrasting views." The Fairness Doctrine thus guards the right to an open discussion and debate of important issues affecting our lives, one that is not one-sided or obviously biased.

To invoke the Fairness Doctrine, the issue must not only be controversial, but of public importance. For instance, the ongoing conflict in the Middle East provokes much controversy and debate, but has little direct effect on the local community. Thus, no matter how strongly a group might feel about a television discussion of Palestinian refugees, they undoubtedly would have a hard time convincing a station to give them time to respond under the Fairness Doctrine. The same holds true for issues of historical, academic, or personal significance that have little or no impact on the local community. To be covered under the Fairness Doctrine, an issue must stir considerable debate within many segments of the community.

The Fairness Doctrine has been affirmed on many occasions dating as far back as 1928, when, in the Great Lakes Broadcasting case, the Federal Regulatory Commission said that if a public issue is dealt with on the airwaves, there must be "ample play for the free and fair competition of opposing views." The move toward the Doctrine actually began with the inclusion in the Radio Act of 1927 of an "equal time" provision for use and purchase of airtime by political candidates. Then, in 1932, Congress passed an amendment to the Radio Act requiring "equal opportunity for the presentation of both sides of public opinion." The next two decades brought many challenges and affirmations until, in 1959, Congress amended the Communications Act to mandate that broadcasters "operate in the public interest and (to) afford reasonable opportunity for discussion of conflicting views on issues of public importance." This legislation legitimized the Fairness Doctrine as had nothing else before. Now only an act of Congress could eliminate it.

Further definition and solidification of the Doctrine came with two landmark cases during the 1960s: the Cullman Broadcasting Company decision and *Red Lion vs. FCC*. In 1963, Cullman Broadcasting asked for an opinion from the FCC on whether it was required to air opposing viewpoints to one of its radio programs. The FCC responded that the station was required to broadcast the opposing view, even if the proponents of that view could not afford to pay for the time.

Such was the birth of the "Cullman Doctrine," which established the right to "balanced" coverage. If a controversial issue, piece of legislation, or initiative campaign is being debated in your community, you have the right to have both sides of the issue aired by your local stations. If a station has been airing your opponents' point of view almost exclusively possibly because they have the money to buy large amounts of air time, your media coalition can rely upon the Fairness Doctrine and the Cullman Doctrine to ask for airtime to respond, whether or not you have the money to pay for that time.

The Red Lion case was similarly supportive of the public's right to access. In 1964, during a "Christian Crusade" program, the Reverend Billy James Hargis attacked investigative journalist Fred Cook for trying to "destroy" Senator Barry Goldwater (who was running for president at the time) in this book *Goldwater: Extremist of the Right*. Among other things, Hargis accused Cook of being a professional mudslinger and stated that he had been dismissed from a New York newspaper for making a false charge against an unnamed official. Cook then asked WGCB, the Red Lion, Pennsylvania station that aired the syndicated show, for time to respond. The station refused. Cook petitioned the FCC, claiming he had the right to respond under the Personal Attack rule in the Fairness Doctrine on the grounds that WGCB had impugned his character during the presentation of a controversial issue of public significance. The FCC ruled in Cook's favor.

WGCB refused to relent, and the matter was turned over to the courts. The U.S. Court of Appeals upheld the FCC ruling. The case was then referred to the Supreme Court for the first constitutional test of the Fairness Doctrine. Citing the First Amendment, the Supreme Court voted unanimously to uphold the FCC decision "to preserve an uninhibited marketplace of ideas in which truth will ultimately prevail." The Court reiterated the public's First Amendment rights and its belief that broadcasters were to operate in the public interest. Most important, the court held that the public's right to "suitable access" could be "constitutionally abridged either by Congress or by the FCC."

The Cullman Doctrine and the Red Lion case should provide ample ammunition for your media coalition in its battle for public access to the airwaves. And the battle has already begun, whether or not local advocates have declared war. The Fairness Doctrine is not only being threatened by the FCC, but by broadcasters and within Congress. Broadcasters often argue that the Fairness Doctrine puts them at an unfair disadvantage to the print media, which have no fairness requirements. From the halls of Congress comes an even bigger threat, especially with a Republican-controlled Senate. Many congressman and senators are quite anxious to erase the Fairness Doctrine from the legislative books. A strong grass roots advocacy effort could make a big difference in the outcome of such a challenge or, for that matter, in whether or not a challenge is even mounted.

Organizing a Senior Media Rights Coalition

A local senior media rights coalition (SMRC) is a grass roots organization made up of representatives of local advocacy, service, and educational organizations and led by such groups as the Gray Panthers, AARP, Area Agency on Aging, and the area senior lobby. The composition should be quite similar to that of the Senior Media Committee (discussed in chapter 8), whose primary purpose is to gain airtime and produce senior-oriented television programming. In fact, it might make organizational sense to have just one group, with a dual assignment: (1) to pursue programming possibilities and (2) to use grass roots advocacy to help the senior community increase its power and control over the airwaves and to create a partnership with local stations to work toward more balanced programming in the public interest.

To organize a SMRC you do not have to be expert in communications or electronic media; you need only be strongly concerned about how television (or radio) airwaves are being used and want to be more actively involved in the decision-making process. You also do not have to have a large group to be effective. A small, but vocal, initial membership can have great impact. And as word gets around, the membership surely will grow.

The task of putting together a SMRC is not an easy one. To press successfully for change in a powerful, sophisticated, and well-organized television industry, you must demonstrate strength, sophistication, and sound organization of your own. Effective organization goes beyond having a coalition of dedicated individuals and groups, although that clearly is the first step to a successful SMRC. Other key ingredients to consider in developing your SMRC include membership, organizational structure, incorporation, leadership, building your base, budget, and best use of meeting time.

Membership

A critical decision in the organization of your SMRC is how to formulate the membership structure. What organizations will you invite to become involved? Should you limit participation to a prescribed number of representatives from these member organizations? Or should you open membership up to interested local citizens? Maybe you should do both.

All three options have good and bad points. By limiting membership to the selected organizations and their representatives, you can consolidate your power base and have more time to concentrate on the interests of the member organizations. In addition, your group will have instant credibility due to the already established reputations of the member groups. By opening membership to the general community, on the other hand, you can promote more widespread community involvement, energy, and input.

The final option—combining organizational representation and general membership—is probably most desirable. You will have the best of both worlds: the established influence of respected community organizations and the involvement of interested community members. Slots can be provided on the steering committee for each member organization, with a proportional share set aside for representatives of the general membership. Both general and organizational members can be actively involved on subcommittees, where most of the work is done anyway.

The core of the organizational membership of your SMRC should be local senior-oriented organizations and groups involved in service and advocacy, such as the local Gray Panthers network, the local AARP chapter, the Area Agency on Aging, the senior legal services program (the legal advice may come in handy), local senior centers and nursing facilities, the local senior lobby group, and other senior or social service groups. But don't stop there. Other like-minded groups, such as the local citizen's utility board or the Ralph Nader-inspired Public Interest Research Group or Common Cause group should also be solicited for group membership. Check carefully into potential groups; ask other organizations for recommendations. Avoid the embarrassing mistake of overlooking an organization that should have been asked to become involved.

You should also wage a strong and continuing effort to recruit general membership from the community. Many of your individual members will come from member organizations. But there are many other potential members in the community who may not belong to any organized group. Recruit them through press releases to local media sources, general community announcements, and speaking engagements before groups and clubs. Membership candidates also may crop up at senior centers, nutrition sites, agency staff meetings, club meetings, and churches and synagogues. The more individual SMRC members you recruit, the more person-power you will have to work on SMRC projects. Likewise, the more potential impact you will have on local television.

Organizational Structure

The structure of your SMRC is important, although not critical. You do not want to be either too formal or too informal. For example, a central steering committee made up of representatives of the major groups in the coalition, the group's leadership, and other active members, should help formulate policy, direction, and the plan of action. Steering committee members typically will shoulder a major part of the workload and provide a positive direction for SMAC involvements. As the SMRC grows, subcommittees may be formed to tackle different tasks. You might have subcommittees for fund raising or publicity or individual projects (Program Watch, Access, Legislative).

Guard against the tendency to become too centralized or too bureaucratic. Either tendency can stifle creativity and cripple the effectiveness of your SMRC. Encourage flexibility and widespread involvement of the membership. Do not require steering committee approval for everything your subcommittees want to do. Major new initiatives, however, should get the approval of the leadership, as well as the membership.

Keep the SMRC membership as actively involved as possible. Too often, most of the workload is shouldered by a few. If motivating the membership becomes too much of a chore, that may be a sign that a new membership drive is called for. New blood can be very refreshing to an organization.

One way to head off general membership boredom and to shore up any weak spots in your coalition is to involve general members in the decision making and problem solving. Any organization needs checks and balances. You are all in this together! From debate and discussion on important issues and projects comes insight and direction. Make sure you have the support of the membership before you begin any major action. If the membership does not feel ownership, the leaders will find themselves standing alone at a critical moment when they need support the most. Spend time developing support among the members for each project. It will pay off. A neglected membership is ripe ground for division in the ranks. A happy membership feels an involvement and ownership in SMRC activities.

Incorporation

You may want to incorporate your SMRC legally for fundraising purposes. Most companies or foundations will not donate money to an organization unless it has nonprofit, tax-exempt status under section 501(c)(3) of the Internal Revenue Service code (otherwise they cannot take the donation as a tax deduction). You can usually get state incorporation from the Secretary of State's office and the 501(c)(3) forms from the local IRS office.

The process for incorporation is relatively simple. You will need to prepare by-laws outlining such matters as membership requirements, purpose and the selection and responsibilities of your leadership. You will also need to make available a list of your steering committee (or board of directors). It is wise to get assistance in incorporation from a friendly practicing or retired lawyer or a local legal services office. Otherwise, you may file incorrectly or end up spending hundreds of dollars for legal assistance.

An alternative to incorporation is to channel funds through one of your member organizations. Whatever your choice, you should make it only after careful thought and investigation of the potential benefits and losses.

Leadership

One of the greatest challenges in organizing your group will be to find effective leadership and spokespersons. There is no easy answer to the age-old question: what constitutes an effective leader? There also is no easy route to finding one. There are, however, some basic qualities to look for:

Commitment. Your leaders must be committed to helping promote a better media image of the elderly. Stay clear of individuals who are jumping on an interesting bandwagon to fulfill an ego need.

Knowledge and Experience. Major leadership responsibilities are best placed on persons who have knowledge of or experience in either media, advocacy, or aging, ideally in at least two out of the three areas. Organizations are often judged by the expertise shown by their spokespersons. You do not want an individual representing your SMRC at press conferences and public speaking engagements who is not fully knowledgeable of the issues being discussed.

Communication Skills. Your spokesperson should have sound communication abilities. Remember this is the person the public and the press will associate with your SMRC. Place your best foot forward by having spokespersons who are equally comfortable in front of a television camera, newspaper reporters, or a live audience.

People Skills. It is extremely difficult to inspire and motivate an organization if the key leaders do not deal well with people. To lead, you must be able to convince people to follow. Individuals who are not "people persons" should serve in leadership positions where there is less direct dealings with people.

Intergenerational. It is imperative that you incorporate both young and old into leadership positions in your SMRC. An overabundance of either young or old leaders will detract from the appearance of intergenerational support. A good first step to set the intergenerational tone is to have co-chairs; one who is old and one who is young.

Finding ideal leaders to fill the chair and the steering committee is not as difficult as it might seem. The cream of the membership inevitably rises to the top. Soon after the SMRC is organized, the natural leaders will show themselves. So will the organizers, those with fund-raising and bookkeeping abilities, and those with lobbying skills.

The real challenge is to mold this raw talent into a core leadership that will make things happen. Balance is the key to meshing talents, personalities, and skills and to avoid stepping on egos or invading anyone's "personal space." Don't expect any leader, even the co-chairs, to be perfect. What you want from the co-chairs is a balance of personal talents and abilities. The same holds true with the leadership on the steering committee and key subcommittees.

Select your chairperson(s) as soon as possible, but avoid hasty decisions that will cause you grief further down the line. Once the chairpersons have been selected, they can shoulder much of the burden of filling the other leadership spots. Whatever the position, select your leadership carefully. The future of your SMRC depends on it.

Building a Base

Much of the success of a SMRC will hinge on how well its efforts are planned and how solid a base is laid. Where is your SMRC heading and what are you going to do when you get there? These questions must be answered at the outset. Will your SMRC concentrate on gaining access to the local television airwaves or on monitoring programming for age stereotyping? Will you focus on supporting legislation to restore regulations wiped out by the FCC or on lobbying against FCC efforts to tear down the Fairness Doctrine? Or maybe will you combine efforts in all these areas—putting equal time and energy into gaining access to the media, preventing stereotypical programming, and lobbying efforts.

Once your goals and objectives have been established, develop one-year action or work plans for each project you plan to undertake. These work plans should map out a step-by-step course of action, with timelines for each step, to chart exactly how each project will be carried out. With careful preparation and planning, your SMRC will be able to hit the ground running and have immediate impact on the local television industry and community.

Budget

The SMRC envisioned in this chapter is a low-budget community action organization. Paid staff is not contemplated, but if you want to try to get the funding for such a position(s), more power to you. For now, however, it is assumed that your SMRC budget will consist mainly of the following line-items:

1. Office rental (if you can find a place that is inexpensive)
2. Office supplies and equipment
3. Printing and duplication
4. Postage

The main financial objective is to have enough money to conduct your activities effectively. How much money you need depends on what you want to accomplish; if you don't have enough, you may find yourself stopped short of your goals. Money should not absorb too much of your time, however. Much can be accomplished with very little. The bottom line is to have the financial backing to put out professional-looking materials such as position papers, issue statements, press releases, proposals. And that hinges on being able to purchase attractive, well-designed stationary, a typewriter, typing paper, note pads, pens and pencils, and other office supplies, as well as being able to make good copies of your work. The cost should not be outrageous. And you can cut it down even more by borrowing equipment or soliciting donations.

A central location for your operation also is important. If necessary, use a member's residence. Ideally, however, you should find actual office space. Inexpensive alternatives often can be found in older buildings, churches, or even in shared office situations with other organizations that have extra space.

The money to make up your budget typically will come from individual donors who are supportive of your efforts or from local corporations that are sympathetic and want to donate to a worthy cause. These donations will not come pouring in just because you are doing effective work in the community, however. You will have to visit local corporation executives or write fund-raising letters to lists of individuals who have supported similar activities in the past. There also is nothing wrong with asking for donations at public speaking engagements. In addition, you might schedule an annual fund-raising event, such as a walk-a-thon, an intergenerational dance, a senior crafts fair and bazaar, or a benefit night at a local movie theater or playhouse.

Although hard times have made the competition stiff, private foundations can provide an excellent source of funding if you happen to strike their fancy. Check the *Foundation Directory* at your local library for potential sources. The best bets are foundations with an interest in aging, media, or community advocacy that are located in your state or region. Write a two-page letter introducing your organization and the project for which you are seeking funding. The foundation will let you know whether to submit a formal proposal.

For more information on budgeting and fundraising for local advocacy organizations, consult some of the many good books on the subject as well as local experts in the public and private sectors, who may well be willing to offer wise counsel.

Best Use of Meeting Time

Hold meetings only as often as needed—no more, no less. You want to keep your group involved and motivated. But the last thing anyone needs is to meet just for the sake of meeting.

When you do meet, use your time efficiently and effectively. Have a firm idea of where you want the meeting to go. Plan a clear agenda, allowing for input from the membership. A sample agenda might look like the following:

1. Introductions (groups, guests, etc.)
2. Reports from the steering committee and subcommittees, with discussion and action by the membership
3. Reports on current SMRC projects or issues, followed by discussion and action by the membership
4. New business, projects, or issues
5. Agenda for the next meeting

Set a time limit for the meeting and do your best to stick to it. Let people have their say, but keep things moving along. Debate is healthy, but endless discussion and rehashing of an issue only breeds impatience. Be sure to keep the discussion on track. Avoid a meeting that gets out of control, where the loudest and strongest personalities take the floor and rarely relinquish it. Finally, make sure all attendees are aware of their assignments before ending the meeting.

The leadership should have a short debriefing period after the meeting to evaluate it and think about how it can be improved. Was the attendance as expected? If not, what can be done to improve it for the next meeting? Did the participants leave the meeting feeling good about what was accomplished? Did everyone get an opportunity to provide input? Which members were being most disruptive and why? This should help make your future meetings—and your overall effort—more efficient and successful.

Gaining Access to the Media

Once your coalition has been formed, the real work begins. As discussed in detail in chapter 8, the best single tool for combatting electronic ageism is to gain access to your own air time. Through your own series, ongoing program, or even public service announcements you can disseminate valuable information and make sure your side of an issue gets aired.

Thus, efforts to obtain television time should be a major focus of your SMRC's work (unless there is a separate committee such as the media committee described earlier to carry out this mission). For details on how to advocate—and win—your own television program, consult chapter 8.

Monitoring against Ageism

Gaining your own show may not always be possible. Even when it is, one show or even a series of shows cannot singlehandedly undo ageism on the airwaves. Thus, an equally important goal for your SMRC is to serve as a watchdog by monitoring the programming of all local television stations and cable systems. You can determine whether the programming is balanced, fair, unbiased, and nonageist. If it is not, you will have the documentation to prove it.

This does not mean that a few dedicated SMRC members must spend the major part of their lives in front of the television. Divide up stations and time segments among a number of individuals, many of whom would likely be watching television at that particular time anyway. Each of the monitors should keep a thorough log of the programming they are watching. This undoubtedly will be the only log you have as stations are no longer obligated to share their program log with the public.

Before you begin monitoring, establish clear goals. There are a number of programming areas your coalition can monitor: on which do you wish to focus?

Maybe you are most concerned about the amount of overall programming geared to the older population. How many—if any—network originated programs are aimed specifically at the elderly? If such programs exist, do they adequately address the problems and needs of older persons?

Maybe your concern is local programming, both public service and commercial. Do local programmers cover issues of concern to older persons? If they do, is the coverage realistic and honest? Are they being balanced in their coverage in accordance with the Fairness Doctrine? Are they disproportionately biased in their programming toward the side that can afford to put a lot of money into advertising?

What about the characterizations of older people? You may want to log the number of older characters you view and whether they are cast in a positive or negative light—with particular emphasis on network comedies, dramas, and movies. How often are older characters seen in programming? What are their roles? Are they characterized in a stereotypical, ageist manner? Are they cast in inferior, less capable roles? Are they more likely to be seen as healthy, or as decrepit and disoriented? Are they stubborn, rigid, and inflexible, or are they dynamic and open to change? Do they have positive relationships with the younger generations, or are they old sticks in the mud? Most important, will average viewers, who likely will have little or no knowledge about the older population, gain a positive or negative perception of the elderly from what they are viewing?

Your monitoring efforts should be ongoing but broken up into phases that last at least a month or two. The exact time span per cycle depends on how many stations are in your local area, how many persons are monitoring, and whether or not they are monitoring morning, afternoon, and evening programming on weekdays or weekends. The more thorough you are, the better position your SMRC will be in to advocate change. It will be hard to convince anyone that a station runs ageist programming or devotes little air time to aging issues without comprehensive data to back up those charges. Thus, before you approach a station to complain about coverage, make sure you are armed with sufficient data from a watchdog effort to leave no doubt about the validity of your complaint.

Dealing with Local Stations

You will have the best chance of having an impact on a station's policies or programming if you maintain cordial, even friendly, relations with it. An adversarial relationship will get you nowhere fast. Remember, the station has the upper hand, especially after the recent FCC deregulation decisions.

In any event, most stations will be inclined to deal with you in a responsible and professional manner if you negotiate with them directly. No one, least of all the station, wants to see a programming dispute become a matter for the FCC or the courts to decide. After all, the station's personnel have to work and live in the community just as you do, and they will undoubtedly be as eager as you to resolve legitimate concerns fairly. Some helpful hints for facilitating this process follow.

Evaluate Your Complaint. However angry you might be at a local station, take the time to evaluate whether you have the grounds for complaint. This can save you wasted time and some embarrassment. Don't imagine that the station is under any obligation to provide you with public affairs programming. Thanks to the FCC, it is not! If you are trying to make a case for greater coverage of senior issues, the burden of proof is on you to convince the station that it would be in the best interest of its viewers (and thus the station) to make a programming change.

It is difficult enough to prove that specific programming aired by a station is "unbalanced" or ageist. If you are trying to prove that a station has an overall bias against the elderly, your task will be that much more difficult. Look at the station's programming as a whole. Build a strong argument based on a number of examples, ideally taken from as many areas of the station's programming as possible.

Be Prepared. Before you make initial contact or meet with a station, be sure you are well prepared. If you believe the station's programming has been ageist in some way, have your facts down pat and have specific suggestions for how to alter the situation. If you believe coverage of an issue was not balanced, be specific as to how it was not and what should be done about it. If you want to gain access to public service time, outline why you think the station should provide the time, backing up your argument with specific data on the lack of such programming and the need within the community. Station personnel are busy people. Do your homework so you can provide information that will be penetrating and will win your case in the shortest time possible.

Try to anticipate the counterarguments the station will raise and be prepared to respond. If you claim that the station did not provide balanced coverage of an issue affecting the elderly, station personnel may counter by saying the issue is not controversial or of enough public importance to warrant coverage under the Fairness Doctrine. They also may claim that your point of view was covered sufficiently in their news and talk or interview programming. Have an adequate response or you will get nowhere with either the station or the FCC if you pursue your case to that point.

Initial Contact. It is generally wisest to first spell out your grievance or recommendation to the station in a letter. Clearly and concisely state your case, suggest alternatives and ask for an opportunity for a face-to-face meeting to discuss the situation. Make sure you know of what you speak. Have a friendly lawyer or knowledgeable member review the letter before sending it. If you are going to accuse a station of not providing balanced discussion under the Fairness Doctrine, you had better be sure of your facts and the law. If you are concerned about the ageist slant of certain programming or commercials, you had better be specific about the times and program(s). A hastily thrown together letter can put you at a great disadvantage before you even meet with the station and can significantly hurt your chances of success.

Meeting with Station Management. Ideally, the station's management will agree with every point you made in your letter and give you everything you want. This is a wonderful fantasy, but not terribly realistic. At best, the station may try to appease you by giving in to some of your requests. If so, the suggested solutions very likely will be inadequate from your standpoint, and a meeting with the station's management will be necessary.

Go into that meeting with your first string: SMRC members who are well versed, knowledgeable, and good communicators. An intergenerational mix is best, if possible. Do a dry run-through in advance to iron out any rough spots.

Be firm but act with class. Do not be antagonistic or confrontational. Be specific with illustrative examples. Try to put yourself in the station managers' shoes. Sell them on how your proposal will benefit the station and increase their public acceptance. Offer to help them in the future on this and other issues.

Above all, do not be unreasonable. If you are attempting to gain access to the airways, do not expect to get your own show in the first meeting. If, however, the station's management offers you a guest appearance on one of their public service programs or offers to work with you on a PSA, accept the offer. Remember, the station is under no obligation to give you anything! A small amount of airtime is better than none, and it will help you engender greater public awareness of your issues and concerns. If you have gained the respect of the station in the process, more victories will follow. In addition, each meeting with a station gives you insight that will prove helpful in future interactions with that and other local stations.

Not all meetings with local station management will have a happy ending, however. If you find yourself in this situation and you think you have a valid complaint under the Fairness Doctrine or any other law or regulation, there are other avenues by which to seek relief.

Taking Further Action

Among ways to obtain fair treatment are press conferences, public demonstrations, or petitions to the FCC or other decision-making bodies. Before you embark on any of these courses, however, think about it carefully. Once you take your problem outside a station, you will jeopardize any future relationship with that station. The current relationship may be so bad that it will make little difference. If it is not, however, you may want to rethink your strategy. Whatever the situation, every action must be carefully thought out. Hasty reactions have a tendency to come back to haunt you. Following are possible options for presenting your case if the station turns you down.

Public Rally or Demonstration. In true Gray Panther style you might hold a rally or demonstration outside a television station. As long as you can attract a large enough crowd, this can be an excellent way to get the station's attention and establish public awareness.

A large crowd in front of a television station, especially one in a populous area, can be a real attention-grabber. But, even more important, a successful demonstration should receive coverage by local newspapers, radio news, and rival television stations. Television stations are very conscious of their public image, especially commercial stations, which depend heavily on local advertising dollars. Advertisers may be a bit turned off if they think the public is displeased, especially if that displeasure runs across the generations, a point that underlines the importance of having a multigenerational gathering.

Organization is the key to success in any public demonstration. Get all SMRC member organizations involved. Get sympathetic speakers who can "move" a crowd. Use guerilla theater. Make sure the press is invited. Arrange transportation for participants. Get colorful signs made. Look for a gimmick; for instance, if you are protesting age stereotyping you might have a "rock-in" in front of the station with a line of people rocking in rocking chairs. Getting adequate numbers of participants is important. Otherwise, you will give the impression of lack of support, which will hurt your cause. If you are having trouble getting a large enough group, you might consider picketing in front of the station. Although picketing involves a longer commitment of time, it requires far fewer participants and can have an equally strong impact.

Petitioning. A petition drive is another vehicle for demonstrating support for your cause. Petition drives are time-consuming, however, and must be used strategically for maximum effect. The signed petitions might be presented to a station official at a rally in front of the station or at a well-attended public meeting (with the press in attendance, of course). Petitions are a way to show significant community support. But make sure they are presented in such a way as to produce large community impact. The process is far too time-consuming to do otherwise.

Boycott. One sure way to cause a stir in the community is for your SMRC to recommend a boycott of a particular station. This is a serious

step, however, and should be implemented only after careful consideration. Try to exhaust all other less onerous remedies first. If you have,
and you are sure a boycott is justified, proceed carefully. If done care-
lessly, a boycott could backfire on you, damaging not only your protest
effort, but your credibility.

Formal Complaint to the FCC. When all else has failed, the option remains of carrying your complaint to the FCC. Before doing so, however,
you need to seek legal and expert advise to make sure you have a convincing case. The FCC receives a tremendous number of complaints,
many of them unjustified. You will have to prove that your case is the exception. Put a lot of energy into the development of your case. Be specific
and have sufficient back-up data. Illustrate precisely how the station's
programming has been unbalanced under the Fairness Doctrine or has
done a disservice to the public. Vague generalizations will not get you far.

Even if you decide to file a complaint with the FCC, your main objective still should be to reach some kind of settlement with the station. Settling the matter outside of the FCC or the courts is best for all involved.

If you do file, your correspondence with the FCC should include a
description of your organization, the station in question with call
numbers and location, the issue(s) that prompted your complaint,
specifics about the programming at issue, exactly where the imbalances
took place and persuasive arguments as to why this programming vio-
lated the intent, if not the letter, of the law. After careful review and,
most likely, many edits, you will be ready to send the correspondence to
the Enforcement Division, Mass Media Bureau, Federal Communications Commission, 1919 M Street, N.W., Washington, D.C. 20554. Send
a copy to the station or cable system as well.

If your complaint meets all the FCC's requirements, a prima facie
case will be established. The station will be asked to respond. The FCC
will then either ask for more information or they will make a ruling. If
the decision is negative, you have 30 days to appeal. The next stop is the
U.S. Court of Appeals in the District of Columbia, which is a level that
few complaints ever reach. At this point, you had better have a good
communications lawyer who knows the technical ropes.

Few complaints to the FCC ever go anywhere. Stations are given a
great deal of discretion in their programming. So if you are going to take
this route, do it well and make it count.

Lobbying

Although working with local stations is your first and in many ways
your most critical task, it also is important not to ignore the larger pic-

ture. The majority of the decisions that affect what you see on your television screen do not come from the operator of the local station, but from power brokers who may be hundreds or thousands of miles away at FCC headquarters in Washington, D.C. or with the networks in New York or California. Your local station can decide whether to give you a half hour of time for your public service program, but it will not make the decisions about the fate of the Fairness Doctrine or other laws and regulations affecting the use of the airwaves. Likewise, your local station may help to dispel some of the negative stereotypes by broadcasting a positive, aging-oriented documentary or series, but it has virtually no control over the network originated entertainment programming that takes up a majority of the airtime.

Thus, at least a portion of your time should be dedicated to lobbying the networks, the FCC, congress, and other decision makers who hold the key to these matters. The greatest weapon you have is people, and the more the better. People can write letters to officials and letters to the editor in area newspapers. They can also pay visits or send telegrams to pertinent officials.

Letter-Writing Campaigns. Writing letters to officials, including your congressperson and television network executives, can have much more impact than you realize. Both parties have a great deal of stake in pleasing the public and a great aversion to public displays of displeasure. As a matter of fact, congressional and senatorial offices keep track of the level of response they receive to issues. The more letters sent, the more impact it will have.

The best letter-writing campaign includes letters from as many individuals as possible, written in their own words. Form letters or postcards also have an impact, but much less so. The letter itself need not be more than a page and should focus on only one issue at a time. To make sure the letter writers have a sound knowledge of the issue or programming they are writing about, it is helpful to provide them information sheets with the facts and persuasive arguments.

If time is of the essence, your group's message can be conveyed quickly through telegrams. This may be the best option if pending legislation comes up suddenly for a vote. The one drawback to telegrams is that your message must be kept to around ten words to keep the cost reasonable.

Letters to the Editor. If you succeed in getting them published, letters to the editor can have excellent impact. But you must plan carefully. Frame your arguments with care. Make sure your facts are correct and up to date. Then, instead of flooding newspapers with letters and taking the chance that a poorly written letter will be printed, have your most knowledgeable and best writers take on the task. Not only will their letters have a greater chance of making it into print, they also will be more likely to get across the point your group wishes to make.

Lobbying your Congressman and/or Senator. When you are trying to promote change at the national level, the most direct route is your own congressperson or senator. He or she has to be reelected every two to six years. What you, the constituent, has to say should thus be important. If your concerns are not taken seriously, you always have the option of raising them again during the next campaign or, ultimately, in the voting booth.

There are a variety of ways to present your views to your congressional representative. One of these is to contact his or her office by letter, phone, or in person. If you can visit the representative in person, all the better. But, remember, these are very busy people and they obviously cannot meet with every group or individual. That is why they assign staff to cover specific issues. Often it is better to talk with staff members, anyway, as they may be more expert in a particular area and may have more time to spend with you. Furthermore, they are likely to end up doing the background work for the senator or congressperson in any event.

Never forget that your message will be even stronger if you have others to back it up. Do not just go to the office. Organize a group to go with you. Do not just send your own letter to the office. Get others to write, as well. One phone call is nice, but fifty are a lot better. It is not that your congressperson or senator does not respect your individual opinion, but he or she represents 550,000 or more people. If the legislator is persuaded that a significant number of constituents share your view, he or she will be more likely to act.

Whatever form it takes, grass roots lobbying is an extremely effective way of affecting policy and it seems to be becoming more so. The outcries of the senior population in 1982 were credited with stopping President Reagan's plans to cut social security. In 1983 a massive letter-writing campaign that dumped hundreds of thousands of letters on Capitol Hill, weighed heavily in the defeat of a law that required banks to withhold 10 percent of individuals' interest earnings. The old adage that the squeaky wheel gets the grease is as true today as the day it was created. And your grass roots media lobbying effort is as good an excuse as any to put it to the test again.

Tying into Successful National Models

There are a number of groups working toward greater public control of the airwaves that serve as excellent examples of effective media advocacy efforts. These groups know the ropes and could be of great assistance to you if they are organized in your area.

The Gray Panthers Media Watch Task Force, led by 80-year-old Lydia Bragger, has been successfully fighting ageist portrayals in the broadcast media for the past decade. Local Gray Panther networks all over the country have been letting their voices be heard loud and clear with regard to how programming is responding to the issue of aging. The Public Interest Research Groups (PIRGs) inspired by Ralph Nader have been actively involved in media-oriented advocacy. One notable example was the formation by the Missouri PIRG of the St. Louis Media Access Group (MAG) and their subsequent efforts to help organize MAGs elsewhere in the country.

The efforts of groups such as the Gray Panthers and the PIRGs should serve as an inspiration to advocates interested in forming media advocacy groups and should provide some comfort in the knowledge that there are other advocates around the country who share your concerns and are attempting to do something about it.

Standing up for our Rights

There is no better time than now to stand up for our rights to the airwaves. The broadcast industry continues to discriminate against the elderly in the way it portrays the older generation and in how it addresses their needs. Older persons and their concerns still receive minimal amount of public service programming time. The FCC, established as the public's guardian of the airwaves, is now leading the charge to deregulate them. Having already eliminated most of the regulations relating to public service requirements, the federal agency now seems bent on destroying the Fairness Doctrine as well, and with it, very possibly, your right to fair coverage of controversial issues of public importance.

Your only hope to stop this erosion of your rights is to organize. A senior media rights coalition (SMRC) made up of local advocacy, service, and educational organizations can monitor existing local and network programming to determine the amount of coverage geared to issues and concerns of the older population. Your SMRC also can advocate for local aging-oriented public service programming, organize local protests against stereotypical or biased programming, and lead lobbying campaigns relating to federal legislation or FCC actions.

The success of your group depends on your ability to formulate a membership structure that involves all interested groups and individuals in the community and is built on solid organization, careful planning, and crackerjack implementation. Another key ingredient to success is to maintain a cordial and professional relationship with local stations. Without it, negotiations regarding the station's policies and programming will be made much more difficult, if not impossible.

In the long run, all your work will be worthwhile if you can make inroads into programming in your local area and have an impact on policy decisions at the local and national level. The airwaves may belong to the public, but unless the public fights for access to them, they will become the exclusive purview of those for whom the bottom line is all that matters.

References

Commonwealth of Pennsylvania Office for the Aging. 1977. The New Older Citizen's Guide: Advocacy and Action. Harrisburg, Pa.: Department of Public Welfare.

Gray Panther Media Watch Task Force. 1983. *Gray Panther Media Guide: Age and Youth in Action for Advocacy, Programming, Production, and Participation.* New York.

Ianacone, Evonne. 1979. *Changing More than the Channel.* Washington, D.C.: National Citizens Committee for Broadcasting.

Public Media Center. 1983. *Talking Back.* San Francisco.

Appendix A
You and Television

This is a study designed to give audiences an opportunity to evaluate television in their lives. Knowing more about the audience it serves will help the broadcasting industry to do the best job it can. Please answer each of the following questions by checking the appropriate answer.

I. **Respondent Data**

1. What is your sex? Male ____ Female ____
2. What is your age? 55 or less ____ 56–65 ____ 66–75 ____ Over 75 ____
3. What is your marital status? Married ____ Single ____ Divorced ____
   Widowed ____ Separated ____
   Did this event occur within the last year? ____ 1–3 years ago? ____
   More than 3 years ago? ____
4. Do you live alone ____, with another person or persons ____, or in a group setting such as a retirement hotel ____? (Please check one.)
5. Pleae circle the highest level of schooling *attained* for both A and B
   A. Pre-college: 1 2 3 4 5 6 7 8 9 10 11 12
   B. College: 0 1 2 3 4 5 6 7 8

II. **Television Use**

1. Generally, how much do you watch television on the average weekday?
   Less than 1 hour ____ 1–3 hours ____ 3–5 hours ____ over 5 hours ____
2. How much do you watch television on the average *Saturday*?
   Less than 1 hour ____ 1–3 hours ____ 3–5 hours ____ over 5 hours ____
3. How much do you watch television on the average *Sunday*?
   Less than 1 hour ____ 1–3 hours ____ 3–5 hours ____ over 5 hours ____

An audience survey by the University of Southern California, Leonard Davis School of Gerontology, in cooperation with the University of Maryland, College Park, Center on Aging.

4. Please check if you subscribe to any special television service such as cable ____ or movie channels ____.
5. If you answered the last question, do you watch this special television service more ____, less ____, the same as ____ regular channels?
6. At which of these times during the fall do you usually watch television? (Check as many spaces as are applicable.)

	6 A.M.–Noon (Morning)	Noon–6 P.M. (Afternoon)	6–9 P.M. (Evening)	9–12 Midnight (Night)	12 Midnight–6 A.M. (Late Night)
Mon.–Fri.					
Sat.					
Sun.					

III. Program Preferences

1. What are the names of your three favorite television programs? (If news, please specify *which* program.)
   A. _____
   B. _____
   C. _____
2. Which types of television programs do you prefer? Check only three preferences.
   ____ Feature films
   ____ General drama
   ____ Informative documentaries
   ____ News
   ____ Situation comedy
   ____ Sports
   ____ Suspense mystery drama
3. Which of the following programs have you viewed more or less regularly during the past year? (Check all that apply.)
   ____ ABC Sunday Night Movie   ____ Magnum PI
   ____ Alice   ____ M*A*S*H
   ____ Archie Bunker's Place   ____ NBC Monday Night Movie
   ____ Football, Baseball, Basketball ____ NBC Sunday Night Movie
   ____ Dallas   ____ One Day at a Time
   ____ Facts of Life   ____ That's Incredible
   ____ Fall Guy   ____ The 5:00 P.M. News (Weekday)
   ____ Hart to Hart   ____ The 6:00 P.M. News (Weekday)
   ____ Jeffersons   ____ The 7:00 P.M. News (Weekday)
   ____ Little House on the Prairie ____ Three's Company
   ____ Love Boat   ____ 60 Minutes

IV. **Audience Opinion**

1. On the whole, the *entertainment* that television offers to you personally is
   ___ Very unsatisfactory
   ___ Somewhat satisfactory
   ___ Somewhat unsatisfactory
   ___ Very satisfactory
2. Television often provides companionship. How would you rate this function of television in your life?
   Strong ___ Moderate ___ Weak ___ Not at all ___
3. Please list the two major sources for your understanding of world events:
   ___ Magazines
   ___ Newspapers
   ___ Other people
   ___ Radio
   ___ Television
4. Do you feel that when older people appear as characters in television *dramatic material*, they are usually presented factually and honestly?
   Yes ___ No ___
5. Do you feel that when older people appear as characters in television *comedy*, they are usually presented factually and honestly?
   Yes ___ No ___
6. Do you feel that when older people appear in television *commercials*, they are usually presented factually and honestly?
   Yes ___ No ___
7. Do you feel that television commercials influence you to buy what is advertised?
   Yes ___ No ___
8. Do you feel that television offers the older adult audience adequate programming to meet their particular needs and interests? (Check one.)
   ___ Yes, television offers adequate programming for older adults.
   ___ No, television does not offer adequate programming for older adults.
9. Please check one of the following:
   ___ Older people are different from other adults in their television viewing needs and interests.
   ___ Older people are no different from other adults in their television viewing needs and interests.
10. If there are any subjects of interest and importance to you that are not presented on television now and you would like to see presented, what are they?

11. Have you seen anything on television (either specials, news, documentaries, etc., or regular programs) which you feel should not have been shown to the general public? If so, what program(s) and why?

_____

_____

_____

Appendix B
Sample Scripts

Sample Script 1
Sexuality and Seniors: Why the Societal Taboos?

Introduction

Good day and welcome to _____, a show dedicated to issues of special concern to senior citizens and their advocates.

Our show today is sponsored by the County Senior Media Committee in conjunction with the County Area Agency on Aging. I am John Smith and I will be your host.

In today's world, young adults are being permitted increasing freedom to express their sexual desires. But for seniors, the rules are different.

Although all major medical studies conducted in recent years have proven that there is no physiological reason why those seniors in reasonably good health should not be able to carry on active and satisfying sex lives, society continues to frown on such activities. And it does so based on one of two myths. The first is that sexuality is not a normal characteristic of senior citizens. The second is that it is somehow wrong, or "dirty," to enjoy sexual activity in later years.

Jim Leader, a noted specialist on senior sexuality, is with us today, and he will discuss these myths and what can be done to explode them.

Welcome to the show, Jim.

Questions

- Most experts who deal with media images of the elderly concede that there is a chicken-and-the-egg kind of dilemma as to what causes stereotypes of this age group to be perpetuated. Are the media merely reflecting the images of older people that already exist in society, or

This script was originally prepared for use on *Senior Perspectives*, a long-running, senior-oriented public service program broadcast on KVAL Television in Eugene, Oregon.

are they actually helping to create these images? Nowhere is this question more relevant than in a discussion of senior sexuality. When television and the movies portray sexuality as being synonymous with youth, beauty, and agility, are they merely reflecting attitudes that already exist, or are they contributing to younger people's intolerance of the sexual interests and needs of the elderly?

- Masters and Johnson concluded that social-psychological factors were more powerful inhibitors of sexual activity than biological aging. These included such factors as preoccupation with work, physical and mental fatigue, overindulgence in food and drink, and reactions to societal taboos about sex in old age. How badly do these factors affect the sex life of seniors?
- While studies show that male sexual interests and abilities diminish with age, there does not seem to be a commensurate loss in interest or ability for women as a result of aging. Why is this?
- What exactly are the sexual capacities of the aging male and female human being?
- Masters and Johnson emphasized regularity of sexual performance through the adult years as important for maintaining sexual capacity and effectiveness. Could you comment?
- More than twice as many older women are widowed than older men. What kind of social and personal problems does this cause?
- Another area within the field of sex and aging that has been colored with myths and misunderstanding is that of menopause. Could you briefly explain the menopause process and how it affects a woman's sex life?
- Is there a male menopause and, if so, what are its effects?
- One area that is still shrouded with shame and guilt is that of masturbation. Is it becoming more acceptable as a sexual outlet?
- Could you go into more detail on how the health factor affects sexual activity in the elderly?
- Do you see the attitudes about sex and aging changing in the near future?

Wrap-up

Thank you, Jim, for being on the show. You've been very informative and, I'm sure, have helped our viewers better understand that sexuality is, and should be, as much a characteristic of the old as it is of the young. It is neither unusual or immoral. What is immoral is the fostering of such myths and the subsequent restrictions they place on the elderly.

Thank you all for watching. I would like to welcome you all to continue to tune in to _____ in the future.

Have a good day!

Sample Script 2
Drugs and the Senior Citizen: A Solution or a Problem?

Introduction

Good day and welcome to _____, a show dedicated to issues of special concern to senior citizens and their advocates.

Our show today is sponsored by the County Senior Media Committee in conjunction with the County Area Agency on Aging. I am John Smith and I will be your moderator.

No one has to be told that we live in a drug-oriented society. Nearly every time you pick up a paper or turn on the news you read or hear something about drugs. But usually the focal point of the story is some young person who has taken, sold, or otherwise been involved with illegal drugs such as marijuana or cocaine.

A story that has not been told so often is about prescription drug use and abuse. But for senior citizens, who provide the biggest market for these drugs, it is a story that should be told. Although seniors make up only 11 percent of the population, they consume around 25 percent of the prescription drugs. Thus, issues of cost, overuse, side-effects, right and wrong combinations of drugs, and the role of the doctor and pharmacists are particularly important to seniors.

Our guest today is Joe Jones, Director of the _____ County Drug Information Center, who will discuss these and other issues related to senior prescription drug usage.

Welcome to the show, Joe.

Questions

- How much more do the elderly use drugs than the general population? Why?
- What drugs are most commonly used by seniors?
- What is the doctors' role in all this? Some seniors are taking over a dozen drugs a day. Do seniors really need all these drugs, or do doctors sometimes overprescribe to avoid dealing with the underlying problems?
- How often are seniors given drugs they don't need?
- Physical and mental disorders are often caused by adverse drug reactions. What, if any, precautions are taken when seniors are prescribed drugs?
- What types of drugs should not be mixed with other drugs?

This script was originally prepared for use on *Senior Perspectives*, broadcast on KVAL Television in Eugene, Oregon.

- Do doctors typically keep an extensive drug history on their patients to avoid the wrong mixture of drugs?
- What questions should seniors be asking of doctors who are prescribing drugs for them?
- Prescription drugs represent a major medical cost to seniors, yet they are not covered under Medicare. Why is this?
- How major a financial burden are drugs and what problems does the lack of coverage by Medicare cause?

Wrap-up

Young people are not the only people in America with drug problems. Although the source and type of problem may be different, senior citizens also have a good deal to worry about when it comes to drugs. With the advice of good people like today's guest, Joe Jones, however, senior citizens and their doctors will make sure that drugs are prescribed only as needed and used only as directed.

Thank you for being on the show, Joe. I'm sure our audience enjoyed it as much as I did.

Thank you all for watching. I hope you'll continue to tune in to

_____.

Have a good day!

Sample Script 3
Gerontophobia in America

Welcome to our _____ Interview, where we try to get to the heart of the issues and concerns that affect the lives of older persons.

Introduction

Our guest today once said: "Ageism is the notion that people become inferior because they have lived a specified number of years." Maggie Kuhn has worked hard to dispel that notion; to illustrate that aged Americans are as skilled, proficient, competent, and productive as any other age group. In fact, they may be more so. After all, they have a life-

---

This script was originally prepared for *Pathways*, a senior-oriented program broadcast on Media General Cable, Channel 30, in Fairfax, Virginia.

time of experience to fall back on, which Maggie Kuhn did in 1970 when she founded the Gray Panthers to help fight ageism.

Points for Discussion

- Americans suffering from "gerontophobia"
  —Why do Americans fear aging?
  —Is ageism as big a problem in our country as it once was?
- Stereotypes of aging
  —Myth of the sexless senior
  —Importance of physical appearance
  —Are wrinkles and gray hair still a badge of distinction?
- Myth of disengagement
  —Youth and age in action contradicts this theory.
  —But what about the "leisure world" concept?
- Myth of uselessness
  —Older persons making their presence felt
- Myth of senility
  —Ramifications of the mental decline stereotype
  —Learning as a part of old age
- Television and radio
  —Are they reaching older persons?
  —Why are older characters rarely used?
  —Advertising to the young
  —Emphasis on 18–49 age group
  —Actually the most disposable income is held by the 50–65 age group
  —The empty nest syndrome
  —Network domination
- Reaching the young
  —Aging curriculum in the elementary and secondary schools
  —Doesn't the fight against ageism need to start with the young?
- Comparing young and old
  —Similar difficulties

Wrap-up

Our society didn't become ageist overnight; and it won't become sensitive to the concerns of the aged overnight. But pioneers like Maggie Kuhn are making inroads, and helping ensure that tomorrow will be a brighter one for older Americans.

Thank you for joining us today, Maggie.

And thank all of you for watching. I hope you'll continue to stay tuned.

Good day!

Sample Script 4
Alzheimer's Disease: Unlocking the Mystery

Welcome to our _____ Interview, where we try to get to the heart of the issues and concerns that affect the lives of older persons.

Introduction

Americans are now coming to the realization that senile dementia—commonly known as senility—is not a normal part of aging, as myth would have it. Only 5 percent of the elderly population have this type of mental impairment. And approximately half of these dementias are caused by a tragic illness called Alzheimer's disease—a disorder that results in the deterioration of memory, language skills, intellect, and emotion.

Alzheimer's disease is the fourth leading cause of death among the elderly, killing 100,000 persons each year. The cost to society is $6 billion. But the cost to victims and their families in anguish and pain is far greater still.

Today we begin a two-part series on Alzheimer's disease. Our hope is to gain a better understanding of the disease, its effects on loved ones, and how they can learn to cope with it.

Guest (Part 1)

- Dr. Bill Smith, Specialist in Alzheimer's disease, Hometown America Medical School

Guests (Part 2)

- Barbara Thine, psychiatric social worker
- Suzy George, member of family with Alzheimer's victim
- Joe Baker, leader, local Alzheimer's victim support group

This script was originally produced for *Pathways*, a Media General Cable, Channel 30, Fairfax, Virginia, production.

Points for Discussion

(Part 1)

- Diagnosis of Alzheimer's disease
  —How difficult is it?
  —Tests used
- Symptoms
  —Differentiating between those with Alzheimer's and individuals exhibiting similar, but unrelated, symptoms
  —Examples of common disorders causing confusion among the elderly
  —Reasons for other forms of dementia
- Cause of Alzheimer's disease
  —Theories being investigated
  —Does any one theory seem more reliable?
- Changes in behavior
  —Behavior changes as disease progresses
  —Are the patients the first to notice changes?
- Response of the patient
  —Verbalizing frustrations
  —Depression in Alzheimer's patients
- Seeking help
  —Does treatment work with certain symptoms, especially in the early stages?
  —Prognosis of the disease
- Caring for the Alzheimer's patient
  —Family care in the early stages
  —Appropriate time for nursing home, or other nonhome, placement
- Duration of disease
  —Average length
  —Does physical health remain fairly good?
- Medical benefits
  —Are Alzheimer's patients eligible for Medicare/Medicaid?
  —Other medical coverage
  —What does it cost to care for an Alzheimer's patient?
  —Where do the major costs come from?
- Research
  —Direction of research
  —Federal research support
  —Future research direction and funding

(Part 2)

- Family member caring for a loved one with Alzheimer's
  —What special skills need to be learned?
  —Where do families obtain information and training?
- Dealing with difficult situation
  —Appropriate responses (examples)
  —Seeking help
  —Importance of verbalizing your feelings to someone who understands
- Role changes within the family
  —Losing the head of the household
  —Response of the family
  —What changes have to be made?
- Maintaining social skills
  —Is it possible to become isolated by friends and family?
  —Or to isolate oneself from others?
- Alzheimer's victims with children still at home
  —How are the children able to cope?
  —Do they have special needs?
- Deciding to place a loved one in a care facility
  —When is the right time?
  —Coping with the guilt
- The value of support groups
  —For Alzheimer's victims
  —For loved ones
  —How are groups structured? Who are the group leaders?
  —Sharing information and ideas
- Individual counseling
  —Does it help, especially with individual problems?
- Alzheimer's disease and related disease associations
  —Group's overall purpose
  —Role in finding support groups for victims and their families
  —Funding
  —Legislative efforts
- Support groups in the local area
  —How can you find them?
- Looking to the future
  —Will a cure be found?
  —Future legislative efforts

Wrap-up

We hope we have provided some insight into Alzheimer's disease. This is a serious disease that has serious consequences for thousands of Americans and their families. Someday maybe we will be so lucky as to see its eradication. But for now, all we can do is help fund research and try to understand the stresses and problems that victims and their families face.

Thank you _____, _____, and _____ for join-
Barbara Thine   Suzy George   Joe Baker
ing me here today.

And thank all of you for watching. I hope you'll continue to stay tuned.

Good day!

Appendix C
Selecting a Topic

The range of possible topics for an aging-oriented television or radio program is virtually unlimited. The following list of suggestions, though hopefully thought-provoking, is only a beginning.

1. Age discrimination
2. Aging in other cultures
3. Alcohol use and abuse in senior citizens
4. Alzheimer's Disease
5. Appearance
6. Area Agencies on Aging
7. Arthritic
8. Bereavement
9. Black elderly
10. Cancer
11. Consumer frauds
12. Condominium conversion
13. Cooking tips
14. Counseling the older adult
15. Crime and the elderly
16. Cultural difference
17. Day care centers
18. Death and dying
19. Demographic information
20. Depression
21. Diabetes
22. Divorce
23. Driving
24. Drug use and abuse
25. Economic influence
26. Elder abuse
27. Emotional problems in the elderly
28. Employment
29. Exercise
30. Fashion
31. Financial problems/planning
32. Foot care
33. Funeral practices
34 Gray Panthers
35. Handicaps
36. Hair care
37. Hearing
38. Higher education
39. Historical perspective on aging
40. Hobbies
41. Home safety/security
42. Housing
43. Institutionalization
44. Intergenerational programs
45. Learning
46. Legal difficulties
47. Legislative issues/process
48. Leisure time
49. Living wills
50. Loneliness/isolation
51. Love
52. Make-up

53. Marriage
54. Media
55. Memory
56. Menopause, female and male
57. Multigenerational family
58. Muscles/strength
59. Nursing homes
60. Nutrition
61. Obesity
62. Organizing
63. Outreach
64. Pension plans
65. Pets/pet therapy
66. Physical changes
67. Physical fitness
68. Physical health
69. Politics and aging
70. Prostate
71. Recreation/entertainment
72. Religion
73. Reminiscences
74. Retirement
75. Retirement communities
76. Review of services (advocacy, protective, health, recreational, legal)
77. Rural versus urban needs
78. Self-help groups
79. Senior advocacy
80. Senior centers
81. Senior life adjustments
82. Senior olympics/sport competition
83. Sensory problems
84. Sexuality and aging
85. Sight
86. Skin conditions
87. Socializing
88. Stereotyping the elderly
89. Stress
90. Successful aging
91. Taxes
92. Technology
93. Television
94. Transportation
95. Travel/vacations
96. Victimization of the elderly
97. Video revolution
98. Vitamins
99. Volunteerism
100. Widowhood and loss
101. Wills
102. Youth and the elderly

Appendix D
Glossary

ABC American Broadcasting Company.

Abstract set A decorative set that suggests no specific location.

Across the board A program or announcement that is aired Monday through Friday at the same time.

Adjacency Consecutive airing of programs or announcements, which are said to be adjacent to each other.

Ad lib Impromptu speech or any unprepared and unscripted material.

Affiliate A local station contracted to carry the programs of a television or radio network.

Angle shot The camera shot taken from above or below a subject instead at the more typical shoulder level.

Animation The process of moving figures or letters. "Simple animation" refers to letters that pop onto the screen to form words. "Full animation" refers to film cartoons.

Ann. (or Anncr.) Abbreviation for announcer.

Aspect ratio The 3 × 4 horizontal radio used in film and video.

Audio The sound portion of television.

Audio cue A sound that is used to "tag" or denote an upcoming production event.

Audio dub The recording of sound only, without disturbing the picture.

Audition The tryout for an acting, announcing, singing, or any other type of performance.

Background The setting of a program where a scene is played.

Background projection The projection of a scenic or informational background on a screen within a set.

Background sound or music The sound or musical effects that are played as back-up to the major action.

Back light Light behind an image to be photographed, used to create depth; if used incorrectly, can cause severe silhouetting or shadows.

Back-to-back Adjacent airing of telecasts.

Balop An opaque projection device.

BCU Big close-up. An extremely close shot of a person or object.

Betamax Sony 1-hour 1/2-inch videocassette recorder.

Beta-2 Sony 2-hour 1/2-inch videocassette recorder.

Block   On television, a set of consecutive time periods. A group of programs that is aired at the same time daily may be referred to as a "block of programs."

Bloop   A defect in the sound track of a film, usually caused by a splice.

Blow   To "blow" a line or "blow" a word, synonymous with "muff" or "flub."

Blow up   Enlargement of a photograph.

Blue   Obscene. A "blue gag" or "blue remark" refers to an off-color joke or remark.

Blurb   A written publicity release. A statement or announcement from a press agent.

Board   A control panel used by technicians to control the picture or sound.

Board fade   A fade-out in a program, either audio, video, or both.

Boom   A device that holds a mike or camera in an overhead position.

Braces   Stage braces used to hold up television scenery, usually held in place at the base by weights.

Break   Time out, taking a "break." Announcement of a station's call letters between two programs is a "station break."

Bridge   A musical and/or pictorial transition used to link episodes or scenes.

Burn   A permanent image that persists in the same position on the target of the camera tube.

Business   Little bits of action or small details that add to characterization or accent a particular sequence or scene.

Busy   Too much detail in a set or background.

Cable TV   Television signals transmitted primarily by cable instead of broadcast through the airwaves via antennas.

Call letters   A station's identification, e.g., WBNS-TV. A legal FCC identification would include the call letters, channel number, city, and state.

Camera   In television, the unit that reproduces the scene or objects before its lenses by means of a light-sensitive pick-up tube, which transforms the picture into electrical impulses.

Camera right or left   To the right or left of the camera as the cameraperson sees it.

Cans   Head sets used in the studio and engineers' booth.

CATV   Cable television.

CBS   Columbia Broadcasting Systems.

Chain   (1) "Camera chain," the camera, its cable, and its control unit. (2) "Film chain," the film cameras, their cables, and their control units.

Channel   The wavelengths or bands of frequencies authorized for telecasting.

Circulation   The number of families in a given coverage area who own television sets and are therefore a potential audience.

Clearance   The use of musical composition or performance, through legal permission, usually from one of the licensing organizations, BMI or ASCAP.

Close shot   A shot of a human that encompasses the upper torso and head, from approximately the waist up.

Closed circuit   A television production that is not telecast but is shown to a selected audience by means of a "wired" circuit.

Close-up   A small portion of the whole picture. A close-up of an actor might include only the eyes.

Close-up shot A close-up of a man would show only his head and shoulders.

Coaxial Cable A special cable used for the transmission of television signals.

Cold copy Script or text that the performers read on camera without having seen it before or rehearsed it.

Color Local atmosphere or description.

Commercial A sponsor's or advertiser's announcement made over the air.

Construction units Stock pieces used in the construction of stage or television settings. Units may contain doors, windows, bookshelves, or other elements.

Continuity (1) The copy or audio portion of a television program. (2) The logical sequence in which a program progresses or flows.

Contrast The ratio of light to dark in the television picture.

Control room A room that usually houses the director, assistant director, audio person, and switches and video control person, from which the director controls the television program.

Copy The written script for a television spot announcement or program.

Courtesy The announcement given at the beginning and end of a preempted program to credit the advertisers who normally buy that time.

Cover A camera shot that "covers" the whole scene.

Coverage area The geographic area around the television station in which a television signal can be received.

Crawl A listing of cast and production credits that slowly "crawls," either vertically or horizontally, into the camera's view.

Credits The identification of performers, directors, producers, writers, and technicians which is given at the beginning or end of a program.

Cross fade A visual transitional device wherein the picture fades momentarily to blackness and a new scene slowly fades in.

Cue A signal, verbal, or visual, for performers or technicians to make their next move.

Cue line The last line before a new cue; the line that motivates or signals the next action.

Cue sheet An outline of specific cues that are to initiate action throughout a given sequence or show.

Cumulative time The "running time" or time accumulated from the program's sheet.

Cushion Extra materials that can be introduced at the end of a program if it runs short.

Cutting The editing of a film or video tape. Also, changing from camera shot to camera shot in a television program.

Cuts Portions of a script that can be omitted from a program. They may be planned in advance as a safeguard against running over.

Cyc Pronounced "cyke," abbreviation for *cyclorama*, a large canvas or cloth backdrop suspended from a track, usually used to create the illusion of space in a studio set.

Dead mike A microphone that is not in use or will not pick up sound.

Disc Phonograph record.

Dissolve A visual transition in which one picture is slowly substituted for another.

Documentary A presentation based on factual material.

Dolly A camera movement toward or away from the subject. Also, the wheeled base of a television camera.

Double spot Two commercial spots or announcements run back-to-back.

Double system A motion picture recording process wherein sound is separately recorded and later matched to, or synchronized with, the picture.

Downstage (1) To move toward the camera. (2) The part of the stage nearest the camera.

Dress The final rehearsal of talent and production crew before a telecast.

Dry run A rehearsal that may be only a "walk-through" or "talk-through" of lines and cues. The technical aspects of production are not involved.

Dubbing Adding sound to a film. Sounds or background music that are added after filming are "dubbed in."

Dupe A negative film that has been made from a positive film.

Effects Usually used interchangeably with "opticals." The technique used in changing from one scene to another. A take, cross fade, dissolve, wipe or any other device used in changing from one picture to another in either film or TV would be called an "effect."

Emcee Master or mistress of ceremonies.

Establish To begin a scene, visually and aurally.

ET Electrical transcription. Usually refers to a 33-1/3 RPM disc commercially recorded, especially for broadcast purposes.

Fade A gradual change in the picture or sound intensity.

Fade-in To gradually increase the intensity of a video picture from dark to full scene.

Fade to black To decrease the intensity of the video picture until the screen is dark.

FCC Federal Communications Commission.

Feed The transmission of either a radio or television signal to another station or to a network of stations.

Fill To use "pad" material when a program runs short or is unable to run at all.

Film chain An optical system whereby an image from a film or slide projector is transferred to a video camera for use in a television system.

Film clip A short piece of film, usually inserted into a program format as a separate feature or as a supplement to live material.

Film cue A perforation or marking on the film, usually in the upper right-hand corner, which signals change-over from one reel to another or warns that film time is running out.

Film loop A short film spliced end-to-end. When the loop is threaded on the projector, the same picture repeats itself until the projector is stopped.

Film strip A strip of 35-millimeter film to be projected in a film strip projector as individual scenes.

Filter mike A microphone designed to give an unnatural sound to the voice, used most frequently to create the effect of speech over a telephone.

First generation The original recording or master tape.

Fixed focus Unchanging focus of camera lens regardless of what movement takes place in front of the camera.

Flare The reflection caused when bright objects catch the lights and reflect into the camera lens.

Flat The scenic background unit that is used to build the television setting. Also, a lack of contrast in screen image.

Flips Card of a specific size used on a special rack or stand in the television studio.

Flood A type of light used to illuminate wide areas.

Floor manager The assistant to the director who works on the studio floor during the telecast relaying the director's signals and cues to performers and stagehands. Also called "floor director."

Focal length The distance between the center of a lens and where the image is in focus, usually the image plane or the camera tube's target plate.

Follow focus The continual adjustment of a lens to keep the subject in focus when the subject and/or lens are moving.

"Follow" shot A camera's following the movement of the subject without necessarily moving itself.

Frame The limits of the video picture. Also, the single picture in a strip of motion picture film.

Frequency The number of times a signal is emitted per second.

Frequency response The ability of an electronic device to reproduce a wide range of frequencies.

From the top Order to start rehearsal from the very beginning of the musical number or script. May also refer to the start of a scene currently being rehearsed.

F-stop A calibration on the lens that indicates the width of the opening of the lens iris.

Full shot A full-length view of actors or talent.

Gain Degree of amplification of an audio circuit.

Generation The number of copies away from the original.

Gimmick A twist that makes a program, commercial, or performance different from others.

Golden time Overtime in filming of a television commercial, so called because of rapidly mounting the costs.

Go to black Gradual fade out of the picture; same as "fade to black."

Grid The overhead metal framework used to hang lights, scenery, microphones, and other props.

ID Station identification; a 10-second spot of television used for station breaks. Time enough for the product name and claim—and a lot of creative ingenuity.

Image enhancer A electronic device that sharpens the picture.

Input The part of electronic equipment into which signals are fed.

Insert A close-up on some object such as a letter, newspaper, map, or book, to be cut into the main scene when the show is edited.

Kill To eliminate, to cut out, to remove, to stop, e.g., to "kill the mike."

Lap A fast dissolve.

Leader Blank film attached to beginning or end of film clip or reel, used to aid threading of film into the projector and may be numbered to show the number of seconds remaining before the picture starts.

Level   The degree of sound volume.

Limbo   An area of the set having a plain, light, nondescript background.

Line   Wires that carry programs.

Live   Equipment that is turned on, e.g., "a live mike." Also, programs done at the moment, not presented from recordings.

Live-on-tape   A program recorded on tape without interruption and presented without editing.

Live recording   Recording of actual sounds in the physical world, as contrasted with re-recording.

Live sound   Dialogue and sound recorded at the time of shooting.

Location   Any place, other than the studio or studio lot, of a film producing organization where one of its production units is shooting pictures.

Log   A detailed chronological listing of a station's complete schedule.

Logo   Symbol or trademark.

Long shot (L.S.)   A shot in which the object of principal interest is, or appears to be, far removed from the camera.

Low-key light   Subdued lighting, which usually emphasizes subject only. Background is dark.

Master   (1) A complete and official script. (2) Authoritative schedule. (3) The fader on the control console with overall regulation of volume.

M.C.   (1) Master or mistress of ceremonies. (2) Master control room.

Mention   Reference to a product, person, or organization on a television program.

Minicam   Lightweight, often self-contained portable cameras.

Mix   To manipulate the faders on the control room console, blending two or more program elements according to desired balance.

Monitor   Television receivers used in studios or control rooms. Also, loudspeakers used for program sound.

Mood music   Music chosen to establish a particular mood or dramatic tone.

Multi-spot plan   A special plan or package rate for announcements.

Music bed   Music used as background only.

NBC   National Broadcasting Company.

NCSA   Abbreviation for Non-Commercial Spot Announcement, term used by the FCC and television stations to designate public service spots for which no change is being made.

Off mike   Not within the pick-up range of the microphone.

On mike   Within the pick-up range of a "live" microphone.

One shot   (1) A single appearance on a program series. (2) Close-up of one person in television.

Out   Cessation of sound or music.

Outline   An outline is a brief presentation of the principal features of the idea of the film or show, in which the producer's intended approach to his subject is roughly sketched.

Output   The terminal point on electrical equipment from which sound or picture or both can be taken.

Out takes   Rejected shots (or takes or a single shot) which do not find a place in the completed version of the film or show.

P.A.   (1) Public address system. (2) Press agent.

Package   A particuar combination of announcements that is put together to earn special note.

Pan; Panning   The movemment of the camera in a horizontal plane.

Pan shot   A shot in which the camera pans horizontally across the scene.

Participating program   A television or radio show in which a number of advertisers have their products featured or mentioned.

Peaks   The highest level of signal strength.

Pick it up   Direction to increase the tempo to speed up the performance.

Picture   The visual image or likeness of an object recorded photographically on film.

Pitch   A high-powered commercial message or other sales appeal.

Pix   Picture.

Playback   An expression used to denote immediate reproduction of a recording. The term "instantaneous" is sometimes applied to playback, so that there is no doubt of the immediacy of the reproduction.

Plug   A commercial message of a mention of a product name or sponsor.

Portapak   A portable video system.

Positive Print   Positive image from processed film.

Preempt   Telecasting time made available for a special event, which takes the place of the regularly scheduled program.

Prime time   A continuous period of not less than three hours of the broadcast day during which the station's audience is the greatest. In television, 7–11 P.M. (East Coast) and 6–11 P.M. (West and Midwest).

Print   A positive still or motion picture processing from the negative.

Producer   The person who carries the ultimate responsibility for the original shaping and final outcome of a show or film.

Production   The general term used to describe the processes involved in making all the original material that is the basis for the finished motion picture.

Production director   The individual in charge of all station production.

Program director   Individual responsible for the planning of the station's program schedule.

Promo   Spot plugging a program, station, or service.

Promotion   A station's own advertising of its programs and projects.

Props   Abbreviation of "properties," the furnishings, fixtures, or objects and devices necessary to the action on the set or location.

Quartz lighting   Very bright and efficient lighting.

Rating   The percentage of a statistical sample of families who have a radio or television set available who reported hearing or viewing a particular program when interviewed.

Receiver   An electronic device used to receive sounds or pictures or both.

Reel   A metal or plastic wheel used to hold tape.

Relay   An electrically operated switch.

Resolution   The amount of resolvable detail in a picture.

Retake   The retaking or reshooting of a scene in which something has gone wrong.

Reverse angle   A shot of the same or similar action taken from a reverse or opposite angle.

Radio frequency adaptor A device that allows video and audio signals from a VTE to play back on a standard television set.

Rolling title A moving title, or foreword, that rolls up from the bottom of the screen.

Roll it The cue given to the projectionist or video tape operator to signal the beginning of the film or tape unit.

Rough-cut The first edit of the film scenes.

RPM Revolutions per minute.

Run down Any listing of cues, props, costumes, or other elements in a production.

Run over To run longer than the time logged for a program.

Run-through A rehearsal with cast, crew, and technical facilities.

Running time Time actually needed for a live program, film, or tape to run at telecast time.

Saturation The intensity of the color.

Script A common ready reference to a production script, shooting script, or screenplay.

Segment A sequence or unit within a show.

Segue An overlapping of two elements as one fades in over another fading out. Sound effects, dialogue, or recorded music may be segued. Also referred to as a "cross fade."

Series A thematically related group of programs telecast in the same time period over a number of weeks or months.

Set An artificial construction that forms the setting or scene for an ongoing program or a motion picture shot or series of shots.

Share of audience In audience surveys, the percentage of an audience watching or listening to a particular station at a particular time. This is a relative figure, as the total audience size does not remain the same every day.

Shooting outline Used in the absence of a shooting script, may consist of a brief sketch of anticipated topics, events, and actions to be captured by the camera crew, or a more thoroughly prepared point-by-point schedule.

Shot The camera picture.

16 mm The film size ordinarily used in local television.

Soft focus A photographic image that is not sharp, frequently used to obliterate the lines caused by aging.

Sound effects (SFX) Various devices or recordings used to simulate lifelike sounds.

Special effects A generic term for trick effects that are artificially constructed, separate from the main shooting stages.

Splicing The joining together of two pieces of film, end-to-end, in such a way that they form one continuous piece of film. The result is called a "splice."

Sponsor The firm or individual that pays for broadcast time and talent.

Spot (1) Spotlight, source of specific and directional light used for key lighting, modeling or back lighting, accent lighting. (2) Announcements/commercials broadcast between scheduled programming.

Spread Time available for stretching a program or any portion of it.

Stage The studio in which shooting takes place. If designed for sound recording, it is called a "sound stage."

Stand by (1) The order to get ready to begin. (2) A substitute program ready to use as a fill-in in case of an emergency.

Still A still photograph of illustrative material that may be used in a television broadcast.

Stretch To slow down a performance to make it last longer.

Strike To clear a studio, restoring everything to its original, stored, neutral position.

Strip A program that runs every weekday at the same time.

Studio At a television station, room from which programs emanate.

Super imp A superimposition in television; the use of two cameras at the same time, each with its own picture, but transmitted as a single.

Sync Synchronization.

Synopsis A brief outline of a television program or film.

Tag Announcement added to the end of a commercial.

Take Each performance of a piece of action in front of a camera that is exposing film. The successive takes of a scene are numbered from one up and are recorded by photographing a numbered slate board.

Take five Direction for a brief break or recess in rehearsal.

Technical director The director of all camera or video facilities from a television station.

Telephoto lens A lens that makes it possible to take a close shot of action that is occurring at a distance.

Teleprompter A prompting device mounted on the camera.

Televise To transmit a picture electronically using televising equipment.

Theme The central idea of a program.

Third generation Two copies removed from the original tape.

Tight shot A picture that fills the screen with a single object of interest so that no background details distract from it.

Tilt To move the camera up or down vertically.

Time check Synchronization of all clocks and watches involved in timing a program.

Titles The performance and production credits that appear at the beginning and end of a program.

Transparency A technique whereby illustrative or written material is placed on a transparent surface through which background material may be seen as the transparency is picked up by the television camera.

Traveler curtain A backdrop or curtain that may be drawn open or shut.

Tripod A simple type of three-legged camera support.

Truck (right or left) A movement of the entire camera and dolly to right or left parallel with the subject.

Turkey A bad show.

Two shot A shot containing two characters, usually a close or medium close shot. The term "three shot" has corresponding meaning.

UHF Ultra high frequency; a connector used for video cables.

Under To run short.

VHF Very high frequency.

Video The visual, pictorial portion of a television program, announcement, or commercial.

Video cartridge A single-reel closed loop of videotape within a closed plastic container.

Video cassette One reel of videotape and one empty reel in a closed plastic container.

Voice-over (VO) The voice of an offscreen narrator that is heard over a scene.

VTR Abbreviation for videotape recording or videotape recorder.

VU Meter Volume unit meter, measures audio levels.

Walk-through A dry run.

Whip shot A fast pan shot, blurring the action on the screen.

Wide-angle shot A shot that makes it possible for the camera to cut a wide scene from a shallow depth.

Wide-shot A shot that covers a large area.

Wind-up The signal indicating that the program is in its final moments.

Winging a show Directing a telecast without rehearsal.

Wire Optical effect in which a line or object appears to move across the screen revealing a new picture.

Work print The positive print with which the final version of a filmed program is edited.

Zoom A zoom shot is made with a zoom lens, a lens of variable magnification that allows a continuous movement from a wide angle shot to a close shot without moving the camera.

Index

About the Authors

Richard H. Davis, a onetime radio actor and high school English teacher, earned a bachelor's degree in English and Speech at the University of Oklahoma and a master's degree in Theater Arts and Broadcasting at the University of California at Los Angeles. He was awarded a doctorate in Communication by the University of Southern California.

Dr. Davis has taught courses in the social psychology of television communication, in television writing, and in production. He now teaches a variety of courses in the Leonard Davis School of Gerontology at USC.

Dr. Davis has conducted numerous studies of audience behavior, and he has published widely on this topic. He regularly acts as an advisor and consultant to the broadcast industry in the special interest area of adult development and aging.

James A. Davis is a gerontologist, psychologist, educator, senior advocate, and television producer. He is currently an administrator and faculty member at the University of Maryland, College Park, serving as assistant director of Experiential Learning Programs, where he coordinates the university's Internship and Volunteer Service Program, Retired Volunteer Service Corps, and the UMCP Elderhostel Program. He is also a member of the faculty at the UMCP Center on Aging and Health Education Department, where he teaches gerontology in health and media, and conducts research in television audience response, mental health, volunteerism and stereotyping.

Dr. Davis has produced and hosted over 350 television and radio shows. Among his on-going television shows for older persons are *Senior Perspectives* (KVAL-TV, Eugene, Oregon)—in its ninth year of production—and *Pathways* (Media General, Fairfax, Virginia), a national finalist for the prestigious Hometown USA Award. An active advocate, Dr. Davis serves as co-chair of the National Program Committee for the Gray Panthers. He received his bachelor degree in political science, masters in administration and gerontology and doctorate in educational psychology from the University of Oregon.